Families and the State

Families and the State
Changing Relationships

Edited by

Sarah Cunningham-Burley
Co-director Centre for Research on Families and Relationships,
Reader, Division of Community Health Sciences,
University of Edinburgh, UK

and

Lynn Jamieson
Co-director Centre for Research on Families and Relationships,
Professor, Sociology, School of Social and Political Studies,
University of Edinburgh, UK

First published 2003 by
PALGRAVE MACMILLAN
Houndmills, Basingstoke, Hampshire RG21 6XS and
175 Fifth Avenue, New York, N. Y. 10010
Companies and representatives throughout the world

PALGRAVE MACMILLAN is the global academic imprint of the Palgrave
Macmillan division of St. Martin's Press, LLC and of Palgrave Macmillan Ltd.
Macmillan® is a registered trademark in the United States, United Kingdom
and other countries. Palgrave is a registered trademark in the European
Union and other countries.

ISBN 0–333–77341–1 hardback

This book is printed on paper suitable for recycling and made from fully
managed and sustained forest sources.

A catalogue record for this book is available from the British Library.

Library of Congress Cataloging-in-Publication Data
Families and the state: changing relationships/ edited by
 Sarah Cunningham-Burley and Lynn Jamieson.
  p. cm.
 Includes bibliographical references and index.
 ISBN 0–333–77341–1 (hardback)
  1. Family policy. I. Cunningham-Burley, Sarah. II. Jamieson, Lynn, 1952–

HQ518.F29699 2003
306.85–dc21   2003053604

10   9   8   7   6   5   4   3   2   1
12   11 10 09 08 07 06 05 04 03

Printed and bound in Great Britain by
Antony Rowe Ltd, Chippenham and Eastbourne

Professor Colin Bell, sociologist, 1942–2003

Contents

List of Tables and Figures

Acknowledgements

We would like to acknowledge all the contributors to the Colloquium on the Family and the State held at the University of Edinburgh in 1997 and those who helped organise this, especially Sarah Nelson and Malcolm Anderson. We should also like to thank all the contributors to this volume for reworking their presentations for this publication and also for their patience during the editing phase. Carolyn Macdougall provided excellent help in preparing the manuscript. Thank you also to Graham Crow for reading the manuscript and providing helpful comments.

Notes on Contributors

Sarah Cunningham-Burley and **Lynn Jamieson** are both co-directors and founder members of the Centre for Research on Families and Relationships (http://www.crfr.ac.uk). CRFR is a consortium across a number of Scottish universities committed to creating links between academics, policy makers and practitioners and to stimulating high quality research on families and relationships in Scotland. Dr Cunningham Burley is a Reader in Community Health Sciences and Professor Lynn Jamieson teaches Sociology, both at the University of Edinburgh.

Karen Clarke is a Senior Lecturer in Social Policy at the University of Manchester, where she has been since 1991. She previously worked as a researcher at the Equal Opportunities Commission and at the Centre for Socio-Legal Studies in Oxford. Her principal research interests are family policy, gender and the labour market and changing family forms and gender roles.

Janet Finch is Vice-Chancellor of Keele University. Before taking up this post in 1995, she was Pro Vice-Chancellor and Professor of Social Relations at Lancaster University. In recognition of her contributions to Social Science and higher education, she has been awarded honorary degrees by six Universities. Her principal research interests are family relationships and relationships across generations. She has held a number of research grants and published extensively on this, and related, topics. Her most recent book is *Passing On: Kinship and Inheritance in England* (2000) with Jennifer Mason.

Beverley Prevatt Goldstein has worked extensively in the fields of social work practice, social work education, community development and training and consultancy. Her publications centre on family placement, identity, black perspectives and evaluation of initiatives in social work education and the voluntary sector. She is Director of the Black Minority Ethnic North East Voluntary Sector Network and a member of the General Social Care Council.

Gill Jones is Professor of Sociology at Keele University. She was Chair of the Advisory Committee to the ESRC's Youth, Citizenship and Social

Change Programme; and Programme Advisor to the Joseph Rowntree Foundation's programme of research on young people's transitions to adulthood. She is mainly known for her empirical research on young people and their families. Recent research includes reviews of social protection systems for young people in the UK and elsewhere in the EU, and an empirical study of parental support for young people. Publications include *Youth, Family and Citizenship* (with Claire Wallace, 1992), *Leaving Home* (1995), *Balancing Acts: Youth Parenting and Public Policy* (with Robert Bell, 2000), and *The Youth Divide* (2002).

Jane Lewis is Professor of Social Policy at the University of Oxford. Her recent books include: *The End of Marriage? Individualism and Intimate Relations* (2001), *Lone Motherhood in Twentieth Century Britain* (with K. Kiernan and H. Land, 1998), *Contesting Concepts in Gender and Social Politics* (ed.) (with B. Hobson and B. Siim, 2002).

John Rodger is a Reader in Social Policy and Sociology at the University of Paisley and currently Head of the Division of Social Policy and Social Work within the School of Social Sciences. He is the author of *Family Life and Social Control* (1996) and *From a Welfare State to a Welfare Society* (2000), both published by Palgrave/Macmillan.

Peter Selman is Reader in Social Policy in the School of Geography, Politics & Sociology at the University of Newcastle upon Tyne. His main areas of research interest are teenage pregnancy, child adoption and demographic change and public policy. His most recent research report is *Monitoring of the DfES Standards Fund Teenage Pregnancy Grant,* Final Report to DfES: 2001 (with Diane Richardson, Alison Hosie & Suzanne Speak) and he is currently co-director (with Nona Dawson) of a study of *Education for Pregnant Young Women and Young Mothers,* funded by the Teenage Pregnancy Unit. He is author of *Intercountry Adoption: Developments, trends and perspectives* (London: BAAF, 2000).

Alan Tapper teaches philosophy at Edith Cowan University in Perth, Australia. He is the author of *The Family in the Welfare State* (Sydney: Allen and Unwin, 1990). His other main interest is eighteenth century intellectual history.

Tom Shakespeare is Director of Outreach for the Policy, Ethics and Life Sciences Research Institute (PEALS), a Newcastle-based project developing research and debate on the social and ethical implications of the new genetics. He is active in the disability movement and community arts. Publications include *Exploring Disability* (Polity, 1999), co-authored with Colin Barnes and Geof Mercer and *The Disability Reader* (Cassell, 1998).

Nick Watson is a Senior Lecturer in the School of Health and Wellbeing at the University of Edinburgh. His current research interests include a study on the socio-technical history of the wheelchair and work on disabled people and end of life decisions. He has published on many aspects of disability and is the joint editor of *Disability and Culture* (with Sheila Riddell, Palgrave, forthcoming), *Reframing the Body* (with Sarah Cunningham Burley, Palgrave, 2001) and *Organizing Bodies: Policy Institutions and Work* (with Linda McKie, Macmillan 2000). He is active in the Disabled People's Movement.

The Family and the State: An Introduction

Lynn Jamieson and Sarah Cunningham-Burley

This collection debates the appropriate relationship between families in all their diversity and the institutions of the state, engaging with claims about the benefits and harms of state actions for personal lives. The collection includes detailed nation-specific studies of aspects of state-family engagement and contributions written in a British, and, in one case, an Australian context using a comparative perspective. Comparison identifies the idiosyncrasies of national contexts, helps clarify the causal underpinnings of arrangements and provides a sense of alternatives, good or bad. Favourite comparators, the USA and the Nordic countries, are sometimes presented as contrasting models in terms of punitive and generous state-welfare regimes. However, authors typically offer nuanced characterisations. Contributors share concerns about the directions of state-family relationships but no one theoretical perspective or political stance prevails. They first came together to give presentations at a series of events held at the University of Edinburgh in the late 1990s around the theme of the Family and the State. Their fears are not typically those of some political scientists who worry that nation states are losing their powers; rather they debate claims of 'best use' and misuse of state powers and resources in relation to families and personal life. This is a difficult task, given diverse views about the role of the state in contemporary democratic societies, and over what constitutes positive family lives and good personal relationships. The popularity of claiming a Third Way for the state to tread provides another backdrop for the staging of these debates.

Popular, academic and political debates include disagreements about what legitimately constitutes a family, what type of family practices, personal and domestic arrangements over a lifetime should be promoted, celebrated or otherwise given support and what should be censured and proscribed. Additionally, some strands of academic writing doubt the ability of the institutions of states to act effectively, even if desirable actions were agreed. Other academic strands weigh up the histories, costs and benefits of different types of welfare regime and specific state policies. Feminists have pointed out that gender inequalities are enshrined in some welfare regimes; those in which social rights flow to particular sorts of 'active citizen': able bodied, 'independent' workers. This renders not only many women but all children, elderly people, unpaid carers, and disabled people as equivalent in dependency, lacking the agency associated with full citizenship.

Much academic writing has been devoted to 'the crisis of welfare', the faltering of political and public sympathy with taxation for social concerns, and the upsurge of market responses to social ills. The proponents of a Third Way have also entered debates over the history and appropriate future of the relationship between citizenship and social rights. While advocating active inclusive citizenship, and giving some support to a view of citizenship that affords agency across the life-course to all, including children, they also distance themselves from advocating elaborate welfare provisions as a social right from the cradle to the grave. This introduction briefly reviews these general debates and the consequent disagreements about whether any attempt by the state to discriminate between and steer towards particular forms of family and personal life necessarily does harm or good. It then introduces the specific contributions to this volume and how they tackle the diverse aspects of the family/state relationship.

Personal life: Demanding or requiring state action?

Family and personal relationships are crucial to the quality of life and health of individuals and the economic and social well being of society. Family issues are matters of government concern in all states and, in welfare states, they are at the heart of key areas of government action, for example in health, education, and employment, as well as within attempts to eradicate poverty and promote social cohesion and inclusion. Most governments would claim to have policies explicitly intended to support families. Some governments proclaim the wish to pay attention to the impact of all state action, from the management of state education systems to spending on weapons, on family and personal life, although practice may often fall short. While many commentators would agree on the value of striving to gather, use and distribute state resources in 'family-friendly' ways, there is often disagreement concerning the meaning of 'the family' or the range of practices and households that should be recognized and supported as families.

In a democratic society, state action, even if targeted at a minority, tends only to be legitimated as being for 'the greater good' or 'in the name of the people' (Poggi, 1990). But, of course, what is, or is not, 'best for all' cannot be taken for granted as straightforwardly self-evident. Typically, competing interests are involved in shaping and contesting versions of 'the greater good', competing constituencies may claim legitimacy, and some groups never get their interests even put on the agenda. A number of authors have talked of the increasing crisis of legitimacy of the state, as it becomes increasingly difficult to conceal or reconcile conflicting interests or to find apparent common ground. What is 'right' or 'good' in family and personal life is the subject of repeated and sometimes vitriolic debate. For some commentators, any suggestion of state support for households that deviate from conventional family arrangements gives succour to undesirable trends. For such conservatives, all moves away from 'traditional family life' are destabilising and undesirable. However, the trends they lament are seen by others see as the slow, overdue and beneficial process of the democratization of family life and the appropriate recognition and celebration of diverse lifestyles.

In the wealthy nations of Europe, North America, Australia and New Zealand, the conduct of personal life across the lifecourse has changed significantly since the early twentieth century. The age structure of populations has changed as extended life expectancy and declining fertility result in an increasing proportion of elderly people, a trend which will continue well into this century. The aging of the population has coincided with other changes that some commentators claim make traditional forms of family support for older people less assured. Lifecourses and types of households have diversified in new ways. Growing up with two parents, leaving home to marry, then having children, who are brought up within marriage, no longer encompasses the majority experience of unfolding life stages. Lowered fertility and marriage rates and increased rates of divorce are a feature of all wealthy nations, but there is considerable variation in the details. Cohabitation before marriage, a rise in the age of marriage, an increase in births outside marriage and an increase in the never married are common patterns across many countries. High rates of dissolution of cohabitation and marriage mean that coupledom is moved into and out of across the lifecourse, a pattern which tends to increase both lone parent households and 'blended families' involving step-children. Gendered divisions of labour in family households have also been somewhat restructured through the pervasive increase in married and partnered women's employment and hence in dual worker households. It is a matter of debate whether any strong normative sense of the 'right way' of conducting personal and family life remains. Attitude surveys and in-depth studies in countries with high cohabitation rates suggest that there is no longer a strong sense of 'right order' in terms of establishing a sexual relationship, marriage and living together. However, stable partner-relationships are generally regarded as the most appropriate context for having children.[1] A sense of 'family oblig-ation', including an obligation to care, remains strong between parents and children, particularly daughters for their ageing parents, and mothers for their children.[2]

Expectations of gender equality in heterosexual partnerships undoubtedly heightened across wealthy nations in the course of the late twentieth century. Economic restructuring during the late twenti-eth century helped partially undermine men's economic advantages over women, as traditional industries declined. However, ideological pressures towards equality stem from much older philosophical debates, as well as 'first wave' and 'second wave' feminist campaigns. From the first advocates of the classic liberal notion that individual men should be proprietors of their own person, there were also femi-nist thinkers using the notion as a critique of women's lack of financial independence and of their legal status as chattel of father and husband. Notions of individual rights and freedoms sit uneasily with appeals to the 'natural' or 'God given' traditional authority of men. However, successful feminist campaigns around women's citizenship, resulting in formal political equality and the right to financial indepen-dence, did not result in straightforward linear progress to gender equal-ity in family households. Gender inequalities in 'family life' have not disappeared by the early 21st century, despite the near equalising of men and women's labour force participation in some countries, making dual-earner couples the norm. Women typically still carry the bulk of responsibility for housework and bringing up children, and their labour force participation is more likely to be part-time and low-paid. Studies in Australia, the USA and the UK suggest that, although attitudes have turned against taking it for granted that gendered divi-sions of labour are how things *should* be done in family homes, gender divisions, in how things *are* done, persist. While some authors see the trend towards further gender equality as an inevitable and inexorable progression (Gershuny, 2000; MacInnes,1998), others talk of a stalled revolution and destabilizing simmering discontent trapped in the bosom of family-households (Hochschild, 1990, 1997).

Decisions in family-households remain influenced by gender inequalities in paid employment. In most capitalist industrial or post-industrial nation states, occupational opportunities remain different for men and women. Women's average wages typically remain lower, although the restructuring of late capitalism has favoured jobs seen as 'women's work', thus aiding the increase in women's paid employment. Women's consequent increased financial independence was a key enabling factor in the late twentieth century shift to delayed marriage and high rates of divorce, although post-divorce or post-cohabiting women are still more likely to be in poverty than their male equivalents. Many commentators who do not seek a return to 'traditional families' call on the state to ease the pressures of balancing family life and employment (for example, by enhancing state support for parental leave provisions, family-friendly work practices, affordable high quality childcare provisions), pressures acutely felt in the long working-hours cultures of the UK and the USA. More conservative commentators, on the other hand, blame the stresses of family life on feminist demands and exhort governments to act to reinforce traditional gender divisions as a solution.

At the same time as expectations of equality have been heightened, so have expectations of intimacy (Jamieson, 1998). Understandings of family relationships have shifted from a focus on the correct performance of duties or the exercise of rights and obligations to showing love and negotiating mutual pleasure. Since the 1950s, family sociologists have labelled this as a shift in emphasis from 'institution' to 'relationship'. An emphasis on the negotiated qualities of relationships rather than on institutionalized rights and obligations complicates the routes by which any governmental body might hope to intervene successfully in personal life. As Janet Finch argues in this volume, the less institutionalized personal relationships are in terms of standard formal rules (set duties, rights and obligations) and the more fluid, varied and personalized they become, the more dangerous it is for a state to codify a specific form of family life as meriting its support. However, not all commentators see the shift 'from institution to relationship' as benign or inevitable, nor indeed one that governments should condone. Rather than locating heightened interest in intimacy within a general democratization and deepening of personal life, some commentators argue that personal life has become shallower, hollowed out by selfish individualism and consumerism that promotes the pursuit of personal pleasure before all else. Such commentators wistfully contrast their perceived present with the dutifully providing traditional fathers and the self-sacrificing altruism of traditional wives and mothers (Bellah et al, 1985). While some see this as a result of the inability or unwilling-ness of governments to shield family life from the market, in both the United States and the United Kingdom, some conservative commenta-tors have blamed welfare provisions for undermining traditional family obligations. Despite a lack of supporting evidence, commentators like Charles Murray argue that safety nets provided by the state, such as income support for lone mothers, hollow out the character forming functions of the family. Such commentators wish state efforts to be devoted to re-imposing a traditional two-parent nuclear family model of family obligations, and to reasserting the hierarchies between male-breadwinner/ female-housewife, father boss/ mother second-in-command and children as subordinates.

We suggest that Janet Finch's arguments against state adoption of a codified model of 'the family' and for the protection of the vulner-able can be generalized from the UK to all 'post-industrial' societies. Moreover, the other chapters in this volume are generally further testimony to this case. A number of contributors document the ways in which interventions, in the name of a narrow conception of the family, do harm rather than good, whether these are the impact of 'family policies' on teenage parents, lone-parent families, black fam-ilies, and disabled persons. While still believing in the possibility of benign state 'social steering', John Rodger warns against the direc-tion of state efforts towards moral regulation. On the other hand, a number of contributors also demonstrate the dangers of the state failing to notice. This danger has long been documented in feminist work on child abuse and domestic violence. In this volume, Beverley Prevatt Goldstein and Jane Lewis note the dangers of failing to work against arrangements and practices that are sources of disadvantage, vulnerability and damage. Prevatt Goldstein also suggests that states have sometimes unintentionally damaged arrangements and prac-tices that are sources of moral strength and social support for black families. Other researchers have also documented ways in which state actions are insensitively at odds with the morality of its citi-zens. For example, Simon Duncan and Rosalind Edwards have shown how UK policies encouraging lone mothers into paid employ-ment founder on the 'gendered moral rationalities' of some lone mothers, whose notions of 'good motherhood' place a moral imperative on 'being there' for children and meeting children's needs (Duncan and Edwards, 1999).

Government claims of vigorous support for families often do not stand up under close scrutiny as several contributors to this volume demonstrate. Gillian Pascall makes this complaint with respect to the UK: 'In UK practice, supporting the family has rarely meant the kind of practical support for family care that Townsend rightly advocated. The clear conclusion from social research, from Townsend's work onwards, is that social services actually go to those who do not have families: they thus substitute for missing families, rather than supporting existing ones. The political emphasis on family responsibility is not reflected in the fiscal and benefit position of those with children. The real meaning of supporting the family is supporting family responsibility, as distinct from state responsibility, for dependants young and old' (Pascall, 1997, 68). Some of the contributions to this volume provide evidence for this lack of support. For example, Gill Jones documents the lack of support for young adults struggling to form their own households in the UK. Karen Clarke and Jane Lewis document the state's capacity for promulgating contradictory messages concerning marriage, fatherhood and motherhood through family policies. Peter Selman demonstrates how UK and US policies on teenage parents draw on and build inaccurate analyses of the problems besetting family life. Beverley Prevatt Goldstein, Tom Shakespeare and Nick Watson document the unevenness of appropriate supports for black families and the families of disabled people. Alan Tapper complains of the lack of support given to families with children in Australia, in favour of a system that supports the later stages of the lifecourse.

In popular debate and academic accounts, family life is often seen as at the receiving end of the macro social changes of capitalist development, which the state tries to modify or manage as mediator or ameliorator rather than as initiator or driving force. Clearly, this linear view of the relationship between the global economy, the nation-state and local family practices, lacks subtlety and a sense of dynamic interaction. Historians and sociologists of the family have periodically objected to the depiction of family practices as passively adaptive rather than as actively constructive of social change (for example, Thompson, 1984; Morgan, 1996). The everyday micro-level decisions of personal life contribute to macro-level bigger pictures, including global and societal distributions of wealth, the stratifications of class and status, the distributions of entrepreneurial activity and the shaping of state policies. In democratic states, the moralities that inflect state policies are advocated, contested and resisted by different constituencies, although, of course, some voices are always stronger than others. Characteristic family types of late capitalism, such as dual-earner parents seeking to bring up no more than two children, increased numbers of childless and single person households, the small but increasingly visible handful of households founded on same-sex partnerships, are both product and contributor to particular economic and cultural conditions, bringing particular demands for state action sometimes inflected with slightly different moral standpoints. If states can encourage truly democratic participation in their policy making, then singular and inappropriate models of family life, parenting practices and 'good relationships' are less likely to inform their polices. Baseline research into the complexities of everyday personal lives potentially provides policy makers and practitioners with insights that might enable maximizing good and minimizing harm. Contributors to this volume go some way towards demonstrating the potential value of more dialogue between academic researchers and state agents empowered with considering whether and which aspects of personal life require or demand state action.

The 'hollowed-out' and third way state

Debate about appropriate state action has also been fuelled by increased uncertainty about the competence and power of the state to ever act effectively, even in its domestic sphere, given the social, economic and political conditions of the late twentieth and early twenty-first centuries. A number of authors write of the 'hollowing out' of the nation state by a displacement of its powers to other organisations both 'above', 'to the side' and 'below' (Jessop, 1994). Global corporations emerged in the late twentieth century as powerful orchestrators of transnational markets and media giants as powerful manipulators of global media and communication. Analysts of the state have noted that the relationship between the state and global capitalism is never an entirely passive one. As states form supra-state organisations in attempts to grapple with transnational issues, they inevitably give up some freedom of manoeuvre. Supra-state agreements and bodies require deference to the agreed terms and sometimes loss of sovereignty to a transnational grouping, such as the European Union. Moreover, it seems that effective resistance to global forces often comes from the 'side-ways' organisations of international pressure groups working across national boundaries, outside of, and often in spite of, statutory bodies. Meanwhile, as well as losing power to 'above', in order to maintain their legitimacy as acting in the best interests of all, many democratic states have also increasingly conceded power to local and regional levels 'below'.

The 'hollowing out' characterization of changes affecting the state can be questioned. It is possible, for example, that the concessions of power to 'above' or 'below' might, in some cases, revitalize the state by enhancing its legitimacy in both directions. States are key players in international agreements and groupings and governments can potentially use such arenas to claim the legitimacy of working both for the common good of the nation and the greater good of larger groupings, even the planet. Moreover, 'small states' in 'open economies' have typically sustained large public activities – e.g. Sweden, Netherlands, Austria (Rodrik, 1996; Hirst and Thompson, 1996). States also remain key mediators of the struggle between local and global forces in their domestic domain, and, as Bob Jessop points out, 'the maintenance of social cohesion still depends on the state's capacities to manage these conflicts' (1994, 27). Similarly conceding power to 'below' can have a range of outcomes. It remains to be seen, for example, whether the devolved government of Scotland or attempts at settlements of land rights for indigenous peoples of Australia are really new chapters in mutually engaged citizenship or belated steps in the decay of the old colonial British state.

It obviously remains absurd to treat individual citizens going about their personal, economic and political lives and those in charge of the complex organisational apparatuses of nation states as equal players. Governments and state organisations may be unable radically to control global financial markets and media moguls but they retain the ability to deploy national resources in ways that are more or less friendly to particular forms of personal life and to quality of life itself. Whether through war making, persecution of sub-populations, the manufacture of weapons of mass destruction or other means of squandering or despoiling resources, states retain the power to do massively more generalized and specific harm than most individuals could ever do. State power over borders, the right to exclude people or deny them citizenship is awesome. All wealthy nation states are partially peopled by workers who have no citizenship and are explicitly denied what might otherwise be regarded as basic human rights. State legislation passed in California in 1995 seeking to deny education and medical care to children of illegal immigrants is an example of a common punitive tendency towards 'illegals'. Current British policy towards asylum seekers echoes similar tendencies. Ironically, in the history of settler states such as the USA, Australia, New Zealand and Canada, the indigenous people were also long excluded from citizenship rights.

The effect of specific state policies on the general well-being of particular populations has been variable, but it is generally accepted that the development of local and national government provisions to enhance health, education and welfare contributed to rising living standards across the twentieth century. Although income and wealth remain very unevenly distributed in most capitalist nation states, there has been an undeniable improvement from nineteenth to twentieth century in levels of health and education, standards of housing and general standards of living. Whether by the regulation of the worst threats to health posed by the relentless pursuit of profit or by positive provision of state facilities, beneficial changes were aided by state policies. In the majority of 'western' wealthy nations, the period since the Second World War involved the massive elaboration of government enacted 'welfare' policies touching more and more aspects of life. States themselves diversified in a kaleidoscope of organisations with specific responsibilities. However, the refrain of the 'hollowed out' state is just one of a number of themes doubting the future role of the state as a provider of such goods in the twenty-first century.

Proponents of the Third Way adopt an approach to the role of the state that apparently side-steps this debate. They advocate a form of social democracy in which the state is an 'enabler' rather than a 'provider'. The Third Way is conceived of as a path between the hands-off approach of the neo-liberal state and the pervasive state involvement in social and economic life of classical social democracy (Giddens, 1998). An 'enabling' democratic state arguably requires less resources and power than a heavily interventionist socialist democratic state. Debate about the appropriate extent of state intervention has characterized most Western democracies in the 1990s, but the term Third Way became the brand name of the policies of the New Democrats under Clinton in the USA and then New Labour under Tony Blair in the UK. In the political rhetoric of the Third Way, the state is supportive and benign, allowing individuals, in the context of their families and communities, to reach their full potential. Nonetheless, the state remains an important influence in the shaping of policies and practices that affect the everyday experience of family life. The resurgence of the New Right, particularly under the presidency of George W. Bush, brings added force to the need to reconsider family/state relationships. As some contributors suggest, the rolling back of the state may not mean less interference in personal matters, but greater moral control of them.

Most of the authors in this volume have little sympathy for a view depicting the organs of nation states as 'hollowed out', nor do they typically place such distance between enabling and providing or intervening. Rather, they continue to see governmental and quasi-governmental organisations as immensely powerful and welfare regimes as an important route through which such power is exercised. John Rodger comes closest to a 'hollowed out' position in his warnings concerning the consequences of states' abandonment of welfare regimes. He suggests that, as welfare apparatus is discarded, a point will be reached in which governments will have no further purchase over family and personal life. The type of purchase that Rodger envisages is not uncontroversial, as is discussed below. However, here we simply note that while it may be plausible that abdication from state welfare systems leads to a 'point-of-no-return', it is also theoretically possible that powers relinquished can be reclaimed.

Types of policy and welfare regimes

Although all governments claim their social policies and welfare regimes are for the 'common good', analysts demonstrate very significant differences in their outcomes for everyday personal lives, reflecting their different state-specific histories, objectives and coherence. Following Richard Titmuss, it is common to explore the extent to which welfare systems can be characterized as 'residual', coming into play to provide short-term rescue for those who have no access to any other solutions, or as more akin to social rights, an integral, normalized and equalizing part of the social fabric. Gosta Esping-Andersen called the latter 'social democratic welfare regimes' (1990). Different policy and welfare systems have adopted or eschewed institutionalizing particular visions of family life as aspects of entitlement. Historically, many welfare regimes incorporated a vision of the 'normal two-parent family' consisting of a male-breadwinner and female housewife (referred to by Rodger in this volume as the 'standard worker family') into entitlement structures, accepting and perpetuating the financial dependence of women and children on men.

In his much cited typology, Esping-Andersen was primarily interested in whether welfare policies reduce or exacerbate class inequalities. He categorized states into three 'worlds of welfare capitalism', with different distributions of effective political forces resulting in three types of welfare arrangements: the 'social democratic' (exemplified by Sweden, Denmark, Norway and Finland), the 'statist corporatist' (exemplified by Germany, Austria, France and Italy), and the 'liberal' (exemplified by the USA, Canada, Australia, New Zealand, and the UK). The first two types are fully institutionalized welfare systems operating through inclusive or universalistic, earnings-related benefits. They are 'de-commodifying' in their effects in that they reduce the individual's reliance upon the labour-market. The 'language' of their policy debates is dominated by conceptions of benefits as rights. The third type, the liberal welfare regime is 'residual' in the Titmuss sense. Welfare provision is typically minimalist and means-tested, which works against any 'de-commodifying' effect. The 'language' of policy under liberal regimes gives ideological preference to the market distinguishing between individuals *responsible* for their own futures and those who are *dependent* upon welfare, celebrating the former and stigmatizing the latter. Esping-Andersen found that underlying principles of universal provision could be subverted in practice when they resulted in such a low level of provision that only the poor rely on the state, with the better off seeking a higher standard of provision from the market. Once such dualism is in operation, cross-class support for an improved welfare regime is weak, since only the poor are its beneficiaries. Esping-Andersen claimed that only the 'social democratic welfare regimes' typical of Denmark, Sweden and Norway came close to thoroughly and equally 'de-commodifying' individuals across all classes by permitting a socially acceptable standard of living without participation in the market.

Feminist scholars were quick to respond to Esping-Andersen by pointing out that women's equality has historically been restricted by economic dependency on familial relationships as much as on the market. Women are over represented among the section of the population with neither economic capital nor paid employment, despite changes in the post-industrial labour market. The way in which welfare regimes assume particular family forms are highly consequential for inequality between men and women; many welfare systems structure entitlement in ways that perpetuate rather than modify gender inequalities (Bryson, 1992; Dahlerup, 1994; Gordon, 1990; Lewis, 1992; Lister, 1997; O'Connor, 1993, 1996; Orloff, 1993; Shaver, 1990). Interest in gender equality has led to classifying welfare regimes by the extent to which they reinforce 'the male breadwinner model' of organizing the relationship between family households and paid employment (Lewis, 1992; Lewis and Ostner, 1995). 'Defamilialization', 'the degree to which individual adults can uphold a socially acceptable standard of living, independently of family relationships' (Lister, 1997, 173; McLaughlin and Glendinning, 1994) has been proposed as a complementary yardstick to Esping-Andersen's 'decommodification'. In general, the regimes which Esping-Andersen called 'social democratic' are more progressive in terms of gender equality because they tend towards treating people as individuals rather than as contributors to particular form of family life. But further scrutiny of 'defamilialization' reveals differences within the grouping. Norway is less progressive than Sweden, for example (Sainsbury, 1996). A more or less clearly defined vision of 'normal family life' at the heart of welfare regimes also has different consequences for children. Child poverty is a particular aspect of liberal residual regimes in which provisions are deliberately ungenerous.

Julia O'Connor, Ann Orloff and Sheila Shaver focus on the ways in which state provisions institutionalize relationships between the state, the family and the market, noting 'there are significant differences in terms of gender and class consequences depending on which of the two forms of private responsibility, market or family, is supported by public policy' (1999, 223). For example, in the United States state support for full-time motherhood has been obliterated by concern to preserve the freedom of the market. Comparing the social policy regimes of Australia, Britain, Canada and the United States, O'Connor, Orloff and Shaver show that welfare systems often have a contradictory character in terms of gender equality. The United States perhaps offers the most extreme example. In some policy areas impacting heavily on women, the United States sets a notorious example of a 'safety net full of holes' resulting in the marked 'feminization of poverty'. The authors explain: 'citizens have no guarantee of housing, food or health care, no entitlement to public assistance in times of destitution, no public employment as a last resort. Single parents' entitlement to assistance has been replaced by time-limited, state-run and discretionary welfare programs built around work requirements rather than around supporting full-time caregiving' (O'Connor, Orloff and Shaver, 1999, 4). On the other hand, they note that the United States 'seems to have made greater inroads in gender integration of occupations than other advanced countries [and] has been an international leader in policies to guarantee women's 'body rights' such as the freedom from domestic violence, sexual assault or sexual harassment at work' (O'Connor, Orloff and Shaver 1999, 4–5).

A thorough evaluation of social policy and welfare regimes should consider the extent to which they foster equality or inequality in the dignity of personal life with respect to other dimensions of structural inequality such as age, racial or ethnic divisions, sexual orientation and able-bodiedness. These are all issues tackled in this volume in different ways. Alan Tapper looks at the differential effects of post war Australian welfare policy on the older versus younger age groups. Gill Jones focuses on the withdrawal of equal treatment from young people in the UK. Beverley Prevatt Goldstein discusses the extent to which state policies in wealthy, predominantly white, western societies, and particularly in the UK, have cut across or enabled ideals and family practices that have contributed to the survival of black families. Tom Shakespeare and Nick Watson assess how the state frames issues of disability and interacts with disabled people.

The type of social policy and welfare system that holds sway within a nation-state affects all lives, even if welfare is only directed to the poorest or most vulnerable citizens. The social policy system, like the penal system (Garland, 1990) and other aspects of the state (Burchell, Gordon and Miller, 1991; Pringle and Watson, 1992; O'Connor, Orloff and Shaver, 1999) is constitutive as well as reflective of the cultural tenor of a society. As noted by Esping-Andersen, different 'worlds' of welfare become different 'languages' or 'words' of welfare. People, relationships and families are characterized in different ways. Particular understandings of moral worth, appropriate, good and bad behaviours and relationships can be promoted through welfare systems. In other words, cultural as well as material resources are mobilized for or against particular styles of personal, familial and domestic life. Governments can lend weight to social change not only by using welfare systems to redistribute resources but also by talking up or down the dignity of some or all of its citizens in the process. The differential stereotyping of those living on benefit is one visible effect of this in welfare regimes. Ian Gough and his colleagues comment on the particularly stigmatizing and divisive nature of welfare in the USA and note that 'the idea of "welfare dependency" creating a new underclass is relatively absent in Australia and New Zealand' (1997, 38). Ebbs and flows of public support for welfare regimes are more than reactions to the claimed purpose, specific target and expected consequences of any state intervention. Arguments about the costs and benefits of state intervention often carry heavy analytical and ideological baggage. The notion that state-provided services and benefits are 'coddling', and 'moral-fibre-spoiling', for example, can only be supported by certain ways of viewing human nature, society and the state. It sits comfortably within a neo-Hobbesian discourse, in which an even-handed state protects the freedom of the market by enforcing the rule of law on selfish human nature and the New Right discourse of rational, economic human behaviour. Different concerns emerge in subordinate counter-discourses, for example, among those who assume the state performs these same tasks, not as a neutral arbiter but an agent of particular interests (white, capitalist, ruling-class, male). The rule of law is not seen as neutral but a conduit for surveillance, management and control; benefits and services may be regarded as hard won and yet compromising, double-edged concessions wrested from controlling agents. None of our contributors endorse a New Right perspective and some offer good reasons to doubt the even-handedness of state-welfare regimes. Overall, however, they hold open the possibility of welfare regimes that support families and relationships in the everyday practices and moralities underpinning well-being without also reinforcing such less obviously desired outcomes as gender inequalities.

Crisis of welfare and contested citizenship

From the 1980s onwards, there has been talk of a crisis of welfare across western industrialized countries. In a number of these wealthy nation states, governments have claimed that demands for welfare improvements have become insatiable and that the state's role cannot be sustained in the face of the economic and demographic conditions of the new millennium. The necessity of cutting back on welfare provision has become a common refrain in a number of national contexts. In both the USA and the UK, governments have made a show of not seeking to use taxes to redistribute income and wealth in order to ensure a decent standard of living for all. In many welfare states in the late twentieth century, generations of elderly people made particular gains from state welfare (Tapper argues in this volume that the older people were beneficiaries at the expense of other groups); as the twenty-first century progresses, subsequent generations of older people will be unlikely to enjoy similar gains. By the 1990s, surveys of change in benefit provision suggested a pattern across a number of states of meaner benefit levels and more stringent conditions of entitlement in comparison to earlier decades (Daly, 1997; Gough et al, 1997).

Analysts do not agree about the underlying causes of this postulated 'crisis of welfare' and there are particular disagreements about the balance between politics and economics. However, it is clear that this is not a process simply driven by 'hard economic facts'. In a number of nation-states, political climates are dominated by free-market discourse, extolling the benefits of private companies selling services rather than services funded through state taxation. This discourse fits a depiction of the ageing population as an unmeetable burden of demand on the backs of a shrinking population of workers or 'wealth creators'. The rhetorical climate makes this persuasive, even when elderly people were previously workers who paid levies to the state all their working lives. Lois Bryson suggests that welfare cuts made in the name of unavoidable economic realities disguises a backlash reaction to the redistributionary effect of welfare regimes: 'resistance by those who have been the traditional beneficiaries of social arrangements, but whose relative position has been, at least marginally, worsened by more recent developments with the welfare state' (Bryson, 1992, 227). While this statement may also be a political position unsupported by good evidence, it is no more partial than appeals to 'economic reality'.

The debate is wide-ranging with different protagonists diverging in their understandings of the global economy, human nature, morality, the underpinnings of social cohesion and division, and the nature of citizenship as well as of welfare and of family life. Writing in Scotland, we are particularly familiar with the vitriol of this debate in the UK and the US, but aware that it has its counterparts elsewhere. In the UK and the US, the relationship of the state to family life, and particularly state support for lone mothers, has become emblematic of positions on wider issues as the chapters by Clarke, Lewis and Selman illustrate. The conservative Right argue that support for lone mothers is typical of state welfare benefits that undermine morality and promote a one sided view of citizenship, emphasising rights without duties. There are also left-wing critics using the terms 'welfare dependency' who fear moral bankruptcy and disintegration of social cohesion. Those untroubled by how to define the 'common good', focus attention on those feared to have put it aside. Here they do not have in mind the officially excluded, the migrants and refugees who are denied the most minimal benefits of citizenship, but those with formal entitlements to civil, political and social rights who are, nevertheless, regarded as problematic in terms of 'good citizenship'. Solutions alternate between official exclusion through the criminal justice system and means of combating de facto exclusion by providing them a 'stake' in the society which will enlist their active citizenship (Field, 1996). The more radical acknowledge the need for a politics which recognizes the problematic nature of defining the 'common good' and 'good citizenship', given differences between people and the lack of underprivileged voices in its definition.

Ann Phillips (1993) has described how, historically, parts of the left have been suspicious of citizenship rights seeing the language of citizenship as a smoke screen of individualist bourgeois claims of equality disguising economic and social class division. Phillips notes that one of the earlier twentieth century retorts to citizenship-talk was the claim that the expansion of citizenship made little difference in terms of social justice or equality between citizens; formal political and legal equality does not necessarily transform structural inequalities – universal suffrage did not quickly result in a more socially and economically equal society, or even more political representation for women or the working-class. As T. H. Marshall (1950) was writing about social rights as an extension of citizenship, so the architects of the welfare state in the UK were giving fewer social rights and benefits to women classified as dependent wives (Pascall, 1997). As already noted, some welfare regimes, and hence the social rights of citizenship, are consciously crafted to retain inequalities (Esping-Andersen, 1990; Lewis, 1992). But at the same time, other sections of the left have embraced the rhetoric of citizenship and struggled for its extension through a more active participatory democracy. The women's movement slogan of the 1970s, 'the personal is political' resonated with a more general politicization of close-to-home issues among radicals of the New Left in that period – sites such as the housing estate, the community centre, the local nursery, the work place were foci of action and mobilization from which to seek influence on wider decision making about housing, communities, childcare and work. This type of politics sought an answer to the left critique of citizenship as at best affording formal equal rights and duties but actually doing nothing to give people equal access to decision-making processes or enjoying the benefits.

As governments seek ways of reducing the financial burden of state welfare, one strategy has been to remove new groups from entitlement. When welfare entitlements have developed historically as social rights, this is not simply about cutting back specific benefits but redrawing the boundaries of citizenship. In the USA and the UK, governments have sought to narrow full citizenship rights among those of working age to participants in paid employment, with particular effect on those who are excluded from or face particular barriers to participating in employment, such as young people, unpaid carers, lone parents and disabled people. In the UK, policy changes towards young people have involved reversing recognition of young people as independent adults from the age of 16, for example, by withdrawing entitlement to direct income support in 1988. Gill Jones and Claire

Wallace then argued, 'adolescents and young adults are in a problematic situation between dependence and independence. Every piece of legislation which extends the period of dependence in childhood, defers not only adult status, but also the status of citizen in the wider social world. The longer full-time paid employment is withheld from young people, the more training schemes they are expected to enrol on, the longer they are expected to remain dependent on their parents – the more the goal of citizenship, with its obligations as well as rights, seems to be retreating into the distance' (1992). This is a theme further developed by Jones in this volume. Karen Clarke, also in this volume, discusses how both the UK and US governments have pursued punitive policies which have attempted to reduce the numbers of lone parents dependent on state benefits. In the US in particular, these polices have been associated with a large proportion of the children of lone parents living in considerable poverty in comparison with average standards of living. Disabled people have also been disadvantaged by a narrow definition of the 'independent citizen'. As Shakespeare and Watson note, when such versions of citizenship underpin policy 'they could be taken to suggest that disabled people who are not capable of work, of producing anything deemed to be of value, do not have a right to full citizenship'.

Debating family state relations

All of the issues discussed above are aspects of debate over the appropriate relationship between families in all their diversity and the institutions of the state. While all chapters contribute to this debate the first three address this debate in general terms. Many governments attempt to steer family life through their welfare policies but, as Finch argues, steering which cuts across everyday practices is unlikely to have notable success. There is little empirical evidence of success in attempts to incite specific forms of family practice; variations can rarely be causally mapped onto variations in state policies. For example, there is no simple correlation between diversity in types of household and the generosity towards 'non-traditional' households among state welfare regimes. It is true that there are particularly high rates of cohabitation and births outside of marriage in Scandinavian countries, where there are relatively generous welfare provisions which do not discriminate against unmarried unions or strongly uphold 'male breadwinner models' of family life. However, the prevalence of lone parent families is lower than in much of the rest of Europe and rates of births outside marriage are high in the UK which has a relatively ungenerous welfare regime. Just as they are not actively discouraging cohabitation, the Swedish state does not have a punitive policy towards lone parenthood, unlike some other states. High rates of lone parenthood, typically lone motherhood, can be, and in some states are, associated with low rates of birth outside marriage, when the majority of lone parents are not young, never married women but women who have had children in partnerships which have then broken down (Drew, 1998), as Peter Selman and Karen Clarke make clear in this volume.

The explicit aims of state policy are not necessarily reflected in their enactment. Authors in this volume make the case that state action taken in the name of 'the family' can multiply social and personal harms rather than act for the common good. Finch opens up the volume with an overview of 'The State and the Family'. In this, Finch sets out the inherent conflicts and contradictions in state/family relations, and the range of ideological positions present amongst different commentators. Her chapter identifies the range of arenas in which the state and the family intersect, ranging from legislation about divorce to the opening hours of retail stores. Directly and indirectly, the state influences the form and processes of family life. However, in the British context, this may take on a specific form because of some of the characteristics of kinship. Drawing on English data, Finch explores individualism in English kinship. This kinship system emphasizes affect and choice, constructed by individuals across the life course. Nevertheless, there may be some underlying principles about family relationships. Drawing on work on inheritance which she and colleagues conducted, Finch shows how 'the family' is defined, in an operational sense, in the everyday decisions people make about who is and is not 'family'. The state, she concludes, should support flexibility rather than legislate for categories of relationship, but also protect the vulnerable.

John Rodger in his chapter 'Family life, moral regulation, and the State: social steering and the personal sphere' is interested in the extent to which control of social and family life is undermined by the transfer of responsibility from the state to civil society. He notes the growing privatization of responsibility and heightened moral tone to welfare debate, where welfare itself is seen as part of the decline of 'social character'. He separates, analytically, the public and personal spheres and considers the relationship between social policy and social behaviour in the context of post-modernity and the welfare state. Social steering, where ideas rather than resources seem to underpin much of the state's activities, seem to characterize the public sphere.

Jane Lewis explores the role that family law might play in promoting family change, thus providing another perspective on the interrelationship between culture and state interventions, introduced by Finch in the first chapter. Lewis notes that family law attempts to come to terms with rapid family change, but there is ambivalence around whether the profound changes in marriage should be legitimated or not. She explores the extent to which the law facilitates and legitimates particular kinds of behaviour. The liberalization of the divorce law in England and Wales in 1969 reflected a shift in thinking towards a new moral code based on love and individualism. However, the reality of divorced lives remains highly gendered, with women and children more likely to be in poverty.

Family and state across the lifecourse

The engagement between the state and personal life varies across the lifecourse in ways that are also structuring of the lifecourse. A number of authors take a lifecourse perspective and some contributors look in detail at different phases of the lifecourse. Karen Clarke, in her chapter 'Lone parents and child support: parental and state responsibilities', focuses on the underlying principles of gender roles and parental responsibilities for children. She argues that the state has redrawn the boundaries of its responsibilities in relation to family welfare, and the focus on the responsibilities of parents is driven by financial as well as moral concerns. There is a paradoxical reduction of state involvement in the family alongside an increase in other forms of state involvement in private family matters. Overall, these trends result in an increase not decrease in women's dependence on men. The emphasis on private responsibility based on biological parenthood has a clear moral as well as cost containing agenda. However, women may not agree that biological paternity itself should mean continuing financial obligations. Once again, there is a need for much more flexible formulae to meet varied needs.

Alan Tapper focuses on the other end of the lifecourse with a chapter on 'Family Change and the Ageing Welfare State', arguing that state welfare systems have prompted family decline. Although state welfare systems in post World War 2 history were aimed to support families, especially those with children, Tapper argues that they can no longer be considered so supportive. Drawing on financial evidence, he critically analyses welfare states by considering how aims and ideals are operationalized. He proposes four stages to a broad welfare analysis: deepen what is counted by taking taxes and assets into account; track trends across time; examine different cohorts' experiences and the experience of different family types. He argues for the need for horizontal as well as vertical redistribution, as welfare states have become unbalanced against households in which the young predominate. However, not all welfare systems are the same and some interesting differences emerge between Britain, Australia and New Zealand.

Challenging the state: Framing of social issues

Many contributors are challenging the way in which state institutions have framed social issues, sometimes undermining the agency and family practices of sectors of society. Beverley Prevatt Goldstein's chapter 'Black Families and Survival' argues that black people are agents in an on-going process of working on and against hostile prevailing ideological and material practices. She looks at the interrelationship between families and the state in the context of complex racism, drawing on archival research and secondary sources. Writing at a general level, she identifies ideals and practices of family life that have aided the survival of black families in the face of racism. These include children being a vital part of a family; family extending across households; family members, including children, having responsibility for each other and continued respect for elders. She highlights some of the inconsistencies and indifference of state support for these ideals and practices, noting that state actions are sometimes part of the hostile environment that black families must survive. However, she notes that the healthy development of black families requires taking steps to ensure that all black children benefit from ideals and practices that contribute to survival. She suggests that roles within the family need to be reconsidered, as well as the particular positioning of the family and the state.

Tom Shakespeare and Nick Watson take a lifecourse perspective in exploring the position and conceptualization of disabled people. Often marginalized in family research, disability is a significant arena for state intervention. The disabled person is decontextualized and abstracted from the family context, or only understood in terms of the effects of having a disabled person in the family has on other family members. Here, the need for support is reified and any concept of interdependency lost. This polemical chapter explores each stage of the lifecourse and examines the processes of exclusion of disabled people. It argues for a civil rights perspective, based on justice and equality.

Peter Selman considers the relationship between the state and the family in his chapter on 'Scapegoating and Moral Panics', focussing attention on young lone mothers. He challenges the framing of social problems and illustrates how the selective use of data, alongside political and media manipulation of public opinion creates a moral panic around young, single mothers. Looking at demographic trends since the 1960s, he observes that it is the cultural and political context that has changed. This further illustrates the relationship between moralizing about family life and political gain and the complex interrelationship between concerns about illegitimacy, teenage sexuality and abortion. The moral panic and scapegoating about young, single mothers deflects attention from more serious debate about welfare and the involvement of the state in family life.

Gill Jones' chapter on 'Youth, Dependence and the Problem of Support' emphasizes youth as a process rather than static stage of life and considers young people as 'semi-citizens'. She notes that policy emphasis is largely on supporting families with young children, a trend that has been reinforced with vigour through increasing interventions in the early years. Policy only focuses on aspects of youth defined as social problems. In this chapter the voices of young people themselves are present. Jones argues that young people today face new problems, and policy must be changed to reflect this. Transitional status is marked by ambiguity and adulthood can no longer be clearly defined. Young people cannot be economically independent, and so they require some subsidy. However, the boundary between the family and the state is being redrawn. If both the state and the family pull back, then young people may fall into poverty, joblessness and homelessness. In this chapter, young people describe how family support is conditional, making their safety nets very fragile indeed.

These contributions use different methods and different theoretical perspectives into order to analyze family/state relationships. Analysis of interview data, such as presented in Jones' chapter, is complemented by analysis of welfare expenditure in Tapper's chapter. There are also examples of analyses of demographic trends as well as media reporting of such trends. The contributors do not share a single theoretical perspective. The majority of contributors are influenced by feminist perspectives to some degree and some are clearly feminist, but they also variously draw on a range of other traditions and political standpoints, including Marxism, postmodernism, radical black perspectives and the disability movement. The focus of this book is not as centrally concerned with gender equality as some recent feminist collections on gender and the state. Our central concern is with the state and intimate relationships of family life; however, family is defined by those who are living it. While we personally consider issues of gender equality as central to this concern, it is the focus on family-state relationships which links the contributors. Not all possible approaches are represented and this is not entirely deliberate but reflects the limits of space and aetiology of the collection. We regret the absence of some radical voices. However, some chapters take a more polemical turn, providing a critique of, for example, existing conceptualizations of disability and the underlying assumptions within social and health policy. The range of substantive issues covered, from family obligations, to young people in transition, gives the volume a broad focus, yet offers in-depth policy analysis on issues affecting specific groups across the lifecourse. Although the choice of topics covered reflects the expertise of the contributors and the agenda of the original colloquium that gave rise to this volume, they also enable a review of family/state relationships that embraces most stages of the lifecourse, including an examination of inter-generational relationships and marginalized groups. However, the field is not exhausted, for example there is little here on early years' interventions, an area of considerable government initiative, and little on education or health.

Not all of our contributors advocate state welfare systems that seek ways of supporting citizens in carrying out their personal and familial lives without attempting to steer them into particular family forms. Rodgers powerfully argues for continued state steering of family and personal life. It is possible to read Rodger's work as calling for a more prescriptive state view of family obligation than that advocated by Finch. While agreeing with Rodger that states should maintain an interest in enabling people to honour mutual obligations and commitments, we agree with Finch that this cannot be done by attempting to fit the family to any one formula. The subsequent chapters provide new demonstrations of the ways in which state welfare systems can do harm in the sphere of personal life as well as good. Moreover, harm can be caused both by inappropriate attempts at 'steering' as Selman shows in his account of the scapegoating of teenage mothers, and by an absence of any attempts at supporting the efforts that individuals and families make on their own account. Lewis shows the counterproductive tension in the UK between the desire of government both to withdraw from the field and also to secure a set of arrangements that will 'save' marriage. We believe that 'saving marriage' is a less appropriate concern than welfare systems that enhance the capacity of individuals to form and live up to commitments to love and care for others.

Notes

1 For example, in a US study of childlessness, Tim Heaton, Cardell Jacobson and Kimberlee Holland conclude 'childbearing continues to show a strong association with family and spousal commitment' (1999, 538). In the UK, studies of young cohabiting couples find many who believe that marriage is 'better for children' than cohabitation (Jamieson et al, 2000; Lewis, 1999; McRae, 1993; Smart and Stevens, 2000).
2 For work demonstrating this in the UK, see Bornat et al, 1999; Finch, 1989; Finch and Mason, 1993.

Bibliography

Bellah, R. N., Madsen, R., Sullivan, W. M., Swidler, A. and Tipton, S. M. (1985) *Habits of the Heart* Berkeley, University of California Press.

Bornat, J., Dimmock, B., Jones, D. and Peace, S. (1999) 'Generational Ties in the 'New' Family: Changing Contexts for Traditional Obligations', *The New Family?* London, Sage.

Braham, P., Rattansi, A. and Skellington, R. (ed.) *Racism and Anti-racism* London, Sage.

Bryson, L. (1992) *Welfare and the State: Who Benefits?* London, Macmillan.

Dahlerup, D. (1994) 'Learning to live with the state – state, market and civil society: Women's need for state intervention East and West', *Women's Studies International Forum* 17 (2/3) 117–27.

Daly, Mary (1992) 'Welfare States under Pressure: Cash Benefits in European Welfare Sates Over the Last Ten Years', *Journal of European Social Policy* 7, 2, 129–144.

Drew, E., Emerek, R. and Mahon, E. (1998) *Women, Work and the Family in Europe* London, Routledge.

Drew, E. (1998) 'Reconceptualising families' in Drew et al (eds.).

Duncan, S. and Edwards, R. (1999) *Lone Mothers, Paid Work and Gendered Moral Rationalities* London, Macmillan.

Esping-Andersen, G. (1990) *The Three Worlds of Welfare Capitalism* Cambridge, Polity Press.

Fields, F. (1996) *Stakeholder Welfare* London, Institute of Economic Affairs.

Finch, J. (1989) *Family Obligations and Social Change* Cambridge, Polity Press.

Finch, J. and Mason, J. (1993) *Negotiating Family Responsibilities* London, Routledge.

Garland, D. (1990) *Punishment and Modern Society: A Study in Social Theory* Oxford, Clarendon.

Gershuny, J. (2000) *Changing Times: Work and Leisure in a Postindustrial Society* Oxford, Oxford UP.

Giddens, A. (1998) *The Third Way: The Renewal of Social Democracy* Cambridge, Polity Press.

Gordon, L. (1990) *Women, the State and Welfare* Madison, University of Wisconsin Press.

Gough, I., Bradshaw, J., Ditch, J., Eaardley, T. and Whiteford, P. (1997) 'Social Assistance in OECD Countries', *Journal of European Social Policy* 7, 1, 17–43.

Hantrais, L. and Mangen, S. (1994) *Family Policy and the Welfare of Women* Loughborough, Cross National Research Group.

Heaton, T., Jacobson, C. K. and Holland, K. (1999) 'Persistence and Change in Decisions to Remain Childless' *Journal of Marriage and the Family* 61, 531–539.

Hirst, P. Q. and Thompson, G. (1996) *Globalization in Question: the International Economy and the Possibilities of Governance* Cambridge, Polity Press.

Hochschild, A. (1990) *The Second Shift: Working Parents and the Revolution at Home* London, Piatkus.

Hochschild, A. (1997) *The Time Bind* New York, Metropolitan Books, Henry Holt and Co.

Jamieson, L. (1998) *Intimacy: Personal Relationships in Modern Societies* Cambridge & Malden, MA, Polity Press.

Jamieson, L. et al 'Couples and Commitment' Edinburgh University Working Paper, 2000.

Jessop, B. (1994) 'The transition to post-Fordism and the Schumpeterian work-fare state' in Burrows and Loader (eds.).

Jones, G. and Wallace, C. (1992) *Youth Family and Citizenship* Buckingham, Open University Press.

Lewis, J. (1992) 'Gender and the development of welfare regimes' *Journal of European Social Policy* 2 (3) 159–173.

Lewis, J. with Datta, J. and Sarre, S. (1999) *Individualism and Commitment in Marriage and Cohabitation* London, Lord Chancellor's Department Research Series No. 8/99.

Lister, R. (1997) *Citizenship: Feminist Perspectives* London, Macmillan.

MacInnes, J. (1998) *The End of Masculinity: the Confusion of Sexual Genesis and Sexual Difference in Modern Society* Buckingham, Open University Press.

McRae, S. (1993) *Cohabiting Mothers: Changing Mothers and Motherhood?* London, Policy Studies Institute.

Mama, A. (1992) 'Black women and the British state' in Braham et al (eds.).

Marshall, T. H. (1950) *Citizenship and Social Class: and other essays* Cambridge, Cambridge University Press.

McLaughlin, E. and Glendinning, C. (1994) 'Paying for care in Europe: is there a feminist approach' in Hantrais and Mangen (eds.).

Morgan, David H. J. (1996) *Family Connections: An Introduction to Family Studies*.

O'Connor, J. S., Orloff, A. S. and Shaver S. (1999) *States, Markets and Families: Gender, Liberalism and Social Policy in Australia, Canada, Great Britain and the United States* Cambridge, Cambridge University Press.

O'Connor, J. S. (1993) 'Gender, class and citizenship in comparative analysis of welfare state regimes: Theoretical and methodological issues' *British Journal of Sociology* 44, 501–518.

O'Connor, J. S. (1996) 'From women in the welfare state to gendering state welfare regimes' *Current Sociology* 42, 1–124.

Orloff, A. S. (1993) 'Gender and social rights of citizenship: State policies and gender relations in comparative perspective' *American Sociological Review* 58, 303–28.

Pascall, G. (1997) *Social Policy: A New Feminist Analysis* London, Routledge.

Phillips, A. (1993) *Democracy and Difference* Cambridge and University Park, Polity and the Pennsylvania State University Press.

Poggi, G. (1978) *Development of the Nation State: A sociological introduction* London, Hutchinson.

Pringle, R. and Watson, S. (1992) '"Women's interest" and the post-structuralist state' in M. Barret and A. Phillips (eds.) *Destablizing Theory*, Stanford, Standford University Press, 53–3.

Rodrik, D. (1996) 'Why do more open economies have bigger governments' *Working Paper No 5537* National Bureau of economic Research, Cambridge, Ma.

Sainsbury, D. (1996) *Gender Equality and the Welfare States* Cambridge, Cambridge University Press.

Shaver, S. (1990) 'Gender, social policy regimes and the welfare state' SPRC Discussion Paper no 16, Sydney, Social Policy Research Centre, University of New South Wales.

Smart, Carol and Stevens, Pippa (2000) *Cohabitation Breakdown* London, Published for the Joseph Rowntree Foundation by the Family Policy Centre.

Thompson, P. (1984) 'The family and child-rearing as forces for economic change: towards fresh approaches' *Sociology* 18, 514–530.

Part One
Debating Family State Relations

1

The State and the Family[1]

Janet Finch

Introduction: Dilemmas for government

The role of the state in regulating family life has been the subject of substantial analysis by social theorists since the 1970s. I do not propose to revisit the well trodden ground. Rather my starting point is a rather simple (perhaps simple minded) question:

> Why does the state have so much trouble in its attempts to regulate family relationships?

Of course, there is a sense in which all policy initiatives are contentious. But I believe that most people would recognize that, where governments try to intervene in the personal lives of their citizens, their plans tend to elicit difficulties of a particularly sensitive kind. We can see this by considering two examples from the UK.

First, and most obviously, there is the example of changes in the last decade of the twentieth century in legislation on divorce and the subsequent care of children in the UK (see also chapters by Lewis and by Clarke). This is the political hot potato when it comes to regulating family life. The Family Law Bill, which passed through its final stages in Parliament in June 1996, is the archetypal example of a difficult piece of legislation for any government. It was not that there was a single principle that was being challenged by opponents. Rather, there were so many different ideological positions on marriage, divorce and child rearing being fought out in this Bill that it was literally impossible to produce a compromise which could even minimally satisfy all of them. The excellent work of Smart and Neale (1997) on the practical impact of this legislation, plus the Children Act 1989 and the Child

Support Act 1991, demonstrate amply the impossibility of producing family law which satisfies all the main constituencies.

My second example – inheritance – is less obviously politically contentious, but nonetheless raises difficulties, which are almost as tricky when governments try to regulate family relationships.[2] The central problem is how to reconcile two areas of government policy, each of which bears on this. The two policies concern the care of elderly people, on the one hand, and the encouragement of property ownership, on the other. As is well known, the rising number of the 'old elderly' in the population has required governments all over the western world to rethink arrangements for the care of those who can no longer be fully independent.

The spread of home ownership would be claimed as one of the great achievements of UK Conservative governments since 1979, part of a core philosophy about the centrality of property-owning to the kind of society which they wished to create. John Major famously said, on being elected leader of the party, that he wanted to ensure that ordinary British families were enabled to accumulate wealth so that it could 'trickle down the generations'. In encouraging home ownership, there is the implication that this will enhance family solidarity. However, it is obvious that there will not be many of these trickles if most people end up financing their last years through use of the resources invested in housing to purchase one of the many schemes for financing which insurance companies are enthusiastically supporting. This whole issue of how elderly people's assets should be used was sufficiently important for the incoming Labour government to establish a Royal Commission on the long term care of the elderly. This reported in 1999, with central recommendations concerning the circumstances under which personal assets should be used to finance needs in old age (Royal Commission on Long Term Care, 1999). However, there has been divergence in the Westminster (London, England) and Holyrood (Edinburgh, Scotland) parliament's response to these recommendations, with only the latter offering funding for long term personal care.

These two policy areas – divorce and inheritance – between them demonstrate the difficulties for governments when they try to formulate social policies or legislation, which have a potential impact on family relationships. The range of policies to which this refers can be quite varied: from those (like my example of divorce legislation) whose specific purpose is to regulate family relationships, to policies in a whole spectrum of apparently unconnected areas (opening hours of

,retail stores, the funding of students in higher education, to name but two) which do in fact have some bearing on family organisation and relationships. The linking theme in all these cases, and many more, is that governments are always in danger of presuming a 'standard model' of family life for which they can legislate, by making the assumption that most families do in fact operate in particular ways.

In reality, it is very difficult to detect a standard model, in either a descriptive sense (what most people do) or normative one (what people should do). There are very few areas of family life in which there are genuine common denominators, or where a normative consensus actually does exist. This lack of consensus about what constitutes a 'standard model' family is not just about the composition of families – who can legitimately 'belong'. It is as much a lack of clearly articulated normative guidelines about the *form* that relationships should take: what responsibilities and obligations should be attached to being a 'son', a 'sister', a 'father' and so on. My observation certainly applies to the responsibilities of family relationships in adult life, though less clearly to responsibilities for young children, where there may be more consensus at least about the role of 'father' and 'mother'. It is not my purpose in this chapter to elaborate on the evidence of a lack of consensus about the form which family relationships should take in adult life and I should like to take that as read for my present purpose. Research that I did with Jennifer Mason in the late 1980s demonstrated this more clearly than I had expected, confirming the conclusions of earlier work (Firth, Hubert and Forge, 1970; Finch and Mason, 1991, 1993).

The real problem, that I want to explore, is the consequences of this for social policy. The lack of a single model of family life about which governments can assume consensus makes policy formation inherently difficult. One might be able to make that particular statement about most industrial democracies, or, if post-industrial is a better description of contemporary economies, post-industrial democracies. However, I shall argue that in the UK, the absence of consensus about a model or models of family life flows from our distinctive cultural orientations to family and kinship.

Perspectives from social science

What does social science have to offer, in developing an understanding both of why there is a wide variation in the form which family relationships take, against a background where government policies tend to reach for more uniformity?

One could draw many different answers to that question from political science, from sociology, from feminist analysis, and from social history. Each, in different ways, would see state regulation of families as the terrain on which wider conflicts are played out and, therefore, as inevitably troublesome. We could, for example, argue that these difficulties are one facet of the historic and continuing tension between state action and individual rights, endemic to all liberal democracies. Or we might choose to see it less as a matter of formal rights and more of acknowledging different spheres of action – the public and the private – represented by the state on the one hand and the family on the other. Or we might see the state-family tension as a manifestation of deeper divisions within the society, especially gender divisions, with state regulation of the family being one of the means through which men's control over women is reinforced.

Each of these perspectives offers important insights into why the regulation of family relationships is such a troublesome area for governments. However, none quite addresses the issue of variability. For this, I suspect that most social scientists would turn to theorising about modernism and postmodernism, associated with writers such as Giddens (1991, 1992), Beck (1992), Beck and Beck-Gernsheim (1995) and Bauman (1990, 1991, 1995). Within that body of literature the concepts of individual selves and identities are very much to the fore, with an acceptance that changes at the level of societies are intimately connected with changes in the lives and experiences of individual people. As Giddens puts it:

> Modernity radically alters the nature of day-to-day social life and affects the most personal aspects of our experience ... the transmutations introduced by modern institutions interlace in a direct way with individual life and therefore with the self. (Giddens, 1991:1)

Individuals are seen as active participants in this process, centrally engaged in 'forging their (own) self identities' (*ibid*: 2). No longer embedded in traditional structures which previously both constrained and supported our lives, we are all now free to choose even the most fundamental aspects of lifestyle, including social ties as well as identities. Biographies are 'elective', created by the individual (Beck, 1992: 128–132; Warde, 1994: 878–879).

There are implications for family relationships in these analyses. Family ties, it is argued, are no longer 'givens' as they were within traditional structures. They are much more open to individual choice and, as with other social ties, may be developed to suit particular identities and biographies. This is a natural consequence of the conditions of late modernity (Cheal, 1991: 132–150).

Whilst I find this line of reasoning extremely interesting and would want to take it seriously as a way of understanding contemporary family relationships, I would also argue that it is flawed in one important respect. It overlooks something much more fundamental about the UK in particular, namely that family life in these islands has demonstrated this highly variable character for a very long time, according to some distinguished historical work, to which I refer shortly. We did not discover variability in family relationships in the late twentieth century. We might wish to argue that the global pressures associated with late modernity have intensified it, but they certainly did not create it.

I believe, therefore, that we have to look at the distinctive features of family and kinship in the UK in order to understand the nature of its variable character. Although all governments in industrial democracies may have to cope with the consequences of late modernity, I would argue that, in the UK, the state-family relationship takes on a particular character because of the distinctive features of our cultural orientations to family and kinship. My purpose for the rest of this chapter is to map out some of those features, and to demonstrate that the difficulties which British governments face in their various attempts to regulate family relationships can only be properly understood once this dimension is introduced into the analysis.

Individualism in English kinship

My central theme here is the individualistic character of English kinship. I should make it clear that the rest of this analysis applies to England, rather than to the whole of the United Kingdom, simply because the empirical evidence upon which I shall draw – including some of my own work – relates to England specifically. I leave open the question of whether or not it would apply equally to contemporary kinship in Scotland, Wales or Ireland.

What is meant by the claim that English kinship is fundamentally individualistic? Obviously that term can be used in a variety of ways, but I am drawing here on a usage to be found in anthropological, sociological and historical research in kinship. There are a number of different strands to this individualism, of which the most important can be summed up in three descriptors: ego-focused; flexible; affective.

The idea that kinship is *ego-focused* concerns the ways in which any individual's place in a kinship universe is constructed. In anthropological terms, English kinship is bi-lateral, that is, descent is reckoned through both mother and father (if the identity of both is known). But more importantly there is no sense of a 'common ancestor', not even a weak sense, though aristocratic families may be a partial exception to this.

The importance of this feature cannot be over-stated. Its significance was demonstrated powerfully and influentially by Alan Macfarlane in his historical work on *The Origins of English Individualism* (1978). He contrasts 'ancestor centred' kinship systems, where an individual's place in a kinship universe is reckoned by tracing lineage back to a common ancestor, with 'ego centred' kinship in which each individual is the centre of his or her own kinship universe, working outwards and delineating a set of relationships which is unique to him or herself. He contrasts this with much of continental Europe, where the ancestor focus was much stronger, underpinning a peasant economy in which rights to land passed from one generation to the next. English individualism, he argues, can be traced to at least the thirteenth century:

> Within the recorded period covered by our documents, it is not possible to find a time when the Englishman did not stand alone. Symbolized and shaped by his ego-centred kinship system, he stood at the centre of his own social world. (*ibid*: 196)

This is complemented by the second feature which I have highlighted, namely *flexibility*. All the best research on kinship in the last half century has noted that there is a highly variable dimension to English kinship meaning, for example, that people who occupy the same genealogical positions may be treated differently – one brother or sister regarded as 'closer' than another, seen more frequently, more likely to be party to exchanges of mutual assistance, and so on. There is a clear choice about which kin to acknowledge actively, who will be included in one's own kinship network, and that people do exercise that choice (Firth, Hubert and Forge, 1970; Finch, 1989).

I can confirm these patterns from the work which I conducted with Jennifer Mason in the late 1980s and early 90s (1991, 1993). Marilyn Strathern, approaching it from the perspective of an anthropologist, also argues that contemporary English kinship is distinctively individualistic – a system in which individuals relate to each other on the basis of 'persons not positions'. She calls this 'the first fact of English kinship' (1992: 14). This focus on 'persons not positions' means that we tend not to relate to each other as 'mother', 'sister', 'son' in the sense of playing out a role whose normative characteristics are pre-defined. If I have more than one sister or son, then my relationship with each will be different. It is personal, not positional. Of course, it is possible to over draw this distinction. In reality, the balance between the personal and positional elements may vary within any given relationship. Moreover the degree of optionality in any relationship does vary to an extent with genealogical position, with clear evidence that there is least flexibility about relationships between parents and children (Firth, Hubert and Forge, 1970; Finch and Mason, 1993, 2000).

The third characteristic of English kinship is the importance of the *affective* dimension. This is possibly a rather clumsy word to express the simple fact that personal chemistry does matter in family life. In this kinship universe, which I have to construct for myself, and where there is a great deal of choice and flexibility, the dynamics of interpersonal relationships play an important part in defining people in or out, into the core or on the margins. This perhaps makes the process sound rather more fickle than it actually is. To understand fully how the kin universe of any adult has been constructed, we need to introduce the perspective of time. In our own work on family obligations and responsibilities, it became very clear that relationships between specific individuals are built up, and develop their particular character, over long periods of time (Finch and Mason, 1993, 2000). In that sense, each of us has our own ego-focused kin network which is a lifetime's accomplishment, a project which is reviewed and revised on a regular basis, and indeed is often built up – like geological strata – out of the materials of our key life events.

These three features – ego-focused, flexible, affective – define the character of English kinship and have important implications for government action in regulating family relationships. The core of the problem is that it is very difficult to regulate relationships which depend on persons, not positions. To legislate for 'positions' is much easier, since one can attach legal obligations to the role of 'father', 'brother' and so on. The relative absence of legal regulation of family relationships in the UK is itself a reflection of the difficulties that this presents to governments. Inheritance law is a key case here. The regulation of inheritance under English law is a very light touch, by comparison with most continental jurisdictions. The latter, operating on the basis of the civil code, specify proportions of the estate that must pass to named 'positions' within the kinship universe, with the major emphasis being on children rather than the surviving spouse. Under English – and indeed Scottish – law the situation is very much more open. This principle of testamentary freedom in both English and Scottish inheritance law could be seen as symbolising the individualistic character of the kinship system. Whilst one can debate whether either the law shapes or follows social life, at the very least it is self-evidently the case that this aspect of the law is *tolerated* in England, and in Scotland.

Managing kinship in practice

British governments are therefore faced with complex problems when they seek to regulate families, against a background in which relationships have this particularly flexible character. But just how flexible are they in practice? Is it possible to detect any underlying principles, or is there simply an infinite variety according to circumstance? Plainly there are some limits to the flexibility of family relationships, even in England. I have already mentioned the stronger normative expectations attached to parent-child relationships throughout life, though even here much variety is tolerated (Finch and Mason, 1993, 2000). There are also some limits as to who can 'count' unproblematically as close family, as people whose family life is based on gay or lesbian relationships would attest.

Beyond delineating limits of that kind, one needs to get quite close up to the detail of how families actually work to detect what one might call 'operating principles' through which relationships are constructed. They are there but they work very subtly and not entirely predictably. In order to illustrate this, I shall draw on some of my own empirical data, collected in collaboration with colleagues on a ESRC funded project on inheritance and family relationships. The project had several different elements, but here I am concentrating on data from a set of 89 in-depth interviews about how inheritance issues are handled with families in practice. The interviewees were selected on the basis that they came from 'ordinary' as opposed to wealthy families, but otherwise they covered a reasonable spread of socio-economic circumstances, including house tenure. Their ages ranged from 18–89. They all lived in England, most but not all in the north of England, at the time of the interview, but their places of origin were quite widely varied and included some from the Indian sub-continent. Thirty-two interviewees were in the study as individuals and the rest had one or more members of their own family who also was interviewed. Our largest family group in the study included eight interviewees.

I am going to focus on data about how inheritance issues are managed in the light of a history of divorce and remarriage. Forty-six people in our study had experience of this, either personally or within their own close kin group. In addition, many other interviewees talked about divorce and remarriage, sometimes on the basis of having experienced it within their wider kin group. My main purpose is to use this example to identify the underlying principles about family relationships which people try to operate in these circumstances. Divorce and remarriage provide a useful vehicle for this, because people's ingenuity is often quite stretched, making the operating principles more visible than they are in less complex circumstances.

In analysing our data about divorce and remarriage, and their impact on inheritance, it becomes clear that the dominant theme – whether from people who have had direct experience or from others – is to avoid money 'passing out of the family', as a consequence of remarriage in particular. This enables us to gain insight into how 'the family' is defined, in an operational sense.

I can develop this best by setting out in narrative form the scenario which our interviewees worry about. This is a composite narrative, built up from stories which people told about their own experiences, about the experiences of others known to them, and from comments which people make about the kinds of situations which they hope to avoid in future. The basic narrative runs like this.

Basic narrative

1. A marries B (A/B marriage)
2. They have children (A/B children)
3. The A/B marriage ends
4. A marries C (A/C marriage)
5. A dies
6. As the surviving spouse, C inherits everything from A
7. C dies
8. Property is distributed in a way which excludes A/B children

Thus A's money has 'passed out of the family'.

As a composite narrative, this is constructed out of people's hopes and fears as much as – usually more than – direct experience. But for my present purpose this does not matter. The ways in which people express their concerns give clear insight into how they think of 'the family' for inheritance purposes, whether or not the precise circumstances described ever have occurred in reality.

I have deliberately constructed this narrative as gender neutral, since women's and men's positions were treated as equivalent in these respects by our interviewees. This reflects in part the bilateral nature of English kinship, but also the fact that women and men are seen as having similar issues to face when they contemplate inheritance. Women, particularly as widows, do of course often turn out to be the ones who dispose of property to the next generation, since women have a tendency to outlive their husbands (Hamnett, Harmer and Williams 1991; Finch and Hayes 1994; Finch et al, 1996).

The first operating principle, which is visible in my narrative, is the priority given to direct descendants. Above all, 'the family' means A's own children. If there is money left by C which could be 'traced' to A's estate, then there is a strong feeling that A/B children should get some benefit. If they do not, money has passed out of the family.

However, the operating principles are by no means as simple as equating 'family' with 'children'. We can take the analysis a little further by probing the relative claims of A/B children, of C (the second spouse), of C's kin, and of any children who may be born to the second marriage. We can do this by examining variants on the basic narrative, also found quite commonly within our dataset.

Variant 1 (Begins as in basic narrative)

1. A marries B (A/B marriage)
2. They have children (A/B children)
3. The A/B marriage ends
4. A marries C (A/C marriage)
   (changes here)
5. A anticipates that he/she may die first, so writes a will which ensures that A/B children benefit.

Thus A's money has not 'passed out of the family' because A/B children eventually inherit some of it.

In Variant 1, the children of the first marriage do not inherit everything, and probably receive less than they would have, had their parent not married a second time, since parent A has taken action to protect the interests both of the children and of the second spouse. This is regarded as reasonable by our interviewees. It is indeed a specific instance of more general patterns visible in our data: there seems to be a relatively weak sense of children's absolute rights to inherit. Testamentary freedom means, among other things, that parents can choose to spend all their assets during their own lifetime, leaving nothing to bequeath to children. The general impression is that children should not feel cheated in these circumstances. They should not 'expect' to benefit, in that sense. What they can expect is that, if their parent does leave assets, they will not be excluded.

The other two variants pose scenarios which are considerably more complex. Variant 2 introduces two more sets of children into the picture, creating complex step-parent and half-sibling relationships.

Variant 2 (Begins as in basic narrative)

1. A marries B (A/B marriage)
2. They have children (A/B children)
3. The A/B marriage ends
4. A marries C (A/C marriage)
   (changes here)
5. C already has children from another marriage (C/X children)
6. A and C have children (A/C children)
7. A dies
8. As the surviving spouse, C inherits everything from A
9. C dies
10. Property is distributed between C's children (C/X and A/C)

Thus A's money has 'passed out of the family', despite the fact that some of A's children (A/C) do inherit, because others A/B do not.

One thing which these complex variants tell us about is that stepchildren may be included as part of 'the family' within which money should be kept. Provided direct descendants (in Variant 2, this means A/B children as well as A/C children) receive something, it is accepted that proportions of A's estate can legitimately go to C/X children, with whom A has no genetic relationship.

The main point is that people see it as legitimate to acknowledge step-children as part of 'the family' for inheritance purposes, depending on the circumstances. The critical factor seems to be whether the step-parent has formed a personal and warm relationship with a step-child, either in the latter's childhood or in adult life. In these circumstances, it appears to be seen as quite natural for that relationship to be acknowledged through inheritance. The essential point is that it is the type of relationship formed with the step child, not the formal link through remarriage, which counts.

The significance of this point about a personal relationship is further reinforced in Variant 3, which represents the ultimate 'horror story' about money passing out of the family.

Variant 3 (Begins as in the basic narrative)

1. A marries B (A/B marriage)
2. They have children (A/B children)
3. The A/B marriage ends
4. A marries C (A/C marriage)
5. A dies
6. As the surviving spouse, C inherits everything from A (changes here)
7. C marries D
8. C dies
9. As the surviving spouse, D inherits everything from C (which includes A's estate
10. D dies
11. D's property is distributed within his/her family

Thus not only has A's money 'passed out of the family', but it has ended up with people who had no personal knowledge of A.

The horror element is that the people who ultimately benefit *never knew* A, from whom the money originates. There is no claim based on a genetic link nor is there any personal relationship between testator and beneficiary. Though our interviewees do not necessarily assume any culpability on the part of D's family, morally they regard it as an aberration that they should inherit any of A's estate, especially if this means that A's children get nothing. In a situation where there are children who could have inherited, it is the lack of personal relationship which constitutes this as the horror story version of money 'passing out of the family'.

What does this excursion into empirical data tell us about the operating principles for determining who counts as family, in the context of English kinship? Certainly I would argue that it confirms the description, which I gave earlier, of an individualistic family structure which is ego-focused, flexible and affective. However, we can also now see that, in determining how anyone may legitimately construct his or her own kin universe, our interviewees implicitly acknowledge three operating principles.

First in determining the composition of each person's kin universe, 'family' in that sense, there may be a selection process but *the selection should be from a range* which does have boundaries. Children are almost always included. A current spouse is also automatically included, but with some conditions attached if it is a second or subsequent marriage, where the nature of the commitment to a second spouse is limited by the need to acknowledge commitments to children. Stepchildren may also be included as members of the family on the same terms as children, though they need not be. These people constitute 'the family' within which major assets should be retained, except of course for people without spouse or children.

The range from which 'family' may be selected is very tight in the case of inheritance (though it may be broader for other purposes) however, *within that range a personal choice can be exercised.* This is the second principle. Although it is accepted that a surviving spouse will be provided for (it is normally assumed that property will be jointly owned), there is no presumption that an individual has an obligation to leave anything to his or her children. All available resources can be used during her own lifetime. That is a matter of personal choice. People are free to work out their own relationships with their children during their adult lives, in ways which may or may not entail a transfer of assets. They are also free to decide how step children should be treated, relative to 'own' children and to each other. In the course of exercising this freedom, it is quite expected that the strengths and weaknesses of personal relationships – the affective element in kinship – will play a part.

The third principle is that it is understood that *definitions of 'my family' will change over time.* Since membership of a family is based on persons not positions, as each of us moves through life, the nature of our relationships changes. The core parent-child element remains relatively fixed: it is expected that children will form part of 'the family' at whatever age or point in the life course. But everything else can and does change. Spouses can change, stepchildren can appear on the scene, thus altering the shape of 'my family', possibly quite radically. The shape and character of the family alters over time precisely because it is a construction unique to each individual. This analysis is powerfully confirmed by Smart and Neale's (1999, 2001) work on families post-divorce, where they demonstrate that individuals (both adults and children) forge their family relationships out of 'fragments' across households, across generations, with both biological and non-biological ties. Family life, they argue, no longer necessarily equates to biological kin who live in the same household, but it can be as meaningful and supportive as those historically more orthodox arrangements.

Conclusion

In conclusion, I shall return to the role of the state in regulating families, and to the specific question with which I began: Why does the British state have so much trouble in its attempts to regulate family relationships?

Although it may be true that all governments have difficulties in this area, save perhaps those who preside over religiously based regimes, I have suggested that the distinctive problems for British governments stem in significant measure from the individualistic nature of family relationships for which they try to legislate. Though, as I have tried to demonstrate, there are recognisable operating principles by which each individual constructs his or her own 'family', the result is highly variable and in many ways unpredictable. This is not simply a manifestation of a universal post-modern condition, but a feature deeply embedded in English culture certainly, and quite possibly in the rest of the UK.

Against this background, in which variability and flexibility in family relationships are not only practised but also regarded as perfectly legitimate, governments are bound to have trouble if they try to legislate for *categories* of relationship (father, daughter, stepmother etc). This is to treat individuals as positions, not persons – the opposite of the way in which relationships work in practice. On the other hand, it is much more difficult to find ways of regulating relationships which are more personal than positional, in ways which are more in tune with realities.

This analysis of the fundamental features of English kinship illuminates, I believe, the difficulties which governments experience in regulating family relationships. To be more speculative, can we draw lessons about forms of regulation which are more appropriate to the British case?

First, governments should concentrate their efforts principally upon those aspects of family life where there is a clear public interest, most obviously in protecting vulnerable people. Essentially this means children, where in any case there is probably something closer to a consensus about family responsibilities than is the case for most adult relationships. In some circumstances, however, it must also include adults – most often women – who may be vulnerable to physical abuse or to economic deprivation. To go beyond that, and to try to regulate the way people relate to each other in adult life, against some presumed background of how families 'ought' to work, is to ask for trouble. The examples with which I began – policies related to divorce, and to old age and inheritance – demonstrate that.

Second, where the state does get involved in regulating relationships beyond protecting vulnerable people, the aim of policies should be to facilitate flexibility in family life, rather than to shape it into a particular form. It is a proper role for the state to ensure that people have maximum opportunity to work out their own relationships as they wish, to suit the circumstances of their own lives. It is not the proper role of governments to presume that certain outcomes would be more desirable than others.

In summary, the temptation to be directive, to use the law and social policies to engineer family life into particular form, should be resisted. In the British context, it does not suit us.

Notes

1 This chapter is based on the lecture given to inaugurate the University of Edinburgh's International Social Sciences Institute's annual theme 'Families and the State'. October 1996.
2 For a more extensive development of the author's work on inheritance see Finch and Mason (2000).

Bibliography

Bauman, Z. (1990) *Thinking Sociologically* Oxford: Blackwell.
Bauman, Z. (1991) *Modernity and Ambivalence* Cambridge: Polity Press.
Bauman, Z. (1995) *Life in Fragments* Oxford: Blackwell.
Beck, U. (1992) *The Risk Society: Towards a New Modernity* London: Sage.
Beck, U. and Beck-Gernsheim, E. (1995) *The Normal Chaos of Love* Cambridge: Polity Press.
Cheal, D. (1991) *The Family and the State of Theory* New York: Harvester Wheatsheaf.
Finch, J. (1989) *Family Obligations and Social Change* Cambridge: Polity Press.
Finch, J. and Hayes, L. (1994) Inheritance, death and the concept of the home. *Sociology* 28: 417–433.
Finch, J. and Mason, J. (1991) Obligations of kinship in contemporary Britain: is there normative agreement? *British Journal of Sociology* 42: 345–367.
Finch, J. and Mason, J. (1993) *Negotiating Family Responsibilities* London: Routledge.
Finch, J. and Mason, J. (2000) *Passing On: Kinship and Inheritance in England* London: Routledge.
Finch, J., Mason, J., Masson, J., Wallis, L. and Hayes, L. (1996) *Wills, Inheritance and Families* Oxford: Clarendon Press.
Firth, R., Hubert, J. and Forge, A. (1970) *Families and their Relatives* London: Routledge and Kegan Paul.
Giddens, A. (1991) *Modernity and Self Identity* Cambridge: Polity Press.
Giddens, A. (1992) *The Transformation of Intimacy* Cambridge: Polity Press.

Hamnett, C., Harmer, M. and Williams, P. (1991) *Safe as Houses: Housing Inheritance in Britain* London: Paul Chapman.

MacFarlane, A. (1978) *The Origins of English Individualism* Oxford: Blackwell.

Smart, C. and Neale, B. (1997) *Family Fragments?* Cambridge: Polity Press.

Smart, C., Neale, B. and Wade, A. (2001) *Changing Experience of Childhood: Families and Divorce* Cambridge: Polity Press.

Strathern, M. (1992) *After Nature: English Kinship in the Twentieth Century.* Cambridge: Cambridge University Press.

Warde, A. (1994) Consumption, identity-formation and uncertainty. *Sociology* 28: 877–898.

Royal Commission on Long Term Care (1999) *With Respect to Old Age* Cm 4192. London: Stationery Office.

2

Family Life, Moral Regulation and the State: Social Steering and the Personal Sphere

John J. Rodger

Introduction

The architects of the modern welfare state including Meidner and Rehn in Sweden, Laroque in France, Marsh in Canada, Van Rhijn in the Netherlands and Beveridge in Britain, had a vision of a society in which the collective resources of the state could be used to create a more just and humane social order (George, 1996). In Britain, Beveridge understood the welfare state project as the eradication of the five giants of idleness, want, disease, ignorance and squalor. He also believed that the instrument to accomplish that task was a welfare state which pooled risk through the principle of social insurance and channelled collective resources into the provision of free healthcare, education and affordable council housing in order to support family life. Part of the purpose behind welfare state intervention in social and family life has been to influence the choices that citizens make about their own and their children's lives. The concept which will be used to examine this notion is *social steering*, action through which a social actor or social system is moved from one position to another by the intentional decisions of a political authority. The central issue to be examined is the degree to which control of the steering process in the field of social policy, particularly that area that deals with family life, is undermined by the transfer of responsibility for welfare from the state to civil society.

The argument to be developed here is, to some extent, tentative because the movements of change upon which it rests are only just beginning to be visible. Postmodern societies are witnessing a conflict over what has been called 'life politics': the concern is about how private decisions made in the areas of sexuality, moral responsibility, family obligations and lifestyle impact on the wider public interest, especially collective welfare support. In particular, as the countries within the European Union gradually weaken their commitment to systems of state welfare and instead embrace variations on the idea of what I would call a *welfare society* (see Rodger, 2000), the capacity to affect the conditions of existence of family life will weaken. *Steering* social behaviour to ends desired by social policy planners and moral entrepreneurs (the reduction in divorce, reducing the numbers of disrupted families, reducing the numbers of teenage pregnancies (see the chapter by Selman) and the maintenance of effective child protection systems) without the incentive of accessing public resources will be problematic. All that will be left will be the power to exhort people not to engage in 'anti-social' activities. The battleground will be in what Habermas (1989) would describe as the 'distorted public sphere' as social and political interests clash over who controls the cultural instruments to secure hegemony for their *particular* moral position. Alternatively, social steering will be abandoned in favour of social and moral regulation by governments adopting an explicitly social control strategy. In the context of social policy and family life, social steering and social control designate different social and political realities. The difference may be defined by distinguishing between *persuasion* and *coercion*. In the case of the United States, specifically since the passing of the Personal Responsibility and Work Act of 1996, a welfare strategy which explicitly stresses social control has been evident from the decision of some states to withdraw optionality from what the public finances offer as welfare support. Strict eligibility rules and time limits on the receipt of welfare support are the two most common features of this approach. And, given the close intellectual affinity between British and American politicians, this could be an approach adopted in Britain, if not the rest of Europe, as the 21st century progresses, signalling the end of the traditional strategy of shaping behaviour by offering fiscal incentives and providing social services.

A note of clarification is called for at the outset of my analysis. I am interested here in a general trend evident in many welfare systems but particularly salient in North Western Europe. Discussion of 'the welfare state' in Europe, particularly among those with only a passing interest in social policy issues, often fails to differentiate between its Nordic, Anglo-Saxon and Catholic-Corporatist variations. It is not appropriate to discuss these models of welfare here. I can only acknowledge that there will be variation in the pace and direction of change in the different countries within the European Union (Glennerster, 1999). What must also be stressed is that *all* national welfare systems have been faced with the problem of how to adjust to changing patterns of family life, employment and the ageing of the population in an increasingly competitive global economy. There is some evidence that the Nordic model is more resilient than the others (see Kvist, 1999) but even in the Scandinavian countries there is a 'moral agenda' shaping debate about the distribution of responsibility for social welfare between the state, the individual and the family (see Sorensen, 1999; Millar and Warman, 1996). I will return to these models of welfare in the last section of this chapter.

The moral tone of that debate has been particularly evident in Britain where dispute about the future of the welfare state has accentuated two themes which I wish to explore. First, the argument from the right, but also detectable in New Labour social policies in Britain and the centre left throughout Europe, is that state welfare provision has had a negative influence on 'social character'. There appears to be a growing acceptance among politicians pursuing the idea of a 'third way' in politics and policy between free market liberalism and state socialism that the purpose of social policies in the 21st century will be to tackle the perverse incentives which 20th century welfare policies have bequeathed to us (see Field, 1996; Giddens, 1998; DSS, 1999). Second, there has been a trend towards reducing the role of the state as a direct provider of social care, a development which is evident in many European countries (see Tester, 1996). This change has been referred to by Ferge (1997) as the 'individualisation of the social' and appears to signal the decline of collectivist forms of solidarity as commercialism and individualism become established in the field of social policy. A descriptive way of conceptualising this change is the *privatisation of responsibility*.

Welfare and the personal sphere

The starting point for reflecting on these concerns is the critical perspective on family welfare developed by Donzelot (1980). However, the concept of the *social sphere* developed by Donzelot in his analysis of 'the policing of families' needs to be developed further. In that work, the *social sphere* emerges as an institutionalized solution to the problem of how the state can control the private sphere of family life without direct intervention: *social* services and *social* work mediate between the public and private domains to ensure that family life can be controlled without the fundamental principles of the liberal state being violated. As we move towards a *welfare society*, what Robertson (1988) calls 'a social system in which welfare assumptions are an organic part of everyday life' or, more prosaically, a society in which private initiative and commercialism rather than the state assume primary responsibility for welfare and away from a *welfare state*, an administrative entity guaranteeing access to goods and services by statutory rights, the separation between state and civil society in the field of social policy becomes more problematic. The boundaries are beginning to blur as the state divests itself of welfare obligations but retains an 'at arms' length' interest in the supervision of the welfare field: community care, family care and stakeholder welfare, where the individual is the owner of her or his own welfare capital, mean that family life and family support are now considered to be of crucial importance in the welfare equations of the future by those responsible for constructing social policy. However, regulation of behaviour by means of a social care strategy devolved to private initiatives and commercialism is problematic. Melanie Phillips, commenting on Charles Murray's views on the underclass (see Murray, 1996), appears to concede that there is only a limited role for the state and public policy with regard to the moral regulation of family life: public policy can have a 'declaratory effect' and can at best 'announce the moral standards which society thinks are desirable'. What can and cannot be altered in family life therefore requires clarification.

For analytical purposes, and to clarify the argument being developed here, a number of conceptual distinctions can be made. In particular it is helpful to differentiate between the various spheres of activity which typically are conflated in the family and welfare debate.

The state sphere

The state sphere is the source of legislative controls which underpin matrimonial law, social service regulations and laws relating to child welfare and consists of the institutional infrastructures of central and local government which organize the *social sphere*.

The social sphere

The social sphere contains those activities of counselling, advocacy and negotiation practised by credentialled welfare state professionals charged with the responsibility of delivering what Jordan (1987) calls 'the final distribution of welfare'. The social sphere is the domain of the social worker, health visitor and community health nurse. These practitioners mediate between the state and the private and personal spheres, organising care packages and advising and negotiating with people in their natural settings over their social duties and obligations within the household.

The private sphere

The private sphere of family welfare, in the particular context of this argument, relates to those activities of family life that revolve around the caring and supportive functions within the household which are performed overwhelmingly by women. This sphere is important for governments because it prevents the need for family members to draw on public resources. In the context of what Sinfield (1978) has called the social division of welfare, or the differentiation of public, fiscal and occupational welfare, this sphere of activity is a gendered addition to that triumvirate and closer to the concept of the 'sexual division of welfare' which Hilary Rose (1981) draws attention to in her re-reading of Titmuss.

The public sphere

The public sphere relates to the arena of public opinion formation and ideological conflict conceptualized by Habermas (1989). It draws our attention to the institutional mechanisms which direct and distort communication through things such as 'public relations', the mass media, political debate and the formulation and presentation of issues in public space. Debate about family life and the formulation and presentation of evidence relating to changes in family structure are, crucially, shaped by the institutions of the mass media which set agendas and generally determine *what is to be known* and *what constitutes evidence* of 'deterioration' or 'moral decline'.

The personal sphere

What I am calling *the personal sphere* relates to activities of self-identity formation and the changing moral economy of people in their everyday lives, in the context of postmodernity. Increasing interest in the self, emotions, intimacy and identity and the obsession with personal development may be threatening to undermine social solidarity by individualism and replace imperative social commitments by lifestyle choice (see Giddens, 1991; and Mestrovic, 1997). The political concern is that 'anti-social' activities, understood in the broadest sense of pursuing personal well-being at the expense of family, community or social responsibilities, may be harming children and elderly dependants by undermining the civic basis of a new welfare settlement. It is the *personal sphere* which is the real focus of the family debate.

Governments can control the *state sphere* because they control the power to enact laws. They can control the *social sphere* because they control the professional direction of social work, health visiting and community nursing. They can even control the *private sphere* of welfare activity because they control the flow of resources which underpins community care, but they cannot easily control the *personal sphere*, or what E. P. Thompson (1970) might have called 'the moral economy of the masses': sexual codes and the situational morality of intimate relationships and 'family values' are difficult to influence (see the discussion by Finch in the previous chapter). The distinction between public and private moral meanings, or between the meanings embodied in policy incentives and the perception of incentives by those at whom they are aimed, has always been evident. Family values which are reified and form part of the ideological rhetoric of the public sphere are not the same as family values that are lived. Morality, we could say, has a societal and formal dimension but also a subcultural and informal dimension and the latter is complex to understand and awkward to control.

Social policy and social behaviour

In Britain, family life became an object of interest when the 19th century philanthropists and moral entrepreneurs felt that it was imperative that the private conduct of the lower social orders should be regulated in the public interest. Public health and moral hygiene were considered at that time to be inextricably bound together. What began as charitable welfare work has ended with the expansion in the numbers of professional health and welfare practitioners licensed by the state to oversee family life in the modern welfare state (see Rodger, 1996). The concern for social and moral hygiene characteristic of the mid-Victorian period remains at the heart of the contemporary family debate. The focus today is not exclusively on working class families, although the increasing concern expressed about 'underclass families' or 'dangerous families' indicates that there remains a continuing interest in the social behaviour of those at the bottom of the social hierarchy. It is the impact of the welfare state on public finances, and what some perceive to be their perverse influence on 'social character' (see Field, 1996), which has stimulated a renewed interest in how social and family life can be subjected to social and moral regulation in the public interest.

The British welfare state has used a variety of mechanisms to shape behaviour. The two main ways of doing this have been through the direct provision of state funded services and the fiscal device known as tax expenditures (child tax allowances, mortgage interest relief, life assurance relief and pension scheme relief).

With respect to the provision of services in the British context, it has been noticeable in recent years that the state has been changing gradually from being a direct provider of social welfare to being an 'enabling authority'. At best this has meant funding and supervising at 'arms' length' quasi-autonomous non-governmental bodies (quangos), but at its worst it has meant the abrogation of responsibility for the provision of welfare services which have been devolved to commercial, voluntary or informal supply. With this alteration in the role of the welfare state, a process of re-negotiation has begun between the state and the citizenry over the limits of collective welfare obligations. The assumptions being made about social behaviour and individual responsibility are changing and the expectation grows that individuals and communities will do more for themselves, while the state does less. In the area of community care the informal support of family and neighbours is increasingly factored in when decisions are being made about the appropriate mix of welfare services to be provided for groups such as elderly people and disabled people in the community. In the British context, the New Labour government has embarked on a reform of the social security system and is exploring ways of devolving responsibility for pensions through the idea of stakeholding in which the individual becomes the owner of her own welfare capital. Social housing has, perhaps, undergone the most radical transformation from being a state provided resource to being either a market or voluntary association commodity. However, the increasing stress on community participation, individual reliance and voluntarism to be found in the succession of annual reports on welfare from the Labour government since 1997 indicates that the traditional conception of the relationship between social policy and social behaviour may be changing (see DSS, 1999).

Tax expenditures have been described as 'public revenue losses which result from tax provisions which give special reliefs to various categories of taxpayer' (Wilkinson, 1986: 23). Of course, the concept of the state treating the non-collection of taxation as a form of welfare is a controversial issue. Nevertheless the sphere of fiscal welfare has been one of the most explicit means used by the welfare state to *steer* people to act in ways considered desirable by the policy makers. However, the *steering control* afforded by these fiscal devices has been unpredictable.

They are uncontrollable and erratic because they are determined by the actions of millions of individuals; they may not lead to the behaviour originally intended and politically they are difficult to withdraw once they have become established. The over consumption of housing in Britain is partly explained by a classic form of tax expenditure, mortgage interest tax relief. The drawn out process of withdrawing mortgage interest tax relief in Britain is a good example of the political and market difficulties which tax expenditures can create for governments (see Hogwood, 1989). Without the instruments of government conventionally associated with welfare systems found in Western Europe since 1945, state *managed* welfare benefits, state funded geriatric and personal social services, social housing, fiscal incentives to marry and support children, *steering power* will be lost and influence on family life may be less responsive to those seeking to shape or alter it.

In order to understand why there is this renewed interest in the moral regulation of family life, we must acknowledge that the 'male-breadwinner/female carer' model of family underlying West European welfare systems fits uneasily with a social reality of rising divorce, lone parenthood, cohabitation, a declining interest in marriage and the rise in female participation in the labour market. During the full employment era from the late 1940s to the early 1970s, male workers made relatively small claims on the welfare state during the active phase of their working life. However, this has given way to large ongoing claims as full employment has been replaced by cyclical phases of mass unemployment and the decline, in particular, of the unskilled and semi-skilled industrial jobs which in the past employed men. Long-term and frequent unemployment among male industrial workers between the ages of 16 and 65 has had an impact on how the welfare state operates. The 'standard worker family' has gone and, as Esping-Andersen (1996) has observed, so too have the assumed 'full-time, lengthy and unbroken male careers' in industrial manufacturing upon which the concept of the *social wage* was largely based.

Accompanying these structural changes in male employment is the reality that patterns of family living are changing rapidly. Increasing numbers of women are no longer full-time carers: their brief and early entry into the labour market followed by permanent exit to manage the household, bear and rear children and care for elderly relatives has also gone. Women now seek work (the economic activity rate of women aged 16–59 in 1998 was 72 per cent according to Labour Market Trends, March 1999 quoted in Family Policy Study Centre, 1999), they also demand compensation for unemployment and today make claims on the welfare state to protect themselves and their children to a far greater extent than was even envisaged as recently as the early 1980s. For example, the financial costs to the welfare state of supporting divorced and re-ordered families has contributed to the expansion of the welfare budget, with the expenditure going to lone parents rising from £2.2 billion in 1981/82 to £9.9 billion 1997/98 (Social Trends, 29, ONS 1999 quoted in Family Policy Study Centre, 1999). Under the strain of meeting escalating demands on the welfare state in a global context of rapidly changing labour markets and family structures, there has been an increasing reliance on means tested benefits and a decline in the importance attached to the work based social insurance principle. However, Field (1996) has argued that the growth of means tested benefits is harmful to social character because they penalize working harder by taking account of income, discourage saving by taking account of savings and encourage dishonesty by asking questions about personal means. The growth of means testing also has tended to fix people in what are called 'poverty' and 'unemployment' traps, making employment financially unattractive for those who experience either their welfare benefits tapering off as they begin to earn, or that their welfare income is equal to that which could be earned from low paid employment. This results in a fear among policy makers and opinion-formers in government that the 'standard worker family' of the past is becoming the 'welfare dependent family' of today.

As the social policy planners cannot rely on the model of 'the standard worker family', some have argued for measures, both fiscal and moral, to encourage and support its return (see Morgan, 1995 and 1997; Phillips, 1997). For example, a number of commentators on contemporary social policy have suggested that many women prefer to exist as lone parents rather than seek long term relationships with unemployed and unemployable men considered to be 'bad prospects'. It is argued that the welfare state, as it is currently constituted, encourages lone parenthood and irresponsible male behaviour by providing the wrong incentives (see Fukuyama, 1997; Dennis, 1997; Dennis and Erdos, 1992; Phillips, 1999). Phillips (1999), for example, wants social policy to be re-directed towards privileging marriage and supporting the traditional family. In *The Sex-Change Society,* she asserts that men and women are equal but different and that women have a key child raising role to perform while men have an invaluable breadwinning role to fulfil which constructs and consolidates their male identity by civilising them and locking them into family units. Through policies designed to get welfare dependent lone mothers back to work, she argues that the state has become both a surrogate father, supporting fatherless families, and a surrogate mother by paying for and, in some instances, providing child care. While Phillips insists she is not opposed to women's right to work, she is displeased that social policies appear to discourage women from fully embracing their 'natural' maternal role. This type of argument represents what Smart (1997) has referred to as 'wishful thinking' in which it is hoped that the family can be 'returned to an idealized state'. Increasingly in family policy the underlying objective is to re-stabilize family life: 'there is a dominant inferential framework into which policy is inscribed, and this is the idea of *getting back* to a specific family form' (Smart, 1997: 303). The main dilemma for the opinion-formers and social policy planners within the state, who see family life deteriorating and not simply changing, is that the *steering power* afforded by social and public policy is always problematic: the right incentives and disincentives to behave in ways regarded as appropriate by the moral entrepreneurs in politics and the media are always difficult to judge. The real issue for polemicists on the family (such as Dennis, 1997; Murray, 1996; Morgan, 1995 & 1997; and Phillips, 1999) is, in any case, to change the mores and moral relativism of contemporary society which, they claim, have encouraged a drift into incivility in general and family deterioration in particular.

Postmodernity and the welfare state

In the areas of service provision and tax expenditures, therefore, the welfare state in Britain, and elsewhere in Europe, is shifting responsibility for social care and welfare security to individuals, families and communities. This process of transferring responsibilities from the state to civil society has been described by the term 'the hollowing out of the state' and is understood as an integral part of the movement from a Fordist to a post-Fordist welfare system. It is not appropriate here to discuss this change in detail. In general, it refers to the decline of the Keynesian welfare state founded on universal social security which some political economists argue was functionally related to the era of mass production and mass consumption Fordism (see Jessop, 2002). The economic and political rigidities associated with the Keynesian welfare state and the Fordist economy have given rise to a new welfare regime characterized by the marginalisation of the principle of universalism in welfare benefits and the marketisation of state social care services (see Burrows and Loader, 1994; Carter, 1998). It is the implications of the movement to a post-Fordist welfare state that are of interest here.

The general response to the problems and contradictions of the Fordist welfare state has been to explore alternative ways of delivering welfare beyond the state. Increasingly, theorists of the welfare state are convinced that we are moving inexorably towards a new welfare model and the postmodern paradigm is gaining credibility as a description of this emerging welfare system (see Ferge, 1997; Burrows & Loader, 1994; Esping-Andersen, 1996; Leonard, 1997; Rodger, 2000). Ferge (1997) has described the central features of this shift:

- A stress is placed on individual responsibility for the purchase of private and freely chosen welfare products rather than reliance on collective welfare solutions (stakeholder welfare).
- Families and family boundaries are increasingly acknowledged as setting the limits to which social responsibility need extend.
- There is a declining interest in social integration, social inequality and the pooling of risks with other members of society: the retention of more earned income is preferred by those in secure employment to yielding taxes to what is increasingly portrayed as an inherently 'profligate tax spending state'.
- Negative civil and political rights which guarantee 'freedoms of choice' are preferred to positive rights which secure access to resources and services underwritten by the state.
- The commercial, voluntary and informal sectors of care become the main social policy instruments supervized by an 'at arms' length' posture by government and the state.
- State welfare is only for the 'truly needy' and based on principles of workfare rather than welfare.

There is, therefore, a greater stress being placed on private responsibilities and self-reliance. Individualism in postmodern societies derives from numerous sources and is generally considered to be endemic. As Giddens (1998) observes 'individualism, in short, is associated with the retreat of tradition and custom from our lives' (Giddens, 1998: 36) and while he may be sanguine about this social change, and generally rejects the view that we are increasingly living in a 'me-first' society, there must be concerns about the relationship between growing individualism and the decline of social solidarity in post-welfare societies (see Rodger, 2003). In the field of social policy, the emphasis being placed on the individual and the family taking responsibility for their own welfare needs may be creating the conditions for 'amoral familism' (Banfield, 1958).

Amoral familism leads to individual and family interests being maximized at the expense of public and community projects. Although originally developed in the context of analysing 'backward societies' it may be relevant today in post-industrial and postmodern societies dominated by markets and the cash nexus. Whatever its causes, individualism leads to lifestyle choices which are often 'anti-social' in that people pursue their personal well-being and interests before those of family, community or society (see Rodger, 2000). An example of amoral familism, and one which is of particular concern to the architects of community care policies, is that of 'granny dumping': a variety of elder abuse which may, in some circumstances, lead to actions such as the abandonment of an elderly relative in a public place in order to avoid the financial and emotional responsibility of caring for them. Having radically reduced state funding in the field of elder care, the policy makers within the state will discover how difficult it is to *steer* social behaviour towards the self-reliance and family obligations desired by the new welfare settlement. In addition, family and community solidarity may be undermined by policies which preach self-reliance and family responsibility without first putting in place the supportive material and service infrastructure to ensure that the goal of community rather than state care can be achieved.

The policy response of affluent countries to the growing individualism has been to begin a process of redefining social citizenship in active rather than passive terms. Evidence for this can be found in Europe and the English speaking world where a new policy context is being constructed based on the concept of *the active society*. The concept of the 'active society' being promoted by the OECD, for example, seeks to transcend passive welfarist assumptions founded on the maintenance of large populations of non-workers outside the labour market by encouraging social policies which make participation in the labour market the norm: active labour market policies and workfare strategies, particularly relating to lone parents who have been welfare dependent for long periods, define this idea (see Walters, 1997; Kildal, 1999; Kerr and Savelsberg, 1999). Working for one's welfare benefits, either through labouring or undertaking skills training, becomes a requirement, therefore, rather than an option for those unwilling to enter the labour market cheaply. Citizenship access to welfare based on social rights characteristic of the traditional Nordic, Catholic-Corporatist and Anglo-Saxon models of welfare, should, the

OECD suggests, be replaced by a stress on 'employmentship' access to security purchased by the individual. Rather than lifelong state guarantees of access to collectively funded resources, what is now being offered is a lifetime guarantee of an opportunity to acquire marketable skills in an increasingly competitive global economy. It is individuals who will be responsible for their social security, rather than the state, in this emerging policy design. This approach to social policy means that passive and compensatory policies which allow long-term dependency on welfare benefits will no longer be considered morally appropriate or economically prudent.

The interesting paradox emerging is that the greater the stress on individualism, in particular the attempt to re-interpret *social citizenship* in terms of the citizen's contribution to society rather than as a 'status' to which welfare rights are attached, the greater the likelihood that the state will have to act coercively, even in matters of family life and parental responsibility, whenever social and economic behaviour is not compliant. The emerging family discourse from the right has become increasingly strident and marked by a vocabulary which talks of *responsibilities* and *obligations* rather than social rights, a view which has gained the ascendancy on the centre left as well. The Labour Government elected in 1997, for example, has been active in promoting the notion of parental responsibility and has embraced policy measures which *strongly encourage* lone parents into the labour market, borrowing directly from the coercive policies being pioneered in the United States which explicitly require work for welfare benefits (see Ellison, 1997; Brivati and Bale, 1997). And the strategy of welfare 'activeness' is increasingly being replaced by welfare 'coercion' in the context of the management of *deviant* families. For example, the targeting of 'anti-social families' in the Crime and Disorder Act 1998, and the taking-over of the main principles of Frank Fields private members Housing (Withholding of Payment) Bill by the Government in proposed legislation to deal further with 'problem families', signals a fundamental departure from a strategy of *social steering* in an era of post-welfarism. Stepney, Lynch and Jordan (1999) suggest that the New Deal policy in Britain will lead to coercion because a 'simplistic and moralistic view of poverty and social exclusion' imported from the USA in the 1980s is influencing contemporary left of centre policies today. This view was reinforced by the evidence from the pilot studies designed to test the 'new deal' to coax lone parents back to work and off welfare benefit were disappointing: *Hansard Written Answers* 16 June 1998 indicated that in the pilot scheme of the 40,000 lone parents in the government's target group only 1678, or 8 per cent, found work. Such a poor outcome from a major policy initiative may in time stimulate a more coercive approach. In Britain fiscal inducements are being offered to low paid working families through the *Working Families Tax Credit,* and other changes to the tax system, but the Labour government's real concern is with the non-working family. The claim is that:

> A proactive welfare system is at the heart of tackling worklessness. Our ambition is to deliver *a change of culture among benefit claimants*, employers and public servants, with rights and responsibilities on all sides. Those making the shift from welfare to work are being provided with positive assistance, not just a benefit payment. (DSS, 1999, chapter 4. *My emphasis*)

The moral agenda signposted by this proactive approach is to focus increasingly on how welfare objectives can be realized with the state acting not as a direct provider of services or, indeed, as a distributor of tax expenditures, but instead as a facilitator of 'partnerships' between private and voluntary groups. That effort is increasingly geared towards changing the attitudes and behaviour of those who governments perceive are drawing most on state welfare resources. The Labour government's annual report *Opportunity for All* (DSS, 1999) provides many examples of local initiatives seeking to tackle the problem of disrupted families and teenage pregnancies by using educative rather than material resources. Indeed Daly (1999) reports that the government's strategy to tackle the high numbers of teenage pregnancies in Britain is actually to threaten to withdraw resources, in particular children's services grants, unless social services departments can demonstrate how they are addressing the issue of teenage pregnancies in their plans. However commendable the many educative projects may be, the official discourse which talks about national campaigns, 'joined-up action', prevention and support, is unclear about how 'arms' length government' can *steer* behaviour towards approved goals (DSS, 1999), or, indeed, deliver a 'change of culture among benefit claimants'.

Social steering or moral regulation?

The problem faced by all European governments in the future will be how to ensure that informal care will be provided in a world of disrupted and re-ordered families, where caring obligations are less clear than they were in the comparatively low divorce era prior to the 1970s

(Finch, 1989). If the state is to shed its responsibility for personal social services in a new 21st century welfare settlement then it seems increasingly likely that it will attempt this through strategies which seek to educate and change behaviour rather than spend public funds. In the area of family life and social policy the absence of concrete resources to alleviate the vast problem of child poverty has not lessened the volumes of research and theory devoted to the explanation of social disadvantage, educational underachievement and the fragility of life as a lone parent, increasingly by searching for answers in behaviourism rather than political economy. Indeed, relatively small amounts of money in government terms, such as the £2 million given by the Labour government to establish a *National Family and Parenting Institute*, give the appearance of action when in reality little is being done to tackle entrenched social problems. And even where there is recognition of the magnitude of a problem such as child poverty, the time scale adopted to bring about significant change is unambitious: the Labour Government are estimating a period of twenty years before the problem is effectively eradicated in Britain partly because redistributive social policies are not being contemplated (see DSS, 1999).

In July 1999, Alistair Darling, the then Secretary of State for Social Security in the UK Labour Government, was widely reported as arguing that 'ministers have a moral duty to reshape the welfare system' and that the 'modernisation' of the welfare state entails helping people to help themselves (Frean and Watson, 1999). However, if the problems underlying the welfare state are fundamentally about changing behaviour, culture and attitudes, how is this to be achieved? In a world where the imperative to 'reconstruct' welfare systems has increasingly meant discouraging demands on the state, the departure from direct service provision has left the drivers of state policy with fewer steering levers. Commercial and voluntary organisations have taken a devolved responsibility for welfare work with families from the state, especially regarding the caring work with elderly people. With the emergence of a contract culture, these organisations supply and arrange care for a price (see Lewis, 1993; Whelan, 1996; Nicholls, 1997). This trend epitomizes the shifting of responsibility for welfare from the state to civil society and it is because of the development of the 'arms' length supervision' accompanying the contract culture that the issue of the state's *social steering* power is now problematic. The dilemma is not only that decision-making power about how resources should be allocated increasingly lies with non-elected quangos and trustees, but also that the nature of the contracts agreed between the state and the commercial and voluntary sector may permit control over the direction and character of service provision to deviate markedly from that ideally desired by politicians and the public. Rummery and Glendenning (1999), for example, describe the situation in the UK as a move from 'universal access to NHS services to discretionary access to residual local authority services'. As indicated earlier in reference to the signs of 'amoral familism' in contemporary society, by forcing families to carry the financial and emotional burden of caring by reducing quality state provision, family obligations can be tested in ways not predicted by the policy architects in government. The contract culture is a policy instrument which makes *social steering* a more imprecise process than ever.

Schenkluhn with Webber (1988), for example, have developed a number of useful distinctions in a comparative study of health systems which can inform our broader interest in the concept of *social steering*. In terms of the models of welfare identified earlier, they focus attention on the contrasting features of *steering* power within the Catholic-Corporatist welfare regimes of Switzerland, Germany and Italy. They introduce the notion of *steering deficit* to conceptualize the margin of slippage between what was intended and what was achievable in health policy objectives. In key areas of service delivery it was discovered that there was comparatively less of a *steering deficit* in Italy compared with Germany and Switzerland because of the greater central political steering afforded by Italy's state health system. The power of medics and the private insurance industry in Switzerland and Germany meant that, in general, policies geared to controlling expenditure and directing health care services towards policy goals were more difficult to achieve. Devolved and decentralized policy systems are more likely to create *steering deficits* because the principle on which they tend to operate is predicated on *self steering*. Contracts carelessly, or indeed cleverly, constructed can maximize the power of *self steering*. In a similar vein, the personal sphere of social and family life presents an interesting policy problem because it too is premised on a principle of individual freedom, of *self steering*, but today it constitutes a pre-eminent concern of policy actors seeking to control and direct the reform of the welfare state. The personal sphere of family life presents, we could say, a major *steering deficit* for contemporary governments.

In the light of these policy issues, the notion of *social steering*, which I am suggesting may be developing in OECD countries, is becoming increasingly complex in a context of growing social individualism. With respect to the Nordic model of welfare, specifically the Swedish welfare state, Therborn (1990) has contributed to a better understanding of that complexity through his examination of the best remaining example of a democratic socialist welfare system geared to collective provision. *Social steering* in the Swedish welfare system has been accepted more readily perhaps than in other systems. Its main objective has been to direct the strivings of the population towards policy goals considered desirable by policy planners and/or moral entrepreneurs seeking to build a solidaristic and humane social order in accordance with democratic socialist goals. However, *social steering* as a form of social engineering in the welfare state has typically treated non-state actors as 'targets' whose behaviour is to be changed by putting in place a battery of benefits and incentives to encourage them to change their behaviour. This appears to have been the case in Sweden. There has been an arrogance associated with this type of social administration, which Therborn criticizes. Populations become subjected to the exercise of invasive surveillance and control by the collation of data which is used to determine how best to bring about their movement towards the policy planner's goals. Steering tends to be a constant process in which the ignorance of the target population is remedied by the dissemination of public information combined with constraints and incentives of a service and fiscal nature to channel its actions along routes designed to meet the principal goals. The notion that there should be feedback from the people being subjected to this process is laudable and is at the heart of Therborn's attempt to sketch an outline in which the macropolitics of welfare state planning and the microsociology of family and community living can be related in a more democratic and accountable way. As Gould (1988) has observed, social control and welfare have been very closely allied in Swedish welfare history, especially in the field of child welfare and family deviance. Indeed, it is because Therborn appears to be committed to Swedish state welfare and aware of these totalitarian tendencies that he attempts to set out a more accountable framework for public policy.

In advancing his analysis, Therborn distinguishes between four aspects of welfare state action. *Social administration* points to the realm of benefits and the efficient economic management of the welfare bureaucracy to better serve the social needs of the population; *social education* involves the varieties of actions initiated by the state in the fields of health promotion and social care; *social reform* is understood as the focus of the political contest surrounding the scope of welfare and in particular the principles and ideologies which shape its rules of eligibility and entitlement. These aspects of welfare states have only limited functions to perform regarding steering power. *Social steering*, however, is an aspect of welfare state action which Therborn considers 'reaches furthest into people's lives'. In the context of the Swedish welfare state in the early 1990s, what Therborn has in mind by *social steering* is the state's attempt to improve the living conditions of households by using the instruments of social policy in the fields of work, social services, housing and leisure. This does not fit well with current developments in the structure of what I have referred to as the Anglo-Saxon model of welfare. Locating Therborn's conceptual distinctions within the spheres of action which I have outlined above, social administration can be located within what I have called the *state sphere*, because it articulates that range of activities connected with social service regulation, management and finance; social reform can be placed within my notion of the *public sphere* because it is in essence the end product of the policy process which is grounded in partisan politics; and social education logically belongs within the *social sphere* because it is ultimately concerned with what Therborn has called those 'exhortatory efforts by public bodies, with regard to hygiene, the use of tobacco, alcohol and narcotics, sexual behaviour with a view to the risks of AIDS and venereal disease' (Therborn, 1990: 375). I have in mind here the activities of health promotion and community health specialists rather than the partisan and ideologically grounded discourses which might find expression in the 'distorted public sphere'. *Social steering* in Therborn's perspective is about households not intimate family relationships and so does not naturally fall into what I have called the *personal sphere*, despite his claim that it reaches furthest into people's lives. His mode of thinking in the context of the Swedish welfare system conceptualizes social steering in terms of resource allocation and wealth redistribution. However, today a postmodern welfare strategy, typified by the notion of *the individualisation of the social* (Ferge, 1997), is no longer about surveying the population in order to better prepare social services to meet their needs but rather about educating, regulating and dampening down popular aspirations to accommodate the population to a new welfare settlement based on individual responsibility and an *active* rather than *passive* concept of citizenship. In short, Therborn does not distinguish social steering from moral regulation, because even in 1990 it was not clear which way welfare politics was moving in a social democratic welfare system existing outside the European Union and yet to experience the full force of a competitive global economy, but this is precisely what needs to be done if the contemporary relationship between social policy and family life within the OECD countries is to be understood. The demise of the 'standard worker family' has so distorted the way welfare systems now actually work that the boundaries between what Therborn calls social administration, social education, social reform and social steering in the Anglo-Saxon and Catholic-Corporatist models of welfare have blurred and the membrane which now binds them together, or perhaps overlays them all, is moral regulation. There is also evidence emerging, since Therborn's original research at the beginning of the 1990s ,that the Nordic model too may be succumbing to a more explicitly moral guidance in its social policy (Sundstrom and Tortosa, 1999). In a context where escalating welfare expenditure is positively feared by governments everywhere, a simpler way to put this is that *social steering* is no longer about effecting the conditions of existence of family life and more to do with altering or changing the *moral* conditions of social behaviour, but without the incentives of collective goods and benefits. It is ideas rather than resources which increasingly appear to be the main thrust of state activities connected with *social steering*: so called moral arguments channelled through community projects for better parenting, supporting individual responsibility for the care of dependent elders and children and encouragement to uphold marriage are not offered so much as supplements to augment state programmes to improve family life but largely instead of resources. The perplexing question is, of course, how can states shape social behaviour and expectations if their *steering power* lacks material resources to distribute or redistribute? If responsibility is privatized and contracted out to volunteers and informal care, how can the 'final distribution of welfare' be ensured: how can we ensure that people care and assist each other and refrain from actions which harm themselves and others? (see Jordan, 1987). What now appears to be at the top of social policy agendas is the tackling of problems without dedicating tax resources to the task. With respect to family life, social exclusion and inclusion, parenting deficits and risk management among 'dangerous families' are some of the projects currently being given priority in various guises throughout the OECD countries. The emerging international hegemony for what has been called the 'the third way', reconciling economic liberalism with notions of social justice and moral duty, appears increasingly to demonize those living at the taxpayers' expense (see Jordan, 1998). Workfare and family mutuality are the themes driving policy.

Some brief indicators of policy effort can be used to illustrate an increasing trend. The Green Paper *Supporting Families* (Home Office, 1998) points to a number of policy trends in the UK: the creation of social mentors for children without a parent or parents; enhancing the role of health visitors to include marriage advice and parenting education; creating a new role for Registrars, effectively making them 'secular vicars' to both advise on the seriousness of marriage and conduct civil naming ceremonies for children. The Teenage Pregnancy Unit within the Social Exclusion Unit has appointed local coordinators to monitor teenage pregnancy rates and prepare educative and publicity initiatives to address the issue (see the chapter by Selman, Arai, 2003). The publication of a booklet *Your Children Matter* (The Scottish Office, 1998) details advice to parents on their responsibilities: on how to talk to and relate to their children. And in Australia, the House of Representatives Standing Committee on Legal and Constitutional Affairs published a report in April 1998 *To Have and to Hold: Strategies to Strengthen Marriage and Relationships* which concerns itself with relationship and family skills education (Bayley, 1998). Its intention is to stimulate action to counter the rising divorce rate and its consequences for the problem of child and household poverty. In the area of social work with families, the strategy is increasingly to engage in what Parton (1998) has called 'risk management' with those families deemed to be 'dangerous' or vulnerable (see Rodger, 1996). In a financial climate of limited resources, and driven by the slippage into managerialism by the social work bureaucracies, it is the social work task to assess risk and to ensure that preventative and supportive services can be provided within budgets. And the growth of the family centre concept ensures that surveillance of 'dangerous' families can be accomplished at minimum cost (Cannan, 1992).

Conclusion

It is appropriate to end an analysis by pointing towards ways in which it can be deepened and extended. It is becoming clear that the focus on 'governance' as opposed to 'government' in contemporary social and political theory is a broad recognition that the issues raised here about *social steering* are of pre-eminent contemporary concern. Stoker (1998) suggests that governance 'is ultimately concerned with creating the conditions for ordered rule and collective action'. Indeed much of the contemporary literature on governance seems to discuss the notion in terms of the 'functional' adjustment of the capitalist state to the new global economic context: the move from the Keynesian National Welfare State to the Schumpetarian International Workfare State (see Jessop, 2002). The argument that is elaborated by Jessop and others is that the relationship between the state and the institutions of civil society is becoming functionally realigned to meet the challenges of a new international social and economic order. The new configuration of power requires the state to look upwards and outwards to international institutions while also devolving power downwards to non-state institutions (see Rhodes, 1997; Pierre, 2000). Governance in the welfare context is, therefore, about replacing hierarchy, centralized political authority and central policy direction with devolved power, dispersed centres of political authority and centres of decision making. It could be suggested that it seeks to resolve difficult problems through the redistribution of administrative responsibilities rather than economic resources; precisely the strategy adopted to deal with family problems (DSS, 1999). The questions raised by this chapter are what are the limits of governance? How does the state and society control the private sphere where social, moral and sexual choices are made by individuals responding to their situational circumstances? What happens when *social steering* no longer works effectively? Eitzen and Baca Zinn (2000), pointing to welfare developments in America, have outlined what happens to families and children when welfare legislation abandons *social steering* in favour of coercion. The removal of the welfare safety net in the United States has meant that the very problems that the American welfare legislation introduced by the Clinton administration in 1996 was designed to address are made worse: teenage pregnancies have increased, child poverty remains high and the correlation between poverty, divorce and the decline of marriage is reinforced. Recent legislative initiatives in the British Parliament to withhold housing benefit from 'anti-social families' (Frank Field's Housing Benefit (Withholding of Payment) Bill, Hansard, July 2002) suggest that, perhaps, the Americans are showing us our welfare future. Moral regulation may become a central goal of future welfare legislation.

Behaviour, especially in the area of 'life politics', has become a major focus for public and ideological debate. The greater the sense of powerlessness governments experience regarding the control of lifestyle choices, and the more persistently social and political interests seek to connect social and sexual behaviour to material outcomes, especially in the field of state welfare, the more likely it is that family policy will be reduced to a political football in what is bound to become a 'distorted *public sphere*': the blurring of the boundaries between social control and social policy will become evident and family policy will be replaced, increasingly, by legislation aimed at behaviour modification.

Bibliography

Arai, L. (2003) 'British Policy on Teenage Preganancy and Childbearing', *Critical Social Policy* 23, 1:89–102.

Banfield, E. (1958) *The Moral Basis of a Backward Society* New York: The Free Press.

Bayley, R. (1998) 'Supporting Marriage the Australian Way', *Family Policy: Bulletin of Family Policy Studies Centre* Autumn.

Brivati, B. and Bale, T. (1997) eds. *New Labour in Power: Precedents and Prospects* London: Routledge.

Burrows, R. and Loader, B. (1994) eds. *Towards a Post-Fordist Welfare State?* London: Routledge.

Cannan, C. (1992) *Changing Families Changing Welfare: Family Centres and the Welfare State* London: Harvester Wheatsheaf.

Carter, J. (1998) *Postmodernity and the Fragmentation of Welfare* London: Routledge.

Daly, N. (1999) 'The Politics of the Big Stick', *Community Care*, No. 1278: 14.

Dennis, N. (1997) *The Invention of Permanent Poverty* London: Institute of Economic Affairs.

Dennis, N. and Erdos, G. (1992) *Families Without Fatherhood* London: Institute of Economic Affairs.

Donzelot, J. (1980) *The Policing of Families* London: Hutchinson.

DSS (1999) *Opportunity for All: Tackling Poverty and Social Exclusion* Cm4445 London: The Stationary Office.

Eitzen, D. S. and Zinn, M. B. (2000) 'The Missing Safety Net and Families: A Progressive Critique of the New Welfare Legislation', *Journal of Sociology and Social Welfare* 27, 1: 53–72.

Ellison, N. (1997) 'From Welfare State to Post-Welfare Society?' in B. Brivati and T. Bale eds., *New Labour in Power: Precedents and Prospects* London: Routledge.

Esping-Andersen, G. (1996) ed. *Welfare States in Transition* Cambridge: Polity.

Etzioni, A. (1993) *The Spirit of Community* New York: Simon and Schuster.

Family Policy Studies Centre (1999) 'Family Policy Index' *Family Policy: Bulletin of Family Policy Studies Centre* Autumn.

Ferge, S. (1997) 'The Changed Welfare Paradigm: The Individualisation of the Social', *Social Policy & Administration* 31: 20–44.

Field, F. (1996) *Stakeholder Welfare* London: Institute of Economic Affairs.

Finch, J. (1989) *Family Obligation and Social Change* Cambridge: Polity.

Frean, A. and Watson, R. (1999) 'Darling Claims Welfare to be a Moral Crusade', *The Times* 19 July.

Fukuyama, F. (1997) *The End of Order* London: Social Market Foundation.

George, V. (1996) 'The Future of the Welfare State' in V. George and P. Taylor-Gooby eds., *European Welfare Policy: Squaring the Welfare Circle.* Basingstoke: Macmillan.

Giddens, A. (1991) *Modernity and Self Identity* Cambridge: Polity.

Giddens, A. (1998) *The Third Way* Cambridge: Polity.

Glennester, H. (1999) 'Which Welfare States Are Most Likely to Survive?' *International Journal of Social Welfare* 8 1: 2–13.

Gould, A. (1988) *Conflict and Control in Welfare Policy: The Swedish Experience* London: Longman.

Habermas, J. (1989) *The Structural Transformation of the Public Sphere* Cambridge: Polity.

Hogwood, B. (1989) 'The Hidden Face of Public Expenditure', *Policy and Politics* 17 2: 111–130.

Home Office (1998) *Supporting Families: A Consultation Document* London: The Stationary Office.

Jessop, B. (2002) *The Future of the Capitalist State*. Cambridge: Polity.

Jordan, B. (1987) 'Counselling, Advocacy and Negotiation', *British Journal of Social Work* 17: 135–146.

Jordan, B. (1998) *The New Politics of Welfare* London: Sage.

Kerr, L. and Savelsberg, H. (1999) 'Unemployment and Civic Responsibility in Australia', *Critical Social Policy* 2: 233–256.

Kildal, N. (1999) 'Justification of Workfare: The Norwegian Case', *Critical Social Policy* 3: 353–370.

Kvist, J. (1999) 'Welfare Reform in the Nordic Countries in the 1990s', *Journal of European Social Policy* 3: 231–252.

Leonard, P. (1997) *Postmodern Welfare* London: Sage.

Lewis, J. (1993) 'Developing the Mixed Economy of Care', *Journal of Social Policy,* 22: 173–192.

Mestrovic, S. (1997) *Postemotional Society* London: Sage.

Millar, J. and Warman, A. (1996) *Family Obligations in Europe* London: Family Policy Studies Centre.

Morgan, P. (1995) *Farewell to the Family* London: Institute of Economic Affairs.

Morgan, P. (1996) *Who Needs Parents?* London: Institute of Economic Affairs.

Murray, C. (1996) *Charles Murray and the Underclass: the developing debate* London: Institute of Economic Affairs.

Nicholls, V. (1997) 'Contracting and the Voluntary Sector: A Critique of the Impact of Markets on Mind Organisations', *Critical Social Policy* 17 2: 101–114.

Parton, N. (1998) 'Risk, Advanced Liberalism and Child Welfare: the Need to Rediscover Uncertainty and Ambiguity', *British Journal of Social Work,* 28: 5–27.

Phillips, M. (1999) *The Sex-Change Society: Feminised Britain and the Neutered Male* London: Social Market Foundation.

Pierre, J. (2000) *Debating Governance: Authority, Steering and Democracy* Oxford: Oxford University Press.

Rhodes, R. (1997) *Understanding Governance: Policy Networks, Governance, Reflexivity and Accountability* Buckingham: Open University Press.

Robertson, A. (1988) 'Welfare State and Welfare Society', *Social Policy and Administration* 22: 222–234.

Rodger, J. (1996) *Family Life and Social Control: A Sociological Perspective* Basingstoke: Macmillan.

Rodger, J. (2000) *From a Welfare State to a Welfare Society: The Changing Context of Social Policy in a Postmodern Era* Basingstoke: Macmillan.

Rodger, J. (2003) 'Social Solidarity, Welfare and Post-Emotionalism', *Journal of Social Policy* 32 (3): 403–421.

Rose, H. (1981) 'Re-reading Titmuss: the Sexual Division of Welfare', *Journal of Social Policy* 10: 477–501.

Rummery, K. and Glendenning, C. (1999) 'Negotiating Needs, Access and Gatekeeping: Developments in Health and Community Care Policies in the UK and the Rights of Disabled and Older Citizens', *Critical Social Policy* 19 3: 335–352.

Schenkluhn, B. with Webber, D. (1988) 'Steering the Health Sector in Switzerland, West Germany and Italy', Paper prepared for workshop on 'Guidance, Control and Co-ordination in the Public Sector' ECPR joint sessions, University of Bologna/Rimini, Italy.

Scottish Office (1998) *Your Children Matter* Edinburgh: The Stationary Office.

Sinfield, A. (1978) 'Analyses in the Social Division of Welfare' *Journal of Social Policy* 7: 129–156.

Sorensen, A. (1998) 'On Kings, Pietism and Rent-Seeking in Scandinavian Welfare States' *Acta Sociologica* 41: 363–375.

Smart, C. (1997) 'Wishful Thinking and Harmful Tinkering? Sociological Reflections on Family Policy' *Journal of Social Policy* 26 3: 301–321.

Stepney, P., Lynch, R. and Jordan, B. (1999) 'Poverty, Exclusion and New Labour', *Critical Social Policy* 19 1: 109–127.

Stoker, G. (1998) 'Governance as Theory: Five Propositions', *International Social Science Journal* 50: 17–28.

Sundstrom, G. and Tortosa, M. A. (1999) 'The Effects of Rationing Home-Help Services in Spain and Sweden: A Comparative Analysis', *Ageing and Society* 19: 343–361.

Tester, S. (1996) *Community Care for Older People: A Comparative Perspective* London: Macmillan.

Therborn, G. (1990) 'Social Steering and Household Strategies: the Macropolitics and the Microsociology of Welfare States', *Journal of Public Policy* 9: 371–397.

Thompson, E. P. (1970) 'The Moral Economy of the English Crowd in the Eighteenth Century', *Past and Present* 50.

Walters, W. (1997) 'The Active Society: New Designs for Social Policy', *Policy and Politics* 25: 221–234.

Whelan, R. (1996) *The Corrosion of Charity: From Moral Renewal to Contract Culture* London: Institute of Economic Affairs.

Wilkinson, M. (1986) 'Tax Expenditure and Public Expenditure in the UK', *Journal of Social Policy* 1: 23–49.

3
Family Breakdown, Individualism and the Issue of the Relationship between Family Law and Behaviour in Post-War Britain

Jane Lewis

The family became a major political issue in the UK during the 1990s as policy makers began to recognize the rapid pace of family change. In the space of a generation the numbers marrying have halved, the numbers divorcing trebled and the proportion of children born outside marriage quadrupled (Scott, Braun and Alwin, 1998). Declining marriage and increased childbearing outside marriage are inextricably linked to the growth of cohabitation, and increases in divorce, cohabitation and extra-marital childbearing have all contributed to the separation of marriage and parenthood. Between 1970 and 1990, the percentage of lone mother families more than doubled. Indeed, it is tempting to write of the 'rise and decline of marriage' in the twentieth century, with marriage becoming virtually universal in the immediate post-war decades and seemingly becoming much less popular in the closing years of the century. Such judgements may be premature, but it is the broad trends associated with the decline of marriage and rise of cohabitation that have promoted the *fin de siecle* anxiety about marriage and the family, now continuing into the twenty-first century.

Pessimism about the family has permeated both political and academic commentary over the last decade, in contrast to the optimistic assessments of the late 1960s and early 1970s (e.g. Fletcher, 1966). In the 1980s, British researchers followed Americans in providing evidence of the detrimental impact of divorce on the educational achievement, employment and personal relationships of children and young adults (e.g. Richards and Dyson, 1982; Maclean and Wadsworth, 1988; Kiernan, 1992). It has been generally agreed that behaviour has become more individualistic. Policy makers clearly expressed their fear of increasing individualism during the 1990s, which they automatically assumed to be selfish and the natural antithesis of inter-dependence (Smart and Neale, 1997). During the course of the debates over the 1996 Family Law Act, Baroness Young expressed the view that 'for one party simple to decide to go off with another person ... reflects the growing self-first disease which is debasing our society' (Hansard, Lords, 29/2/96). This kind of assumption about the nature of the impulse behind the changes in behaviour in respect of the family has not gone unquestioned, for example Giddens (1992) has accepted the idea of growing individualism but has interpreted it as a more democratic development. However, for politicians, men's failure to maintain, on the one hand, together with women's increased economic autonomy, on the other, have been sufficient to inspire concern about the fate of the traditional, male breadwinner family, rather than optimism about its transformation. This has led to questions being asked about the role that family law might play in promoting family change.

This chapter reviews ideas about the nature of the relationship between English law and behaviour (the position in Scotland is different), prior to examining the trends in family law. It is argued that the major reform of family law in the 1960s did play a significant role in legitimizing a trend towards greater individualism in intimate relationships. The story since divorce law reform in 1969 has broadly been one of an attempt to separate the treatment of men and women as husbands and wives, which has become increasingly individualized, from their position as fathers and mothers, which has increasingly emphasized the importance of parental responsibility. However, it is argued that such a separation is not easy to achieve. The broad trend in family law represents an attempt to come to terms with rapid family change, but ambivalence remains as to whether to recognize the profound changes in the marriage system, or to try and put the clock back.

The relationship between law and behaviour

The anxiety about the role played by family law in respect of relationship breakdown is similar to that about the effect of the public law of social security and the increase in female employment on family structure: that is, it is feared that it has permitted certain kinds of behaviour and thus promoted family breakdown. This view has been argued particularly strongly in the case of social policies by American academics and polemicists, who have charged that these have exacerbated women's move towards individualism and away from 'familialism' (e.g. Murray, 1985; Popenoe, 1988). However, both American and British research has effectively demolished the argument that there is a causal relationship between social provision and family change (Garfinkel and McLanahan, 1986; Ellwood and Bane, 1985; Bane and Jargowsky, 1988; Bane and Ellwood, 1994; Ford, Marsh and Mackay, 1995). State benefits and access to social housing might *facilitate* the formation of lone mother families, but they do not cause it. The possibility of being able to achieve autonomous living via wages or benefits is crucial, but is unlikely to be the only or even the decisive factor influencing behaviour.

The Parliamentary Debate over the Family Law Act in the mid-1990s showed that similar fears about the role of family law exist in Britain. Baroness Young argued for the retention of fault in the law of divorce because she believed that 'law influences behaviour and it sends out a very clear message. There would be no point in legislating at all if law did not influence behaviour' (Hansard, Lords 29/2/96, c. 1638). In her speech, Baroness Young began with a discussion of values and the growth of an individualism that she believed to be selfish – the 'self-first disease'(*ibid.*) – and went on to posit a causal connection between law and behaviour.

However, the evidence from social science is complicated in this regard. Most have put more emphasis on variables other than legal change when seeking explanations of the rising divorce rate. Rheinstein's (1972) comparative socio-legal study argued that marital breakdown could be high even in the absence of divorce. In his comparative historical study of divorce, Phillips (1988) also insisted that levels of marital breakdown have not been dependent on legal change. Rheinstein called attention to the importance of the 'cultural climate', arguing that the incidence of marital breakdown increased in times of accelerating social change 'with the unsettling tendencies towards anomie' (p. 311). It is possible to see parallels between this line of argument and the idea of individualism as a primary cause of breakdown. Burgoyne, Ormerod and Richards (1987) concluded rather that economic variables, such as increased female labour market participation; demographic variables, such as young marriage, premarital pregnancy; and individual characteristics, such as emotional immaturity, were more important than legal change. However, as Gottman (1994) has pointed out, demonstrating a strong association between any of these variables and a high divorce rate does not expose the marital processes that lead to dissolution. For example, an increase in women's employment may be understood very differently at different points in time and in different countries, and may therefore also be expected to have different effects on intimate relationships.

In respect of family law, most ink has been spilt on the effects of the liberalization of divorce law which took place in most western countries towards the end of the 1960s and in the early 1970s. In their cross-national study of divorce, Castles and Flood (1993) concluded that the presence or absence of liberal divorce law reform was the most important variable explaining differences in divorce rates between 1976 and 1983. However, the debate over the effects of the introduction of no-fault divorce has been fierce. Peters' (1986) investigation of divorce in the United States found that the rate was not significantly different in unilateral (that is pure no-fault) as opposed to mutual consent states, whereas Nakonezny et al (1995) came to the opposite conclusion. In Britain, Haskey (1996) has concluded that the divorce legislation of 1969 and 1984 allowed a number of people who had previously been unable to obtain divorce to petition successfully for it, with the result that there was an immediate, but one-off, surge in divorces. Beyond this, the argument that the movement towards no-fault divorce caused a rise in the divorce rate is subject to the same objections rehearsed by those looking at a longer time period.

However, the introduction of no-fault divorce (which in the British case was of course partial in 1969[1]) has been blamed for a increase in opportunistic behaviour on the part of men especially in the US (Cohen, 1987), because of the way in which it permits easier exit from a marriage (Hirschman, 1986). Weitzman's (1985) research in California highlighted how much men gained financially on divorce under the new rules, and women and children lost. This proved extremely influential in policy terms, encouraging governments on both sides of the Atlantic to pursue absent fathers for maintenance. Peters' (1986) American research, which did not find any significant effect of no-fault legislation on divorce rates, nevertheless concluded that women received lower settlements in unilateral states. Again, this research has not gone unquestioned (Jacob, 1992). Weitzman's own figures were substantially modified by Duncan and Hoffman (1985), although a series of studies in Britain documented the very real extent of poverty among lone mothers (Eekelaar and Maclean, 1986; Bradshaw and Millar, 1991). However, it is unclear as to how far the position of women and children was worsened by the introduction of no-fault divorce. They had rarely fared well under the old divorce law and Singer's (1989) Californian research showed that the percentage of women getting alimony actually increased under the no-fault legislation.

All this raises in broad terms how far people take the state of the law into consideration before they act, even if the extent to which there is a direct relationship between law and behaviour is a matter of some debate. Mnookin (1979) argued that in the case of divorce, couples bargain in 'the shadow of the law'. This idea captured both the notion of the greater private ordering of divorce that accompanied the introduction of no-fault, and the extent to which law continued to provide the framework within which couples negotiate. However, Baker and Emry's (1993) research among applicants for marriage licences and law students showed the extent of ignorance that prevailed about the law even in these groups, and on the basis of a limited qualitative study (96 interviews) Jacob (1992) suggested that the influence of social networks was much more important than that of lawyers. He concluded that the shadow of the law was dim indeed. However, the ways in which the law affects behaviour may be more complicated. Richards (1982) showed that fathers tended not to ask for the custody of their children because they thought that the state of the law was such that they were unlikely to be successful. While a simple causal relationship between law and family change is as difficult to establish as that between the latter and changes in women's employment or in the availability of state benefits, it is just as likely that the law *facilitates* and, additionally, *legitimates* particular kinds of behaviour.

Certainly, the 1956 Royal Commission on divorce feared that relaxing the divorce law would result in an increase of what it called 'divorce mindedness'. This idea was rejected by Rowntree (1964) on the basis of her survey of 300 men and women in 1959–60. She found no evidence that the idea of divorce as the obvious solution to marital disharmony was spreading from generation to generation. However, Chester (1971) argued strongly that there was evidence of a new value-orientation towards various aspects of personal behaviour, including divorce. Phillips (1988, p. 617) also concluded that 'it seems probable that divorce does breed divorce', because divorce becomes part of the cultural climate within which marriages exist which allows the stigma once associated with divorce to disappear. In many respects, fault-based divorce had already been converted into consensual divorce via the practice of collusion prior to legal reform at the end of the 1960s (Rheinstein, 1972; Glendon, 1976). Nevertheless, the abolition of fault made it socially more acceptable to divorce. As Weitzman (1985) observed, when the rules change about what is expected of husbands and wives on divorce, so new norms for marriage are created. It is law that plays a major part in establishing these new norms, and, as recent research has demonstrated, cultural variables are particularly important to a full understanding of family change (Oppenheim, Mason and Jensen, 1995).

The importance of law in setting the socially acceptable standards for behaviour is immediately apparent in other areas. For example, while the direct effect of equal opportunities legislation on pay differentials between men and women is a matter of considerable debate, there is little doubt that the legislation has made it more difficult to admit to 'a taste for discrimination'. There may also be a feedback loop to consider in terms of motivation. Le Grand (1997) has suggested that policies designed to treat public employees as if they operate entirely as rational economic actors, responding to financial incentives and disincentives, may only succeed in increasing their self-seeking behaviour. In intimate relationships, Cohen (1987) and Posner (1992) have suggested that in so far as no-fault divorce fails to elicit proper compensation from men who behave badly, it feeds such behaviour.

The liberalization of the divorce law in 1969 was symptomatic of a major shift in thinking about the extent to which law could or should impose certain standards of behaviour in intimate relationships. The importance of this shift is widely accepted. In the US, Schneider (1985) has traced the move away from a universalist moral discourse towards the idea that every case is different. He has identified the engines of the shift as changing moral beliefs with an increased tolerance for pluralism, the rise of a psychological view of personal affairs, and the increased emphasis on individual rights. In Britain, churchmen and politicians reformulated ideas about morality in the 1960s such that they were used by others to justify more radical, hedonistic and individualistic behaviour, while they themselves became advocates of further relaxation of the divorce laws. The search was for a higher morality from within to replace the traditional moral code imposed from without. Thus, most influentially, the Bishop of Woolwich advocated a position 'based on love', whereby nothing could be labelled as 'wrong' – not divorce, nor premarital sex – unless it lacked love (Robinson, 1963). It was the spread of this profound shift in thinking that made possible the move from a conservative position on divorce, reiterated in evidence to the 1956 Royal Commission, to one that favoured reform by the late 1960s.

There is a strong case for arguing that this shift in the moral underpinnings of family law played a major part in legitimating a more individualist approach to the moral dimensions of intimate relationships. Posner (1992), a confirmed disciple of neo-classical economic theory, has allowed that moral theories of sexuality represent the only serious challenge to economic theories. In the end, he rejects the case for their influence on behaviour, but he does not explore their important role in changing mentalities. As the demographers Lesthaeghe and Surkym (1988, p. 13) have observed: 'without institutional assertion more latitude is given to individual morality and diversifications of the moral code are at the heart of pluralist societies'. It can be argued that putting more of the responsibility for moral choice on the individual results either in more moral earnestness (this is the position of Bauman, 1993, 1995) or in more self-seeking behaviour. Gibson (1996) argued strongly for the latter in his survey of contemporary divorce patterns, when he commented: 'Hedonism has become a legitimate pursuit within a free enterprise society structured on market forces and materialism' (p. 33). No matter the precise nature of the effect, it seems likely that in regard to changing mentalities, if not behaviour, the liberalization of family law in the late 1960s led rather than followed popular opinion. But, this does not necessarily mean that legal change was instrumental in bringing about the more individualistic approach to the moral dilemmas of personal relationships. That may owe just as much, for example, to the rise of 'psychologic man' (Schneider, 1985), or what Bellah et al (1985) termed the 'therapeutic relationship'.

Nevertheless, the change in the nature of law played a significant role in legitimising the trend. In the US, Thornton's (1989) review of opinion polls from the late 1950s to the late 1980s showed that there had been a significant decline in acceptance of normative imperatives about marriage, divorce and childbearing. In Britain too there has been a liberalization in gender-role attitudes during the 1980s and 1990s, although the pace of change has been slower and less consistent than in the USA or Germany (Scott, Alwin and Braun, 1996).

Towards self-determining adults and responsible parents[2]

The trend in terms of the way in which family law has actually treated men and women as husbands and wives had been towards increasing individualization, with increased amounts of remedial action to shore up their responsibilities as parents. Indeed, the move towards no-fault divorce has been widely characterized as a part of a process of 'deregulating' family law. Glendon's (1981) thesis on deregulation has been the most influential. She argued that while 'the legal ties among family members are becoming loosened, the web of relationships that bind an individual to his job (and his job to him) is becoming tighter and more highly structured' (p. 1).

However, Glendon's analysis of deregulation in the private sphere and more regulation in the public world of work and welfare no longer looks convincing in the twenty-first century. In regard to the public sphere, the restructuring of welfare states, such that the mixed economy of welfare has shifted firmly towards market principles and a greater emphasis on private provision, means that the certainties Glendon ascribed to the public sphere have in large part disappeared. The flexible labour markets of the 1990s with their short-term contracts and part-time hours, and the diminishing role played by social insurance in the provision of unemployment benefits and pensions have resulted in considerable uncertainty. In regard to the private sphere, even when Glendon wrote, to characterize the legal changes that resulted from rethinking their moral underpinnings as a process of deregulation was somewhat problematic. Certainly, as Davis and Murch (1988, p. 13) have observed, after 1969 the interest of the state in the reasons for ending a marriage receded to 'vanishing point'. The absence of fault made it impossible to allocate blame and then, as matter of course to award long-term financial support to 'innocent' female spouses (Smart, 1984). However, in neither the USA nor the UK was it intended that the state should abnegate responsibility for ensuring the welfare of children and their carers.

Reform of family law meant that the state ceased to regulate the dissolution of marriage and concentrated on adjustment between the parties (Eekelaar, 1978). Under a no-fault regime, a marriage without children was effectively terminable at will. The import of the process of liberalization since 1969, culminating in the 1996 Family Law Act, has been to let men and women as husbands and wives order their own affairs, in other words to assume the existence of a degree of individualization, while also putting in place measures that seek to regulate them as fathers and mothers. The problem is that it has been difficult to make a neat separation between these two sets of roles, not least because of the need of children for caretakers and the tendency for women to perform more of this (unpaid) work. The trend towards increasing individualization is also reflected in the recent legislation on 'pension-splitting' on divorce.

When the Archbishop of Canterbury was asked in 1956 about the moral principles underlying justifiable divorce by the members of the Royal Commission on the subject he said:

'I think one would say that the moral principle is that in each ground for divorce there is a frustration of one or more of the purposes of marriage. The purposes of marriage are the procreation of children, natural relations and the comfort that one ought to have of the other. Adultery breaks the union of man and wife. Desertion deprives him of the partner, one of the purposes of marriage. Cruelty frustrates one of them, also insanity, and sodomy and bestiality. I think you could say, could you not, that all frustrate one or more of the purposes of marriage'. (Royal Commission on Marriage and Divorce, 1956, p. 155)

But once the idea of love as the true moral basis of marriage had become paramount, then only the couple could determine the state of their marriage and the purpose of marriage became the welfare of the couple. In her account of divorce law liberalization in the US, Hill Kay (1987) pointed out that initially no-fault divorce law reform was seen as progressive. The idea that divorcing couples should be treated in exactly the same way, thereby ignoring the different nature of their contributions to the marriage and the inequalities resulting from women's greater investment in childbearing and rearing, came later in both the United States and in Britain. Indeed, the separation of the roles of husband and wife, who were presumed equal, from that of mother and father was never as complete in Britain, although the 1984 Matrimonial and Family Proceedings Act took a substantial step further down this road. The reformed law of divorce tended towards treating husbands and wives as equal members of a partnership. This ignored the substantive inequalities that meant *both* that the view of the more powerful party as to the desirability of continuing the relationship might prevail, and that the outcomes for the economically weaker women and children were likely to be poor. Glendon (1981, p. 82) commented that in retrospect, it seemed that the partnership ideologies underpinning much of modern divorce law 'have served the comforting function of appearing to be in control of a constantly deteriorating situation'. In fact, the idea of partnership in which the parties had been assumed to make equal but different contributions, became one whereby it was assumed that both parties were equal.

As is well known, the 1969 Divorce Act in Britain was a compromise (Winnett, 1968). Marital breakdown became the sole ground for divorce, but divorcing couples persisted in using the more traditional grounds of unreasonable behaviour and adultery rather than separation in order to secure a quicker divorce. There was strong opposition to the legislation in Parliament, on the grounds that no-fault divorce without consent after five years of separation would open up the possibility for opportunistic behaviour on the part of men which would prove particularly damaging for women in traditional marriages (House of Lords, 30/6/69, c. 308–11). The position of children *per se* raised little comment. The Law Commission (Cmnd. 3123, 1966, p. 49) reflected the prevailing view of the time when it commented that it was the quarrels preceding divorce that did the harm and the final break would 'lessen the bitterness' and 'facilitate the establishment of a new stable environment which is the child's greatest need'. As Cretney (1996) has remarked, it is unlikely that the 1969 legislation would have passed if Parliament had known that the 'Special Procedure', which obviated the need for a court appearance , would be introduced in 1973 for childless couples and extended to all undefended cases in 1977.

The Lord Chancellor promised to deal with the financial consequences of divorce for women and children (Davis, Cretney and Collins, 1994), and the 1970 Matrimonial Proceedings and Property Act required the court to have regard to all the circumstances of the case and to place the parties in the position that they would have been in had divorce not taken place. Had this been possible to implement, it would have addressed the problem of male opportunistic behaviour and the adverse financial outcomes for women and children. However, in practice solicitors and the courts often faced the problem of the demands of the husband's second family and took a pragmatic, needs-based approach to the division of assets, an approach that has persisted despite changes in the law (Jackson et al, 1993). Increasingly, the courts took into consideration the part that might be played in supporting women and children by public law in the form of social security provision. As Ingleby (1988, p. 49) commented, in a welfare state the role of public law was part and parcel of bargaining 'in the shadow of the law'.

Reliance on social security to provide an income for divorced women caring for children became explicit after the 1984 Matrimonial and Family Procedings Act (Davis, Cretney and Collins, 1994), which moved further in the direction of separating the position of the divorcing adults as husbands and wives from their position as parents (see also the next chapter by Clarke). The attempt to leave the parties to the divorce in the same position as they would have been in had the marriage not broken down, which arguably involved some notion of compensation for women as unpaid carers, was abandoned. In the debates leading up to the 1984 legislation, no mention was made of the problem of securing the economic well-being of women and children after divorce (Eekelaar, 1991). The aim for the adults was to promote a 'clean break' and to facilitate remarriage (Alcock, 1984). This entailed the assumption that men and women could be independent (Douglas, 1990), which translated into the assumption that both could support themselves in the labour market (Maclean, 1991). Smart and Neale (1997) have commented on the way in which this legislation in fact assumed that marriages had become more individualistic. However, in fact the legislation endeavoured to put the child welfare principle first. Primary consideration was to be given to the children 'of the marriage'. Nevertheless, Maclean and Eekelaar (1986) have commented on the extent to which the debate around the 1984 legislation proceeded without much reference to children. In the House of Commons, the Attorney General expressed the hope that if priority was given to children it was more likely that absent fathers would contribute to their maintenance (Hansard, Commons, 16/2/84, c. 397). But, given the social reality in which men tend to support the family they currently live with, this provision served only to make the courts' recognition of the role of social security in supporting the first family explicit.

As O'Donovan (1993) has observed, the focus in the 1980s was above all on adults as the 'consumers' of divorce. The Law Commission (HC 479, 1988, para. 2.22) referred to the need to make the divorce process more consumer-friendly. But at the same time, academic research was beginning to sound the alarm about the effects of divorce on children, which was also noted by the Law Commission (*ibid.*, para. 3.27). The result was a renewed effort to regulate the roles of men and women as fathers and mothers, focusing particularly on fathers. Academics and government documents stated a preference for joint custody arrangements (Richards and Dyson, 1982; Mitchell, 1985; LCD, 1985). The 1987 Family Law Reform Act enabled an unmarried father to apply for a parental rights order, characterized by sceptical commentators as an effort to attach a father to every child (Deech, 1980). It may be argued that this trend was in line with public opinion in so far as this was represented by vociferous fathers' pressure groups (e.g. Families Need Fathers, founded in 1974). Beck and Beck Gernsheim (1995) have suggested that the greater individualism that has accompanied high divorce rates has also resulted in a greater desire for attachment, and that this has focused on children. However, as Smart and Neale (1997) have pointed out, men's desire for contact with children has seemingly been confined to the point of family breakdown; there is little evidence of significantly changed patterns of fathering within marriage. The hope on the part of policy makers was that more contact would result in more child support being paid (Brophy, 1985, p. 238). In the case of unmarried fathers, as Deech (1993) has observed, this showed an over-optimistic belief in the stability of cohabiting relationships.

Finally, the 1989 Children Act sought to promote 'parental responsibility', which contained the double meaning of responsibility towards children on the one hand, and a preference for parental responsibility over state responsibility on the other. Eekelaar (1991) has convincingly traced the way in which the second of these came to predominate. In 1991 the Child Support Act reinforced the financial responsibility of fathers for all their biological children. By the end of the 1980s research had shown clearly that very few women and children received regular maintenance payments from absent fathers, and for those who did, the amounts paid were low (Maclean and Eekelaar, 1986; Bradshaw and Millar, 1991). Having liberalized the law dealing with adult relationships, some attempt had to be made to deal with the problems posed by the care and support of children. But as Smart (1991) and Brophy (1985) have pointed out, the definition of what constitutes child welfare has changed dramatically over time, crudely, from the need of the child for its mother to its need for its father, which may say as much about the struggles between adults as about children *per se*. The child support principle that was articulated in 1991 rested squarely on biological parenthood.

However, it was not easy to deal with children separately from their carers. As Cretney (1996) and Fineman (1993) have commented, there has been a complete absence of principles regarding the maintenance of spouses, and yet the care of children depends in large measure on the welfare and support of their carers. No-fault divorce removed the link between the grounds for divorce and maintenance without substituting any alternative principle to justify the latter. The child support formula implemented by the 1991 legislation contained an element of support for the child's carer, but as a result of the furious opposition by men and their second families to the Act, this was singled out for forceful attack and the formula was modified in 1994 and again in 1995. Given the recent research findings that men (much more than women) feel that obligations to their children depend on social circumstance and connection (Maclean and Eekelaar, 1997), it is not surprising that the 1991 legislation has been modified to take account of this.

The relaxation of the divorce law took place in western liberal democracies which felt that it was neither possible nor desirable to regulate the marriage system such that men's right to remarry and further to reproduce was curtailed. This made it supremely difficult to enforce the responsibilities of men in relation to their biological children, and by extension, those children's carers. Social security law had long recognized this problem. As early as 1953, the National Assistance Board had commented in its Annual Report that 'extracting money from husbands to maintain wives from whom they are separated is at best an uncertain business; it is easier to enforce the maintenance of those with whom the man is living than of those from whom he is parted and the man is more likely to exert himself to maintain the former' (Cmd. 9210, 1954, pp. 18–19). In the case of divorced couples, once the grounds for divorce were separated from the ancillary issues of support for spouses and children, it became very difficult to legislate on the basis on biology.

The attempt to continue to liberalize family law in respect of adults while prioritising children also characterized the proposal finally to introduce full no-fault divorce in the mid-1990s. The initial justification for what became the 1996 Family Law Act was that the use of fault bred conflict and 'ritualized hostility', which was unlikely to foster the post-divorce contact necessary to ensure the welfare of children. Thus the Law Commission (HC 479, 1988; HC 636, 1990) recommended that divorce be treated more as a process and that a 'consideration and reflection' model be employed. The welfare of children was tied to proposals further to liberalize divorce by making it more amicable, but without addressing the central tensions around the division of unpaid work and resources that bedevilled the issue of providing care and support for children. In fact, in 1999 the Labour Government decided not to implement the part of the Family Law Act dealing with divorce. Policy makers remain favourably disposed to mediation, but research findings on this issue have been mixed (Greatbach and Dingwall, 1989, 1997; Walker et al, 1994). Piper (1993, p. 201) has argued that mediation buttresses the 'uneasy masking' of the different gendered meanings of responsibility.

Conclusion

The model underpinning the developments in family law since the beginning of the move towards no-fault divorce has assumed that men and women can be treated the same and, as in the 1996 legislation, that they are able and willing to engage in face-to-face communication and negotiation (Walker and Hornick, 1996). This model of marriage assumes that husbands and wives are able to take responsibility for sorting out their own difficulties. To this extent, the legislation assumes husbands and wives to be fully 'individualized'. However, there is little evidence that this is the case. The family sociology of the 1970s assumed that relationships were becoming more 'symmetrical' (Young and Willmott, 1973), but sociologists in the 1980s documented in detail the unequal division of both resources (e.g. Pahl, 1989) and labour in families. In respect of the latter, Gershuny et al's (1994) longitudinal data showed an increase in men's participation in domestic work over the period 1975–87, but from a very low base. Men do relatively more domestic work in dual-earner households, but mainly because women do less. If earnings are a source of power, then women do not seem to have used them as a bargaining counter. Thompson and Walker (1989) concluded that this is because gender is in fact the key independent variable; the meaning of paid and unpaid work is different for men and for women. Qualitative research has suggested that a majority of couples manage to reconcile gender inequalities by pretending that their relationships are more equal than they are (Backett, 1982; Hochschild, 1990). As Jamieson (1998) has observed, there is little empirical evidence to suggest that relationships are much more egalitarian and, on an optimistic interpretation, more open and democratic, or, on a pessimistic interpretation, more selfish.

Family law has increasingly privatized the affairs of divorcing couples in their capacity as husbands and wives, and the 1996 legislation anticipates that they will take responsibility for issues that arise from their position as parents as well, with the child support legislation acting as a backstop in respect of maintenance. But this mitigates against the achievement of social justice between men and women in the family, which Okin (1989) has argued to be a socially important goal. The consequences of failure to achieve it have been extensively documented in respect of female and child poverty. While both the extent of their poverty and the role of no-fault divorce in causing it have been questioned, the fact that women and children do worse after marriage breakdown than men has not. It is therefore debatable as to how far the adult relationship of men and women as husbands and wives can be separated from their position as parents. It may not be possible to square the desire to treat adult relationships in a gender neutral, egalitarian fashion on the one hand, with the desire to provide properly for children on the other.

As it is, recent legislation effectively assumes that the traditional family responsibilities of men and women will endure when their relationships do not (Hale, 1998), which is in and of itself at odds with assumptions regarding their greater equality in marriage. In a very real sense, law makers have resisted abandoning support for marriage. Indeed, the Parliamentary debates during the passage of the Family Law Act were noteworthy for the way in which 'marriage-saving' was insisted upon as an aim of the legislation. The New Labour Government promoted the support of 'families' rather than 'the family' in its 1998 Consultative Paper (Home Office, 1998), but also declared that marital relationships provide the best form of support for children. This attempt to acknowledge the new and yet not to abandon the old is both understandable and perhaps inevitable. Moreover, it is far from clear that moving to a purely contractual model in respect of intimate relationships, such as (American) feminists argued for during the 1980s (Weitzman, 1981; Schultz, 1982), would be an improvement. It again runs the risk of treating men and women the same, when their relationship to paid and unpaid work is patently different. It may be that the limitations of family law to tread the tightrope between making inappropriate assumptions about the social reality in terms of an imagined equality between men and women, and making assumptions that act to reinforce dependency relationships within families must be more explicitly recognized. The reality of dependency relationships (Fineman, 1993, 1994, 1995) demands collective as well as individual support of children, something that was increasingly neglected in Britain during the 1980s and 1990s.

Notes

1 The 1969 legislation made marital breakdown the sole ground for divorce, but breakdown had to be established by reference to one of five 'facts': adultery, unreasonable behaviour, two years' desertion, two years' separation if both parties agreed, or five years' separation if one party did not. A majority of divorcing couples continued to use evidence of fault, that is adultery or unreasonable behaviour, as the proof of marital breakdown in order to get a quick divorce.

2 A longer discussion of these issues can be found in Lewis (2001).

Bibliography

Alcock, P. (1984) Remuneration or Remarriage? The Matrimonial and Family Proceedings Act, 1984. *Journal of Law and Society* 11: 357–66.

Backett, K. C. (1982) *Mothers and Fathers. A Study of the Development and Negotiation of Parental Behaviour* London: Macmillan.

Baker, L. A. and Emry, R. E. (1993) When every Relationship is above Average. Perceptions and Expectations of Divorce at the Time of Marriage. *Law and Human Behavior* 17: 439–50.

Bane, J. and Ellwood, D. (1994) *Welfare Realities from Rhetoric to Reform* Cambridge, Mass: Harvard University Press.

Bane, J. and Jargowsky, P. A. (1988) The Links between Government Policy and Family Structure: What Matters and What Doesn't. In A. Cherlin ed., *The Changing American Family and Public Policy* Washington DC: Urban Institute Press.

Bauman, Z. (1993) *Postmodern Ethics* Oxford: Blackwell.

Bauman, Z. (1993) *Life in Fragments* Oxford: Blackwell.

Beck, U. and Beck Gernsheim, E. (1995) *The Normal Chaos of Love* Cambridge: Polity Press.

Bellah, R., Madsen, R., Sullivan, W., Swidler, A. and Tipton, S. M. (1985) *Habits of the Heart. Middle America Observed* Berkley: University of California Press.

Bradshaw, J. and Millar, J. (1991). *Lone Parent Families in the UK* Department of Social Security Research Report No. 6. London: HMSO.

Brophy, B. (1985) *Law State and the Family: The Politics of Child Custody*, unpublished PhD. Thesis, University of Sheffield.

Burgoyne, J., Ormrod, R. and Richards, M. P. M. (1987) *Divorce Matters* Harmondworth: Penguin.

Castles, F. G. and Flood, M. (1993) Why Divorce Rates Differ: Law, Religion, Belief and Modernity. In F. G. Castles ed. *Families of Nations. Patterns of Public Policy in Western Democracies* Aldershot: Dartmouth.

Chester, R. (1971) Contemporary Trends in the Stability of English Marriage. *Journal of Biosocial Science* 3: 389–402.

Cmd. 9210, Ministry of National Insurance (1954) *Report of the National Assistance Board for the Year ended December 1953* London: HMSO.

Cmnd. 3123 (1966) *Reform of the Grounds of Divorce. The Field of Choice* London: HMSO.

Cohen, L. (1987) Marriage, Divorce and Quasi-Rents; or 'I gave him the best years of my life'. *Journal of Legal Studies* XVI: 267–304.

Cretney, S. (1996) Divorce Reform in England: Humbug and Hypocrisy or a Smooth Transition? In M. Freeman ed. *Divorce where Next?* Aldershot: Dartmouth.

Davis, G., Cretney, S. and Collins, J. (1994) *Simple Quarrels* Oxford: Clarendon.

Davis, G. and Murch, M. (1988) *Grounds of Divorce* Oxford: Clarendon Press.

Deech, R. (1980) The Case against Legal Recognition of Cohabitation. In J. M. Eekelaar and S. N. Katz eds. *Marriage and Cohabitation in Contemporary Societies.* Toronto: Butterworths.

Deech, R. (1993) The Rights of Fathers: Social and Biological Concepts of Parenthood. In J. Eekelaar and P. Sarcevic eds. *Parenthood in Modern Society. Legal and Social Issues for the 21st Century.* Dordrecht: Martinus Nijhoff Pubs.

Douglas, G. (1990) Family Law under the Thatcher Government. *Journal of Law and Society* 17: 411–26.

Duncan, G. J. and Hoffman, S. D. (1985) A Reconsideration of the Economic Consequences of Marital Dissolution *Demography* 22: 485–97.

Eekelaar, J. (1978) *Family Law and Social Policy* London: Weidenfeld and Nicolson.

Eekelaar, J. (1991) *Regulating Divorce* Oxford: Clarendon.

Eekelaar, J. and Maclean, M. (1986) *Maintenance after Divorce* Oxford: Clarendon.

Ellwood, D. and Bane, M. J. (1985) The Impact of AFDC on Family Structure and Living Arrangements. In R. G. Ehrenberg ed. *Research in Labor Economics VII.* Grennwich, Conn: JAI Press.

Fineman, M. A. (1993) Our Sacred Institution: The Ideal of the Family in American Law and Society. *Utah Law Review* 766:387–405.

Fineman, M. A. (1994) The End of Family Law? Intimacy in the Twenty-First Century. In S. Ingber ed. *Changing Perspectives of the Family, Proceedings of the 5th Annual Symposium of the Constitutional Law Resource Center* Des Moines, Iowa: Drake University Law School.

Fineman, M. A. (1995) *The Neutered Mother, the Sexual Family and other Twentieth Century Tragedies* London: Routledge.

Fletcher, R. (1966) *Family and Marriage in Britain* Harmondsworth: Penguin.

Ford, R., March, A. and McKay, S. (1995) *Changes in Lone Parenthood* Department of Social Security Research Report, No. 40 London: HMSO.

Garfinkel, I. and McLanahan, S. (1986) *Single Mothers and their Children: A New American Dilemma* Washington DC: Urban Institute.

Gershuny, J., Godwin, M. and Jones, S. (1994) The Domestic Labour Revolution: A Process of Lagged Adaptation? In M. Anderson, F. Bechhofer and J. Gershuny eds. *The Social and Political Economy of the Household* Oxford: Oxford University Press.

Gibson, C. (1996) Contemporary Divorce and Changing Family Patterns. In M. Freeman ed. *Divorce, Where Next?* Aldershot: Dartmouth.

Giddens, A. (1992) *The Transformation of Intimacy, Sexuality, Love and Eroticism in Modern Societies* Cambridge: Polity Press.

Glendon, M. A. (1976) Marriage and the State: the Withering away of Marriage? *Virginia Law Review* 62: 663–720.

Glendon, M. A. (1981) *The New Family and the New Property* Toronto: Butterworths.

Gottman, J. M. (1994) *What Predicts Divorce? The Relationship between Marital Processes and Marital Outcomes* Hillsdale, New Jersey: Lawrence Erlbaum Associates.

Greatbatch, D. and Dingwall, R. (1989) Selective Facilitation: Some Preliminary Observations on a Strategy used by Divorce Mediators. *Law and Society Review* 23: 613–41.

Greatbatch, D. and Dingwall, R. (1997) Argumentative Talk in Divorce Mediation Sessions. *American Sociological Review* 62: 151–70.

Hale, B. (1998) Private Lives and Public Duties: What is Family Law for? *Journal of Social Welfare and Family Law* 20: 125–136.

Haskey, J. (1996) The Proportions of Married Couples who Divorce: Past Patterns and Current Prospects. *Population Trends* 83: 25–36.

HC 479 (1988) *Facing the Future. A Discussion Paper on the Ground for Divorce* Law Commission London: HMSO.

HC 636 (1990) *Family Law. The Ground for Divorce* Law Commission London: HMSO.

Hirschman, A. O. (1986) *Rival Views of Market Society and Other Recent Essays* New York: Viking.

Hochschild, A. (1990)*The Second Shift* 2nd edn. London: Piatkus.

Home Office (1998) *Supporting Families.* London: Home Office.

Ingleby, R. (1988) The Solicitor as Intermediary. In R. Dingwall and J. Eekelaar eds. *Divorce and Mediation in the Legal Process*. Oxford: Clarendon Press.

Jackson, E., Wasoff, F., with Maclean M. and Dobash, R. E. (1993) Financial Support on Divorce: The Right Mixture of Rules and Discretion. *International Journal of Law and the Family* 7: 230–254.

Jacob, H. (1989) The Elusive Shadow of the Law, *Law and Society Review* 26: 565–90.

Jamieson, L. (1998) *Intimacy: Personal Relationships in Modern Society* Cambridge: Polity Press.

Kay, H. H. (1987) Equality and Difference: A Perspective on No-Fault Divorce and its Aftermath. *University of Cincinnati Law Review* 56: 1–90.

Kiernan, K. (1992) The Impact of Family Disruption in Childhood on Transitions made in Young Adult Life. *Population Studies* 46: 213–34.

LCD Lord Chancellors Department (1985) *Report of the Matrimonial Causes Procedure Committee*. London: HMSO.

Le Grand, J. (1997) Knights, Knaves or Pawns? Human Behaviour and Social Policy. *Journal of Social Policy* 26: 149–70.

Lesthaeghe, R. and Surkyn, J. (1988) Cultural Dynamics and Economic Theories of Fertility Change. *Population and Development Review* 14: 20–47.

Lewis, J. (2001) *The End of Marriage: Individualism and Intimate Relations* Cheltenham, Edward Elgar.

Maclean, M. and Eekelaar, J. (1988) The Evolution of Private Law Maintenance obligations: The Common Law. In M. T. Meulders-Klein and J. Eedkelaar eds. *Family, State and Individual Economic Security* Vol.I Brussels: Story Scientia.

Maclean, M. and Eekelaar, J. (1997) *The Parental Obligation: A Study of Parenthood across Households*. Oxford: Hart.

Maclean, M. and Wadsworth, M. E. J. (1988) The Interests of Children after Parental Divorce: A Long Term Perspective. *International Journal of Law and the Family* 2: 155–66.

Mitchell, A. (1985) *Children in the Middle. Living through Divorce* London: Tavistock.

Mnookin, R. H. (1979) *Bargaining in the Shadow of the Law: the Case of Divorce*. Working Paper no. 3 London: Law Commission.

Murray, C. (1985) *Losing Ground: American Social Policy 1950–1980* New York: Basic Books.

Nakonezny, P., Shull, A. R. D. and Rodgers, J. L. (1995) The Effect of No-Fault Divorce Law on the Divorce Rate across the 50 States and its Relation to Income, Education and Religiosity. *Journal of Marriage and the Family* 57: 477–88.

O'Donovan, K. (1993) *Family Law Matters* London: Pluto Press.

Okin, S. M. (1989) *Justice, Gender and the Family* New York: Basic Books.

Oppenheim Mason, K. and Jensen, A-M. (1995) Introduction. In K. Oppenheim Mason and A-M Jensen eds. *Gender and Family Change in Industrialized Countries* Oxford: Clarendon Press.

Pahl, J. (1989) *Money and Marriage* London: Macmillan.

Peters, H. E. (1986) Marriage and Divorce: Informational Constraints and Private Contractingä. *American Economic Review* 76: 437–54.

Phillips, R. (1988) *Putting Asunder. A History of Divorce in Western Society*. Cambridge: Cambridge University Press.

Piper, C. (1993) *The Responsible Parent. A Study in Divorce Mediation* Brighton: Harvester Wheatsheaf.

Popenoe, D. (1988) Disturbing the Nest. Family Change and Decline in Modern Societies. New York: Aldine de Gruyter.

Popenoe, D. (1993) American Family Decline, 1960–990: A Review and Appraisal. *Journal of Marriage and the Family* 55: 527–55.

Posner, R. (1992) *Sex and Reason* Cambridge: Harvard University Press.

Rheinstein, M. (1972) *Marriage, Stability, Divorce and the Law.* Chicago: University of Chicago Press.

Richards, M. P. M. (1982) Post-Divorce Arrangements for Children: A Psychological Perspective. *Journal of Social Welfare Law.* May 133–51.

Richards, M. P. M. and Dyson, M. (1982) *Separation, Divorce and the Development of Children: A Review* London: DHSS.

Robinson, J. A. T. (1963) *Honest to God* London: SCM Press.

Rowntree, G. (1964) Some Aspects of Marriage Breakdown in Britain During the Last Thirty Years. *Population Studies* XVIII: 147–63.

Royal Commission on Marriage and Divorce (1956) *Minutes of Evidence* London: HMSO.

Schultz, M. (1982) Contractual Ordering of Marriage: A New Model for State Policy. *California Law Review* 70: 204–334.

Schneider, C. (1985) Moral Discourse and the Transformation of American Family Law. *Michigan Law Review* 83: 1803–79.

Scott, J., Alwin, D. F. and Braun, M. (1996) Generational Changes in Gender-Role Attitudes in a Cross-National Perspective. *Sociology* 30: 471–92.

Scott, J., Braun, M. and Alwin, D. (1998) Partner, Parent, Worker: Family and Gender Roles. In *British Social Attitudes, 15th Report* forthcoming.

Singer, J. B. (1989) Divorce Reform and Gender Justice. *North Carolina Law Review* 67: 1103–1121.

Smart, C. (1984) *The Ties that Bind* London: Routledge.

Smart, C. (1991) The Legal and Moral Ordering of Child Custody. *Journal of Law and Society* 18: 485–501.

Smart, C. and Neale, B. (1997) Wishful Thinking and Harmful Tinkering? Sociological Reflections of Family Policy. *Journal of Social Policy* 26: 301–21.

Thompson, L. and Walker, A. J. (1989) Gender in Families: Women and Men in Marriage, Work and Parenthood. *Journal of Marriage and the Family* 5: 845–71.

Thornton, A. (1989) 'Changing Attitudes Towards Family Issues in the United States'. *Journal of Marriage and the Family* 51: 873–93

Walker, J., McCarthy, P. and Timms, N. (1994) *Mediation: the Making and Re-making of Cooperative Relations. An Evaluation of the Effectiveness of Comprehensive Mediation* Newcastle: Relate Centre for Family Studies.

Weitzman, L. J. (1985) *The Marriage Contract. Spouses, Lovers and the Law.* New York: Free Press.

Winnett, A. R. (1968) *The Church and Divorce.* London: A. R. Mowbray.

Young, M. and Willmott, P. (1973) *The Symmetrical Family* London: Routledge and Kegan Paul.

Part Two

The Family and the State across the Lifecourse

4
Lone Parents and Child Support: Parental and State Responsibilities

Karen Clarke

Introduction

In the context of a more general re-orientation of 'western' governments' commitments to state welfare, there has been a radical shift of policy in Britain on the financial support of lone parents and their children. These changes appear to have been maintained despite a radical change of government in the UK in 1997 from New Right Conservative to New Labour. State policies directed at lone parents are particularly interesting because they involve the articulation of underlying principles of family responsibilities and gender roles. This chapter examines these principles as they were enacted in policy and experienced by lone mothers in the UK during the 1990s. It looks at the extent to which the concept of paternal responsibility, which underlies it, is one which reflects the beliefs of separated parents and, finally considers the significance of the modifications proposed by the Labour Government to the original policies of the Conservative Government, in terms of the relative responsibilities of state and family for children which they imply.

The 1991 Child Support Act which came into effect in April 1993 was one of a number of policy measures aimed at redrawing the boundaries of state responsibility for family welfare. The Act, together with changes to the social security system, aimed to increase the extent to which *parents*, rather than the state, took responsibility for supporting children in lone parent families. This was to be done first by increasing the proportion of 'absent'[1] parents making some financial contribution to their children's support (and increasing the level of that contribution); and second, by increasing the financial incentives for lone parents to contribute to their own and their children's support through

91

employment. This two-pronged approach to the problem of the financial support of the increasing number of lone parent families was driven both by *fiscal* and by *moral* concerns. The policy objectives were similarly two-fold: to reduce state expenditure on lone parents and to encourage greater self-reliance and a greater sense of responsibility among parents for the support of their children. It should be seen as part of a much broader policy programme to reduce state involvement in the family, but as will be discussed below, it involves a rather paradoxical increase in other forms of state involvement and coercion in private family matters, which in turn involves increasing women's dependence on men. At the same time, the exhortation to lone mothers to enter the labour market and become financially self-supporting has taken place with little acknowledgement of the social and employment infrastructure necessary to support lone mothers in the labour market. Until very recently, childcare has been a largely private responsibility, universal employment rights for parents have been limited to the right to maternity leave, while the deregulation of the labour market, leading to an increase in insecure and low paid employment, has made it difficult for those lone mothers not already in employment to find employment which is financially worthwhile. Although the Labour Government elected in 1997 has taken steps to address these issues through measures such as the introduction of a minimum wage, significant investment in the provision of child care and assistance with meeting its cost, lone mothers, along with other women, continue to face real difficulties in finding paid work which will lift them out of dependence on welfare benefits (Finlayson and Marsh, 1998).

Growth in lone parenthood and lone parent poverty

The number of lone parent families in Britain has increased very rapidly over the past 25 years from 570,000 in 1971 to approximately 1.3 million in 1991, with the number estimated to have reached about 1.6 million by the late 1990s (Marsh et al, 1997; Rowlingson and McKay, 2002). Lone parent families now account for about a quarter of all families with dependent children and there are estimated to be 2.8 million children currently living in a household headed by a lone parent (Rowlingson and McKay, 2002; Haskey, 1998). The overwhelming majority of such households are headed by a lone mother and these households are disproportionately represented among the poorest households in Britain. Fifty two per cent of all lone parents in the late 1990s were dependent on Income Support, and the proportion rose to 68 per cent for single lone mothers (Marsh et al, 2001).

According to the government's official measure of low income (Households Below Average Income (HBAI)) 62 per cent of children in lone parent households, approximately 1.8 million children, live in poverty (defined as households with incomes below half of average income, after housing costs) (Rowlingson and McKay, 2002). Surveys of lone parents have repeatedly shown the financial hardship suffered by lone parents, with the well-known implications of this for parents' and children's health and children's educational achievement and therefore their long-term prospects in the labour market (Marsh, Ford and Finlayson, 1997). In Marsh et al's study (1997) lone parents' incomes were less than half those of two parent families. One fifth had a weekly income after housing costs of less than £80 per week. Median earnings of those lone parents who were working were low: £75 per week. A significant proportion of families had housing problems, such as damp, lack of central heating, outstanding repairs and problems with vermin. Three in ten lone parents who were not working reported a limiting or long-term illness or disability and for half of this group this affected their ability to get a job or limited the kind or amount of work they could do. A quarter of lone parents said that they had a child with a long-term illness or disability, which for some affected school attendance and would also therefore affect the possibility of the parent working. More than two fifths of the lone parents in Marsh et al's study had debt problems of some kind and almost half the lone parents interviewed said that they worried about money almost all the time (Marsh et al, 1997, Chap. 3). The problems and disadvantages experienced by lone parents were particularly concentrated among those who were wholly dependent on welfare benefits for their income. This group were younger than the lone parent population generally, were significantly less likely to have any qualifications, much less likely to be receiving maintenance and more likely to be experiencing severe hardship. They were also the largest single group of lone parents. As this chapter will demonstrate, the Conservative Government's child support policy completely failed to address the underlying causes of the increase in poverty among lone parents and instead focused entirely on the implications of welfare dependency for state expenditure, taking a narrowly fiscal and short-term approach to the problem.

The fiscal and moral imperative for change

Lone mothers' increasing dependence during the 1980s on means-tested benefits as their main source of income reflected two changes.

First, the proportion of lone mothers in employment had remained constant or fallen slightly, at the same time as married mothers' employment rates were increasing. By 1990 only 39 per cent of lone mothers were in employment, compared with 60 per cent of married mothers. Second, there was a decline in the proportion of lone mothers receiving maintenance from a former partner. In the period immediately preceding the introduction of the Child Support Act only 30 per cent of lone mothers were receiving regular maintenance payments. The proportion of those on Income Support (IS) receiving maintenance was much lower than that for those not on IS (22 per cent and 40 per cent respectively [DSS 1990]). As a consequence of this combination of an increase in the numbers of lone mothers, the decrease in the proportion in employment and the decrease in the proportion receiving maintenance, the costs to the state of supporting lone parents escalated rapidly during the 1980s, from £1.4 billion in 1981 to £3.2 billion by 1988/9 (DSS 1990). Whereas in the 1980s it had been accepted by the courts and lawyers that the state should cover the gap in resources available to support two households after separation, by lone mothers relying on the social security system, this became increasingly unacceptable to the then Conservative Government by the end of the decade (Davis et al, 1998, pp. 2–4).

The increase in the costs to the state of supporting lone parents also reflected the changing composition of the lone parent population. Whereas the growth in the numbers of lone mothers in the 1970s was largely the result of an increase in the number of married couples separating and divorcing, in the 1980s the most rapidly increasing group among lone mothers was women who had never married (Haskey, 1998). Never-married lone mothers differ from divorced and separated lone mothers in a number of important ways: they are on average younger and less well-qualified and they are less likely to be receiving maintenance from the father of their child (Rowlingson and McKay, 1998).

The growth in the number of lone parents during the 1980s was seen as a problem not only because of the implications for the Treasury, but also because that growth was seen as a symptom of the decline in traditional family and the values of independence, self-reliance and responsibility for which it stood. It was the combination of these two factors – the escalating costs to the state and the anxiety about the decline of the traditional family – which shaped the measures introduced in the Child Support Act and to a lesser extent the social security changes designed to increase work incentives which accompanied it.

The New Right Conservative Government was persuaded by the arguments of writers such as Murray (1994) and Morgan (1995) that state
policies towards lone parents had actively encouraged and facilitated
child-bearing outside marriage and placed lone parents at an advantage
relative to two parent families. The success of arguments of this kind is
reflected in the measures to remove additional benefits for lone
parents, proposed in 1996 by the Conservative Government and implemented by the succeeding Labour Government. In April 1998 One
Parent Benefit and the lone parent premium within Income Support
were abolished for new lone parents (Ford and Millar, 1998, p. 15).

The problem which the 1991 Child Support Act was intended to
address was defined as one of failure on the part of men to acknowledge and meet their responsibilities towards their children, with the
concern about the problem driven by the fiscal implications for the
state of this failure to behave responsibly. Underlying the legislation
was a highly gendered notion of what constitutes responsible behaviour. Responsibility as far as absent parents (fathers) are concerned
originated in biological paternity, which was seen as establishing
universal and unconditional obligations towards children, and was
defined entirely in terms of financial responsibility, without regard to
other forms of parental responsibility towards children. This resulted in
a policy aimed at maximising the amount of child support recovered
from fathers, which did not take into account any obligations towards
step-children resulting from 'social' paternity, nor did it allow for the
costs of meeting paternal responsibilities in other ways, such as providing emotional support for children and maintaining contact.

The identification of what constituted responsible behaviour on the
part of lone mothers was perhaps more ambiguous. Policy on lone
mothers' employment has traditionally been neutral, with lone
mothers not required to satisfy a test of availability for work as a
condition of claiming income support, unlike other claimants
(Kiernan et al, 1998). Recent policy, however, indicates that there has
been a shift towards an expectation that lone mothers should work.
This initially involved establishing greater financial incentives to work
and a limited range of other policy measures, such as the provision of
individual guidance and advice on employment, in order to encourage lone parents to take paid work. The continuing inadequacy of
benefit levels for those lone parents who do not work also constitutes
a less direct pressure to enter the labour market. The White Paper
which preceded the 1991 Child Support Act, in putting forward the
case for change, referred to the gap between the employment rates of

lone mothers and married mothers and the wish expressed by three-quarters of lone mothers on income support to work at some time in the future (DSS 1990, p. 3). Among the aims of the new system it listed:

- Ensuring that parents meet the cost of their children's maintenance whenever they can without removing the parents' own incentive to work and to go on working.
- Enabling caring parents who wish to work to do so as soon as they feel ready and able (DSS 1990, p. 5).

It could be argued therefore that there has been a change in what is expected of responsible lone mothers, from their principal role being that of caring for their children to one where this is to be combined with making some contribution towards their own and their children's financial support through paid work.

The policy package: the Child Support Act and social security changes

The problem of lone parents' increasing dependence on the state for support was addressed through two related sets of measures. The 1991 Child Support Act was intended to ensure that absent parents (fathers) made a much greater financial contribution to their children's support. Changes made simultaneously to Family Credit (FC) were intended to increase lone mothers' incentives to enter the labour market. The shaping of the Child Support Act by the fiscal and moral concerns outlined above, and the lack of concern about lone parent poverty, is apparent both in the provisions of the Act and the way in which it was implemented.

The main provisions of the Act and its associated regulations were:

- The establishment of the Child Support Agency (CSA), responsible for the assessment of all child maintenance payments and their collection where requested.
- The creation of a universally applicable but complex formula to calculate liability for child maintenance.
- An **obligation** on all 'parents with care' claiming means-tested benefits to seek maintenance from the 'absent parent'.[2] Parents with care who were not dependent on means-tested benefits could choose whether or not to use the CSA to claim child support.

- Unmarried fathers' liability for child support payments rested entirely on biological paternity, regardless of the nature or duration of the relationship with the lone mother.
- Step children in 'second' families were not regarded as having any claim on the resources of their step-father, when calculating the level of child support which he was required to pay for children in a 'first' family.
- The requirement to seek child support was only waived if the 'parent with care' could demonstrate 'reasonable grounds' for believing that this would cause her or a child to suffer 'harm or undue distress'.
- Refusal to co-operate, where 'harm or undue distress' was not accepted, was penalized by a significant reduction in the lone mother's benefit.
- 'Parents with care' on Income Support has all maintenance deducted £ for £ from their benefit; 'parents with care' on Family Credit had the first £15 of any maintenance disregarded.

The fact that the requirement to co-operate only applied to lone parents on means-tested benefits and that the maintenance collected was offset against IS on a pound for pound basis demonstrates clearly the pre-eminence of the fiscal objectives which underlay the legislation. This is further borne out by the way in which the legislation was implemented in the first year of operation of the Agency, with the setting of very ambitious performance targets for the Agency both in terms of the number of assessments to be made and the savings in benefit payments to be achieved (Clarke, Craig and Glendinning, 1996; Barnes, Day and Cronin, 1998).

At the same time, a number of changes were introduced to Family Credit (FC) with the intention of increasing the incentives for lone mothers to take up paid work or to increase their hours of work, and so reduce their dependence on benefits:

- The minimum number of hours worked in order to qualify for FC was reduced from 24 hours per week to 16 from April 1992.
- An allowance for childcare costs for children under 11 was introduced for FC claimants from October 1994 for children cared for by a registered childminder or in a nursery.
- The first £15 of maintenance paid to lone parents was not deducted from the FC payments they received.

The Child Support Act passed through Parliament with relatively little discussion and with no significant political divisions. It followed the pattern of much contemporary British social security legislation in containing only the broad outline of the measures to be introduced, with most of the detail being published later in the form of regulations. This also restricted the opportunity to debate amendments made by the Conservative Government in response to the very hostile response to the legislation from absent parents (Clarke et al, 1996; Davis et al, 1998, p. 9–12).

Criticism of and hostility to the Child Support Act and the Agency

After the Act came into effect in April 1993 it was the subject of almost unprecedented hostility from those directly affected by it and repeated criticism both from within and outside Parliament. The unpopularity of the legislation had a number of components:

- The administrative inefficiency of the Agency
- The lack of financial gain for the majority of lone parents who had maintenance assessed by the Agency
- The principles which it sought to apply

These will be examined in turn.

Administrative inefficiency

The administrative problems faced by the Agency became apparent almost as soon as it began its work in April 1993. The Agency was repeatedly criticized in reports from a number of different sources for its delay in processing applications, the inaccuracies in the assessments which it made and its inefficiency in collecting and delivering the maintenance due (Barnes et al, 1998, pp. 16–18). These administrative problems undoubtedly compounded the hostility to the Agency stemming from the other two sources mentioned above – the lack of financial gain to lone mothers and their children, and, for some lone mothers and many 'absent' fathers, the lack of support for the principles of parental responsibility which were implicit in the legislation.

The financial impact of the Child Support Act on lone mothers

The Child Support Act had little effect on lone parent poverty. Because lone mothers on income support had child support deducted from their benefit on a £ for £ basis they could only gain financially if their income from child support lifted them off IS altogether. Where the level of child support took lone mothers off IS, they lost access to other benefits which were attached to the receipt of IS ('passported' benefits), such as free school meals, and might, therefore, paradoxically end up worse off. Lone mothers' financial security, once off IS, depended critically on the regularity of maintenance payments, and the effect of a substantial maintenance award was to make them financially dependent once more on the former partner from whom they had separated.

Lone mothers on family credit were entitled to keep the first £15 per week of maintenance and therefore potentially stood to gain financially from child support payments. However, unlike payments for those on IS, maintenance payments for FC recipients were not guaranteed by the Agency and the extent to which lone mothers on FC gained from maintenance awards in practice depended crucially on the regularity with which the former partner made his child support payments either directly or through the Agency. Where payments were made via the Agency, lone mothers' financial security was dependent on the promptness with which these payments were then passed on to her. The lack of direct co-ordination between the Agency and the procedures for assessing family credit added further to financial uncertainty for lone mothers on FC. Because FC was only reassessed every six months, any change in the circumstances of the absent parent leading to a reduction in the amount of child support paid could not be adjusted for in her FC entitlement in the interim. An early qualitative study of the effects of the legislation on lone mothers, found that four out of 15 mothers on FC had lost financially because payments were being made erratically or not at all, and also because of insufficient co-ordination between the assessment of FC and the assessment of child support (Clarke et al, 1996, p. 20).

The insecurity of income from maintenance potentially worked against the second strand of policy towards lone parents, that of increasing the extent to which they supported themselves and their children through employment. As Millar (1996) pointed out, lone mothers on family credit faced an insecure and complex income package, involving multiple means testing by different agencies, with the most complex combination of income sources occurring at the lowest earnings levels, which were most typical for women in part-time employment. The complexity and uncertainty created by this combination of different sources of income for women on family credit were exacerbated by the Child Support Agency's poor administrative performance in its early years. A more recent report from the Social Security Select Committee showed that there had been a considerable reduction in the delays experienced by lone mothers, so that in 1995/6 98 per cent of payments were passed on to parents with care within 10 working days. However, it is important to note that what may have been an acceptable level of speed and efficiency to a large bureaucracy such as the Child Support Agency may nonetheless still have constituted an unacceptable delay to lone mothers living on very low and precarious levels of income from a number of different sources. A two-week delay (10 working days) in receiving a payment of £40 per week (the average full assessment for an employee in February 1997), potentially represented a significant proportion of total income for a lone mother on Family Credit.

One group of mothers which lost a substantial proportion of their income under the Child Support Act were those mothers on benefits who refused to cooperate with the CSA in seeking child support and so were subject to a reduced benefit direction.[3] Between April 1993 and June 1996 about 50,000 reduced benefit directions were issued. The Agency took an increasingly hard line on what constituted 'good cause', with 27,500 reduced benefit directions issued in 1995/6 alone (Social Security Select Committee 4th Report 1995/6). Such a measure clearly inflicted very considerable hardship not only on the lone mother, but also on the children and it is hard to see how this was consistent with the principle articulated in the 1989 Children Act that the welfare of the child should be the paramount consideration in decisions relating to them.

From October 1996, the benefit penalty involved a reduction by 40 per cent of the adult income support allowance for a period of three years, renewable indefinitely. This amounts to a reduction in weekly income of over £20. Further measures were introduced since September 1997 to compel early co-operation with the Agency by making entitlement to benefit conditional on assisting with seeking child support (Social Security Committee 5th Report 1997, para. 2). Both these changes are likely to result in very severe hardship to lone mothers who feel unable to co-operate for some reason, and to children living in such households.

The financial impact of the Child Support Act has been examined so far only in terms of its effects on lone mothers' income. But it is important to note that this is not the only way in which lone mothers' material situation was affected. A significant increase in the amount of maintenance being paid meant that former partners were, in some cases, no longer able or willing to provide other forms of help in kind, such as help with buying essential clothing for the children, with meeting household bills or contributing to the cost of holidays for the children (Clarke et al, 1996).

For a significant minority of lone mothers interviewed in this qualitative study there had been serious disruption of relationships both between the parents and, either directly or indirectly, between absent parents and children. Ironically, in terms of the Act's moral agenda, these effects were most pronounced in families where the father was in regular contact and had been paying maintenance prior to the Agency's involvement (Clarke et al, 1996).

Attitudes to principles of parental responsibility underlying the Child Support Act

The 1991 Child Support Act is informed by a concept of parental responsibility on the part of the 'absent' parent, which focuses exclusively on financial responsibility, where responsibility derives from biological paternity (or in the case of married fathers from the presumption of biological paternity). How far does this notion of parental responsibility, and paternal responsibility in particular, accord with the views of parents who have separated? Beliefs about non-resident fathers' responsibilities towards children vary by gender and also by circumstances. Normative values also differ from individuals' beliefs about the obligations which apply in their particular circumstances. The picture is therefore much more complex and nuanced than the application of the principle that fathers have universal and exclusive financial responsibility for their biological offspring, which is contained in the Child Support Act. Although a number of studies have found almost universal support, among absent fathers, lone mothers and those in 'second families' for the principle that the absent parent has a continuing financial obligation to his children (Bennett, 1997), this universal support is qualified in different ways for different groups of interested parties. The notion of a single, formula-determined process for determining the level of financial obligation on the basis of simple biological parenthood is not something which commands nearly the same level of support as the simpler principle that there is some degree of continuing financial obligation.

For lone mothers, financial dependence on a former partner, even indirectly, is complex, because of the way in which the payment of maintenance is felt to give a former partner the right to demand accountability for the way in which the money is spent and a right to continuing contact with the child. As one mother put it:

> *If they pay, you feel like you owe them something, that you have to co-operate because they are giving you their money, that they're keeping you ... we would still be joined at the ankles.* (Clarke et al, 1996, p. 34)

This mother preferred to be dependent on the state rather than on her child's father, because of the freedom from personal obligation to him which this allowed her. She saw the costs to the state as temporary and socially justifiable:

> *I'm bringing up the next generation, so I think the state should pay, it's an investment. And I'm not going to be in this situation forever ... I'm going to put back what I've taken – and I've been doing voluntary work for seven years ...* (*Ibid.*)

Where a child is born into an established relationship, the difficulties created by the mother's continued dependence on the father can be set against the belief that the father has a continuing obligation towards the child. Where, however, the child is the result of a brief relationship which ended before or shortly after the child was born, and there is no continuing contact with, or expression of, interest from the father, there is no consensus that men have a continuing financial responsibility for the child (Clarke et al, 1996, pp. 32–33). The principle that biological paternity *per se* brings with it obligations, which the Child Support Act asserts, is not one with which all lone mothers would agree and this led some women to believe that they, rather than the state, should be the ones to determine under what circumstances maintenance should be pursued.

Maclean and Eekelaar's study of parental obligation found that men's views about parental obligation were less strongly based on biological parenthood than women's and were more likely to give equal weight to the obligations created by social parenthood (1997, pp. 140–142), such as themselves becoming a step-father in a new relationship, or the remarriage of a former partner. Bradshaw et al (1999) found that the sense of obligation which fathers felt in relation to paying maintenance for children was contingent on a variety of social circumstances and on mothers facilitating and supporting contact with the children.

The structure of the formula itself, in which a substantial proportion of the child's maintenance requirement derived from the inclusion of a carer's allowance was problematic both for lone mothers and for absent fathers . Although it can be seen as an acknowledgement by the state of the real costs to women of caring for children, in terms of the restriction of opportunities for financial independence through employment, it also supported and perpetuated the traditional gender division of labour between men as breadwinners and women as financially dependent carers. It appears to be at odds with the 'clean break' approach to spousal maintenance adopted in the 1984 Matrimonial and Family Proceedings Act – although the carer's allowance within the formula was technically not spousal maintenance, but part of the child's maintenance requirement.

For absent parents even the indirect support of their former partner may be a source of resentment, where, for example, they feel that it was she who was responsible for the break-up of the relationship (Burgoyne and Millar, 1994; Bradshaw et al, 1997).

New Labour and Child Support

The Labour Government elected in 1997 reviewed the Child Support Act and published its proposals for change in July 1998 (Department of Social Security 1998). The proposed changes were included in the Child Support, Pensions and Social Security Act 2000, which was implemented in March 2003. It is clear that the Blair administration has a very similar perspective on the principles that should govern child support and also shares the moral objectives which informed the 1991 Child Support Act. But while the objectives and governing principles are the same, there are important and significant differences in the means proposed to achieve them, which I would argue, change the nature of the relationship between families and the state, and which incorporate some limited acknowledgement of the problems for lone mothers of their continued financial dependency on a former partner.

The dominance of the short-term objective of reducing government expenditure has been removed, at least in part, by allowing lone parents on IS to keep the first £10 of any maintenance paid. This is intended to provide incentives to co-operate with the Child Support Agency for both mothers, who will gain directly, and fathers, who will see some additional financial support going to their child and may therefore be more willing to make their payments.

Although the obligation to pay maintenance remains a universal one based on biological paternity, there is some acknowledgement of social parenthood and the obligations which that also carries. The presence of step-children in a second family is taken into account in the calculation of maintenance, so that biological and social responsibility for children is given equal recognition. On the other hand, the exemption from paying the minimum payment of £5 which currently applies to men on means-tested benefits with children (as opposed to step-children) in a second family, has been removed. The implication of this change is that attaching some financial cost to biological parenthood remains an important element in the moral agenda to make men feel their responsibilities financially.

Encouraging men to fulfil parental responsibilities in ways other than the provision of financial support was a central theme in the 1998 Green Paper in which the Labour Government's amendments to the legislation were proposed. This stands in marked contrast to the *Children Come First* White Paper (DSS 1990) which preceded the 1991 Child Support Act. The White Paper asserted that maintenance and contact could and should remain totally unconnected issues – an assertion which seems to be refuted by the empirical evidence of a number of studies (Clarke et al, 1996; Maclean and Eekelaar, 1997; Bradshaw et al, 1999). Maintenance in the Labour Government's Green Paper was seen as a means of bringing about greater paternal involvement in other ways and is described as an element in 'an active family policy' (DSS 1998, Chap. 3). 'Child support can play an important part in helping people understand the rights and responsibilities of parenthood' (Chap. 3, para. 11). The Green Paper even went so far as to suggest that the child support system should have a role in identifying and referring on those who need assistance with wider parenting problems.

The formula itself has been simplified, with the carer support element being removed completely. Child support is instead based on a percentage of net income, which varies according to the number of dependent children in both first and second families. Thus the *structure* of the formula has removed women's financial dependency on their former partner, although the material reality of dependency remains.

The emphasis on lone mothers reducing their financial dependency on the state, through employment has increased under the Labour Government. The responsible lone mother under New Labour is more than ever before expected to be a worker as well as a carer. There have been increasing moves through the New Deal for Lone Parents, introduced by the 1997 Labour Government and implemented nationally in October 1998, for this encouragement to work to move towards compulsion, when the youngest child is of school age. However, in contrast with the previous Conservative Government there is much greater recognition of the need for the state to play a part through measures such as the introduction of the minimum wage and more generous financial support for working parents in the form of the Working Families Tax Credit; through extension of parental employment rights (paternity leave, parental leave and extension of maternity leave); and through state investment in childcare both in increased provision and in financial help with meeting the costs of childcare through the childcare tax credit, introduced in October 1999 (Home Office, 1998; Department of Social Security, 1999).

Conclusion

Policy on the support of lone parent families in Britain underwent a radical shift in the early 1990s from a situation where principal responsibility for financial support was accepted by the state, to one where the state's role is intended to be residual, leaving absent fathers and lone mothers with the principal responsibility. Under the policies introduced by the Conservative government, women who were unable to work themselves and whose former partners could not or would not pay maintenance were left at an increased risk of poverty. Underlying these new policies was a highly gendered concept of what it is to be a responsible parent. The concept of responsible fatherhood focused entirely on the obligation to provide financial support, deriving from biological paternity. The concept of maternal responsibility, which is underlying child support policy, appeared increasingly to involve the expectation that lone mothers would be both carers and workers.

The concept of paternal responsibility, which was implicit in the legislation, although it appeared to have widespread support among both lone mothers and non-resident fathers, did not, on closer inspection, reflect the beliefs of separated parents. For both mothers and fathers, social parenthood plays a very important part in creating responsibilities for children and the failure of the Child Support Act to give adequate acknowledgement of this appears to have contributed to the unpopularity of the Agency and the legislation.

The effect of these changes in child support policy was to reinforce women's financial dependency on men. Although the policy was expressed in terms of children's need for and right to financial support, in practice the child support system established by the 1991 Child Support Act was unavoidably mediated through women's financial dependence on men. There is evidence that this dependence was unwelcome to lone mothers and complex in its effects on former partners, because they remained financially bound together, even though the relationship between the two adults involved was over.

While the 1991 Child Support Act may have had some limited success in increasing the level of maintenance paid, the shift of resources which took place was not a shift from men to women, but a shift in the source of the low level of resources going to lone mothers from the state to individual men. The legislation did nothing to address the problem of poverty which very large numbers of lone parent families suffered.

The apparently radical change which took place with the election of a Labour Government in May 1997 has not fundamentally changed policy in relation to child support. There remains an emphasis on private responsibility, deriving from biological parenthood and a clear moral agenda, involving the use of financial obligations as a means of encouraging greater parental responsibility. There has, however, been an important broadening of the view of fathers' responsibility to include the social and emotional support of children, as well as financial support. While the insistence that biological paternity automatically brings paternal responsibilities has not been modified, recognition has been accorded to social fatherhood, through the equal acknowledgement of men's responsibilities to step-children in second families. The modifications to the child support system and the wider welfare reforms introduced will also go some way to reducing women's dependence on men, by providing a greater degree of assistance for entering the labour market. It appears that the relationship between the state and families under the current Labour government involves a greater degree of partnership and some recognition that families are unable to be self-sufficient without the existence of a state provided infra-structure of employment rights and services such as daycare.

Notes

1 'Absent' parent is the term used in the legislation to refer to the parent with whom the child is not permanently resident. The co-resident parent is referred to as the 'parent with care'.

2 The terms 'absent parent' and 'parent with care' have now been replaced with the terms non-resident and co-resident parent in policy documents produced by the post-1997 Labour Government.

3 A reduced benefit direction could be made either if a lone mother refused to co-operate with the Agency by completing the Maintenance Application Form, or if her claim to be exempted from co-operation for 'good cause' (on

the grounds that she or her child would suffer 'harm or undue distress') was not accepted by the Agency.

Bibliography

Barnes, H., Day, P. and Cronin, N. (1998) *Trial and Error: a review of UK child support policy.* London: Family Policy Studies Centre.

Bennett, F. (1997) *Child Support. Issues for the Future.* London: CPAG.

Bradshaw, J. and Millar, J. (1991) *Lone Parent Families in the UK.* DSS Research Report No. 6. London: HMSO.

Bradshaw, J. Stimson, C., Skinner, C. and Williams, J. (1999) *Absent Fathers?* London: Routledge.

Burgoyne, C. and Millar, J. (1994) 'Enforcing child support obligations: the attitudes of separated fathers', *Policy and Politics* 22: 95–104.

Clarke, K., Craig, G. and Glendinning, C. (1996) *Small Change. The impact of the Child Support Act on lone mothers and children.* London: Family Policy Studies Centre.

Davis, G., Wikeley, N. and Young, R. (1998) *Child Support in Action* Oxford: Hart Publishing.

Department of Social Security (1990) *Children Come First. The Government's Proposals on the Maintenance of Children.* London: HMSO.

Department of Social Security (1997) *Social Security Statistics 1997.* London: The Stationery Office.

Department of Social Security (1997) *Child Support Agency Quarterly Summary of Statistics, November 1996.* London: The Stationery Office,

Department of Social Security (1998) *Children First.* Cm 3992 London: HMSO.

Department of Social Security (1999) *Opportunity for All. Tackling Poverty and Social Exclusion. First Annual Report 1999.* Cm 4445. London: The Stationery Office.

Finlayson, L. and Marsh, A. (1998) *Lone Parents on the Margins of Work.* Department of Social Security Research Report No. 80. London: Corporate Document Services.

Ford, R. and Millar, J. (1998) Lone parenthood in the UK: Policy dilemmas and solutions. In Reuben Ford and Jane Millar eds. *Private Lives and Public Responses. Lone Parenthood and Future Policy in the UK.* London: Policy Studies Institute.

Haskey, J. (1998) One-parent families and their dependent children in Great Britain. In Reuben Ford and Jane Millar eds. *Private Lives and Public Responses. Lone Parenthood and Future Policy in the UK.* London: Policy Studies Institute.

Home Office (1998) *Supporting Families. A Consultation Document.* London: The Stationery Office.

House of Commons Social Security Committee Fourth Report (1996) *Child Support: Good Cause and the Benefit Penalty.* House of Commons Session 1995–6. HC 440.

House of Commons Social Security Committee Fifth Report (1997) *Child Support.* House of Commons Session 1996–7. HC 282.

Kiernan, K., Land, H. and Lewis, J. (1998) *Lone Motherhood in Twentieth Century Britain.* Oxford: Oxford University Press.

Maclean, M. and Eekelaar, J. (1997) *The Parental Obligation. A Study of Parenthood across Households.* Oxford: Hart Publishing.

Marsh, A., Ford, R. and Finalyson, L. (1997) *Lone Parents, Work and Benefits*. DSS Research Report No. 61 London: HMSO.

Marsh, A., McKay, S., Smith, A. and Stephenson, A. (2001) *Low Income Families in Britain: Work, Welfare and Social Security in 1999*. London: Policy Studies Institute.

Morgan, P. (1995) *Farewell to the Family? Public Policy and Family Breakdown in Britain and the USA*. London: Institute of Economic Affairs.

Murray, C. (1994) *Underclass: the Crisis Deepens*. London: Institute of Economic Affairs.

Rowlingson, K. and McKay, S. (1998) *The Growth of Lone Parenthood: Diversity and Dynamics*. London: Policy Studies Institute.

Rowlingson, K. and McKay, S. (2002) *Lone Parent Families. Gender, Class and State*. London: Prentice Hall.

Speed, M. and Kent, N. (1996) *Child Support Agency: National Client Satisfaction Survey 1995*. DSS Research Report No. 51 London: HMSO.

5
Family Change and the Ageing Welfare State

Alan Tapper

It is often claimed that, where state welfare systems have grown and matured, so too have family systems become more fragile and troubled. Another common thesis is that state welfare systems today are unfriendly settings for family life, particularly for the family's principal social task, the raising and socialization of children. Not everyone agrees with the first of these claims. Fewer still will agree with the suggestion that the growth of state welfare has prompted family decline. Nevertheless, there is much in these propositions that requires careful thought.

Successful argument needs much more than the contention that A (welfare) has prospered while B (the family) has declined, for A and B might be quite unrelated phenomena. In the present case, A and B are certainly intimately related, for, by any account, state welfare does play a large part in contemporary family life in all modern societies. But that intimate involvement may not be an adverse one. Indeed, if the divorce rate or the fertility rate are taken as indicators of family flourishing, the welfare state must have been a benign influence in the first few decades of post-war history, until about 1970. And it is true that in that period state welfare supported, and saw itself as about supporting, families with children, financially and in other ways. Indeed, in its origins, the welfare state was sometimes conceived of as the extension of altruistic family attitudes to all and sundry. But, in the early twenty-first century, it is clearly a major issue whether welfare systems continue to be so supportive. The evidence, as I see it, suggests that they are not. In this discussion, I will focus only on financial matters, not on the success or failure of welfare systems or families in other ways.

Welfare systems are complex, of course. Commonly they are analyzed under three main headings: aims and ideals; forms and structures; and the operationalization of the aims and ideals. Most typologies concentrate on forms and structures. Aims and ideals are given less emphasis because they are assumed to be relatively clear; namely, vertical redistribution from rich to poor, or a safety net for the disadvantaged and vulnerable, or horizontal redistribution from one stage of life to another. But it is the operationalization issue that is most neglected – that is, the devising of practically applicable criteria for these broad and vague ideals and aims – and it is upon questions of operationalization that my argument will focus.

The welfare state, I shall contend, is enmeshed in problems of measurement, and these are not merely administrative difficulties; they involve matters of basic principle, and they are, in my view, quite intractable. Public policies aimed at vertical or horizontal redistribution must be able to identify, in measurable ways, different persons as rich and poor and different life-stages as affluent and needy. Can this be done? Is it administratively feasible? Has it been done successfully? Or has the welfare state, in its many forms and types, failed to translate correctly its aims and ideals into action?

No-one can hope to scan the performance of all welfare systems. We should refuse to accept welfare ideals as evidence of welfare realities, but once we make this refusal, it immediately becomes difficult to follow closely the reality of even one or two such systems. My argument will depend upon evidence from four cases: Australia, New Zealand, the United States, and Britain. In the standard typologies, Australia and the United States are seen as minimalist, 'lean and mean' systems, devoting only about 13–15 per cent of GDP to welfare, social security and public health funding. Recent liberalization and privatization notwithstanding, New Zealand and Britain spend around 20 per cent of GDP, making them middle-ranking welfare systems, still well behind European states like Sweden and the Netherlands, where 30 per cent is the norm (Jones, 1996, Table 3.1, p. 34). No analysis of the kind to be used here has been applied to the mainland European systems, so my argument applies to them only by extension.

My argument is an attempt to broaden the horizons of welfare analysis, and will proceed in four stages. The first way of broadening the picture is to deepen what is counted, taking taxes and assets and other economic factors as seriously as incomes have commonly been taken. The second is to track trends across time in social policy, with the distinction between 'young' and 'old' as focal concepts. The third is to examine the lifetime experience of different cohorts under the welfare state. The fourth is to look at the treatment of different family types.

Measuring need

Start with the simplest questions about measurement. Put aside the problem of measurement across time. Put aside moral questions about the relation between 'need' and 'desert' and 'contribution'. Can we successfully identify 'neediness', so that we can redistribute resources to prevent or alleviate it? And have welfare systems succeeded in devising suitable ways of operationalizing 'need'?

Measurements are required, and there are many ways of attempting them. All agree in starting with monetary incomes. But income takes many forms. Some, such as salaries and wages, are readily measurable; others, such as investment incomes and informal economy earnings, are very difficult to ascertain, even when there is a willingness to disclose them. There is no need to press that kind of point, since the difficulties with these types of income are the least of our problems.

Taxes too are multiform. Personal income taxes seem straightforward, except that deductions and rebates are often large and variable from case to case. In a few societies – notably Australia and (until recently) New Zealand – income taxes are the main source of government revenue; in most others, consumer taxes bulk large, supplemented by property and payroll taxes (Jones, 1996, p. 42). Taxes paid materially affect 'neediness' and thus eligibility for social support. But how are taxes to be measured at the individual level?

In practice, in the design of eligibility criteria, welfare policy usually dodges the problem by simply not measuring taxes at all. The effect is to build in a bias against those who pay higher levels of taxation. It is commonly assumed that this produces no distortion, since in practice those who are heavily taxed are those who are generally well off. Thus, it might seem, not counting taxes really strengthens the vertical component of the tax/transfer equation. This is at least very debatable. Paying high levels of tax is by no means well correlated with affluence. Expenditure taxes bear most heavily on those with most dependants, usually children. Income taxes fall most heavily on those aged 20 to 60, most of which years are the peak child-rearing period (ages 25 to 50). Not counting taxes thus builds in a bias against families with children, the larger the family the stronger the bias.

A third element to be measured in welfare calculations, and the most troublesome, is assets. Historically, those political thinkers and activists (mainly socialists and social democrats, but also some liberals) who sought 'vertical' equalization commonly thought of assets, not incomes, as the key component of class differences. They had in mind the ownership of land or industrial investments. When, however, the post-war welfare regimes were constructed, the equalization of assets as such played little part. The focus was on redistribution from the income-rich to the income-poor, as though affluence could be equated with high incomes. One obvious difficulty with this assumption is that to be asset-rich is not to need a high monetary income, while to be asset-poor often means having to work long and hard to raise one's standard of living. A second difficulty is that assets normally increase with age. To ignore assets is thus to build in a bias in favour of the asset-rich older half of the population. Both of these difficulties were dodged in most state welfare systems.

Australia is an exceptional case in having an assets test on age pensions, but even it illustrates my point. A retired home-owning couple (the most common elderly family type) may have assets other than the family home worth about $A206,500 (four-to-five times full-time average yearly earnings) before their pension begins to taper off; they can still receive part-pensions on assets up to $A453,500. There is no assets test on the family home. In addition, they can earn $A204 per week (or nearly 30 per cent of after tax Average Weekly Earnings) before the income test applies. The generosity of these terms is illustrated if these asset values are converted to annual cash payments. Assets of $A400,000 ($A200,000 in an average-value family home, $A200,000 in other forms) might easily yield an annual income of $A20,000, a sum roughly equal to the current couples pension. Thus, for couples with such assets the basic state pension doubles their income capacity, or, to put it differently, the pension protects their assets. Tax-funded retirement income provision thus serves mainly as a private asset protection scheme even in Australia's means tested system. Australian support for the elderly is more strictly assets tested than is the case in most other welfare regimes. Other systems, where assets testing is weaker, will tend to be even more favourable to the claims of the elderly and unfavourable to those of the younger half of the population. They will avoid being so only by adopting special countervailing policies.

All else being equal, the effect of this tendency to ignore assets in welfare calculations is to redistribute from those who are income-rich but asset-poor to those who are asset-rich but income-poor. Such a transfer has no clear connection with vertical equalization. To make it serve that purpose would require a workable formula that balances income, assets and the costs of dependants, and no system that I know of has even attempted this. Could it be seen as horizontal equalization across the life cycle? No, for the same reason. Only with a well-developed formula of the kind mentioned could it be clear which stages of life are most in need of support.

But perhaps as a matter of fact those who are asset-rich but income-poor are generally needier than those who are income-rich and asset-poor? The evidence is against this proposition. Studies which count both income and assets have found that the elderly are better off than the nonelderly. In the United States, for instance, Stephen Crystal and Dennis Shea have shown that, when household size, under-reporting of unearned income, and the annuitized value of assets are taken into account, 'the elderly are 124 percent as well off as the nonelderly' (Crystal and Shea, 1990, p. 227). This is a very different figure from that obtained from a simple income calculation. The unadjusted mean income of elderly households is only 63 per cent of that for all households. Taking account of household size, under-reporting and asset values thus makes a large difference. If these measurements are the appropriate ones, then there is no horizontal or vertical equity case for large-scale redistribution to the elderly of the sort seen in the US system.

Even more striking is Crystal and Shea's comparisons between the elderly and families with young children. They find that, on their measures, the elderly are on average 83 per cent better off than households with children under age six. Thus if the American welfare state is attempting to bring about horizontal equalization of income, in this case it is failing very markedly. It seems, on the contrary, to be redistributing from penurious to affluent stages of life. Upward redistribution from young to old is undeniable. Two specialists in American 'generational accounting', Kotlikoff and Gokhale, found that in 1990 net transfer payments (after counting income tax and sales and excise tax) to a typical 70 year old women amounted to $US3025, while the net figure for 10 year old girls was – $US389 (Kotlikoff and Gokhale, 1994, p. 76).

The generalizability of Crystal and Shea's findings might be questioned. Australian evidence, however, offers clear support for their analysis. Analysing an Australian living standards survey that took into account income, taxes, assets, government expenditures on health housing and education, leisure, and household size, Peter Travers and Sue Richardson found that the probability of avoiding poverty increases steadily with age. From age 35 on, they say, 'chances of being in poverty decline continuously with age, to the point that they are negligible around age 65. This difference arises from the fact that people accumulate assets over their working lives. Young people start out with few such assets, whereas asset ownership is likely to be at a peak around retirement age' (Travers and Richardson, 1993, p. 101). Counting all the above components, the sum of which they called 'full income', they showed that typically young adults start out at 0.8 of median full income; that the median is reached around age 40; that full income peaks at age 60 at about 1.3 of the median; and that on average the elderly at no stage fall below the median (Travers and Richardson, 1993, Figure 1.2, p. 40).

Assets are difficult to measure, but that does not invalidate the claim that they need to be measured. Even if they are not measured directly, they can be imputed. The elderly (60 and over) in any modern society are likely to constitute about 15 per cent of the population. If all cohorts were of equal size, and all incomes equal, and everyone saves five per cent of income and invests at five per cent compound interest, the oldest 15 per cent of the population will automatically own 61 per cent of the society's total private wealth. If everyone retires at age 60, and thereafter ceases to save, the over-60s will still own 60 per cent of private wealth. If, in addition, the costs of raising children are factored in by supposing that everyone aged 25 to 44 ceases to save, the over-60s will hold 63 per cent of private wealth. If it is further supposed that in this little social model there is inheritance, and that those who die at 75 pass their worldly goods down to their children aged 50, the over-60s will then own 70 per cent of private wealth. Those aged 18 to 40 will own 2 per cent of private wealth. This model is not entirely unrealistic, and changes to the savings rate make no huge difference to the outcomes. At a 3 per cent savings rate, the over-60s get 54 per cent and the 18–40 group gets 10 per cent. At 7 per cent, the figures are 68 per cent and 5 per cent. Were we to factor in the life cycle of income earning (beginning low and reaching a plateau around age 45) the relative shares of the under-40s would be smaller still. This is of course only a modelling exercise. Possibly actual savings and investment patterns do not follow this model. But if they do not that can only be because consumption has replaced savings. More generally, capacities for savings and consumption increase with age. Yet it is standard for welfare states to compel transfers from those with a lower capacity to others with a higher capacity.

Even when assets are left out of the equation, today's elderly do not appear to be particularly needy. David Thomson's analysis of official

New Zealand figures shows that the elderly have gross incomes per adult-equivalent about four-fifths those of all others aged 25 to 64 (Thomson, 1996, Table 5.2, p. 127). Since income taxes fall heavily on the 25–64 age group, and constitute about 20–25 per cent of income, the elderly are likely to be equal to or better off than the others are when after-tax equivalent incomes are measured. That is not counting hidden incomes, which are highest amongst the elderly. And it is not counting assets at all. Those under age 25 are particularly disadvantaged, having very few assets while paying high tax rates. The New Zealand elderly are clearly far better off than their younger compatriots. The same seems to be true in Sweden. In 1991, Swedish men aged over 70 had gross incomes 20 per cent higher than those of men aged 20–24 (Thomson, 1996, p. 129). Britain, where adult-equivalent incomes and expenditures of the elderly are about two-thirds those of the 30–64 age group, may be somewhat of an exception (Thomson, 1996, p. 131). But even this does not invalidate the claim that transfers in Britain are from poorer to richer age categories, since many relevant factors are not being counted here: assets, taxes, the value of social expenditures on health, housing and education, the value of leisure, the costs of earning an income, all of which should be considered in attempting comparisons between these age groupings.

Perhaps, despite all the evidence above, it might be objected that it has not been shown that the welfare state does in fact transfer resources from the nonelderly to the elderly. A study by the Australian Bureau of Statistics which analysed the incidence of direct and indirect taxes and of public expenditures on health, education, housing and welfare is clear on this point. Amongst ten categories defined in terms of life cycle stages, only singles and couples aged over 65 are net beneficiaries. The strongest net contributors are married couples aged under 35 without children, followed by singles under 35, married couples with non-dependent children only, and married couples with children under age five. Taken as a whole, couples with children were net contributors (ABS 1992, Figure 3, p. 7).

In sum, the bias of income taxes against workers, the bias of expenditure taxes against those with dependants, and the near impossibility of measuring assets or hidden incomes or the value of social expenditures or leisure or the costs of working all have the effect of making welfare realities very different from welfare ideals. I know of no counter-example to the claim that, when all the appropriate factors are counted, today's elderly turn out to be materially better off than the average nonelderly. Yet it is the elderly who are the main beneficiaries of today's welfare policies. Welfare states transfer resources from those who are starting careers, beginning families and buying homes to those who have completed these common life tasks. The challenge for the theorist who wishes to defend existing welfare systems is to find an actual welfare state in which transfers are not from the needy younger half of the population to the non-needy elderly. Welfare systems have no procedures for preventing upward redistribution of this sort. To prevent it would require processes of measurement that few societies have engaged in even at the census level, and which none have built into their assessments of individual welfare entitlements.

Taxing and spending trends

So far I have taken the usual static, snapshot approach that, as I shall now argue, is itself highly distorted. Welfare states do not stand still; policies and priorities change over time, and the changes are not random. Looked at dynamically, they tend to become, and have actually become, unbalanced most especially against those households in which the young predominate, families with children.

In a very general sense, the ideals of the welfare state have changed little over the past half-century. The goal of vertical and horizontal redistribution is still today much as it was fifty years ago. In many countries government spending on welfare and health as a fraction of gross domestic product rose steadily up to the 1990s; in some, the trend has levelled off in the last decade (OECD 1994, pp. 57–61). Despite an appearance of fixed principles, in practice welfare systems have undergone radical transformations, usually without acknowledgement. In those cases where such matters have been studied, it is clear that the main such transformation is a shift from a focus on the young in the welfare state's early decades to its present elderly-favouring form. This shift has been so great that David Thomson, who has drawn attention to it in the New Zealand case, thinks we should talk not about the *welfare state* but about the *Youth State* and the *Elder State*.

Thomson's point can be seen by comparing across time standard benefits for an average-income family of two adults and two children with pensions and benefits for the elderly. Table 5.1 shows the trend, decade by decade, for Australia.

Thus, across the history of the Australian welfare state, standard family benefits have fallen to roughly one-tenth of their original relative value, compared with age pensions. The New Zealand trend is similar, though a little less steep. In 1961, tax relief and payments for

Table 5.1   The ratio of state support for families with children to the single age pension, Australia: 1950–1990

Year	1950	1960	1970	1980	1990
Ratio	1.30	0.75	0.53	0.13	0.13

Note: Calculation is of tax concessions and child allowances for a 'standard family' of two adults and two children. The Dependent Spouse Allowance is not included in the calculation of family support; only support specifically for children has been counted.
Source: Based on figures in Reserve Bank of Australia 1997, Table 2.25.

two children were worth 41 per cent of a single age pension; by 1991, it was 23 per cent (Thomson, 1996, Table 3.3, p. 70). In Britain the 1960 figure was 88 per cent; by 1990 this had fallen to 49 per cent (Thomson, 1996, Table 3.5, p. 74).

These comparisons are only part of the story. Eligibility for pensions and family allowances have also changed over time. In 1950, Australian age pensions went to only 40 per cent of the elderly. In 1960, the coverage ratio had increased to 49 per cent; by 1970 to 60 per cent; by 1980 to 77 per cent; by 1990 there had been a fall to 58 per cent but veterans pensions for the elderly kept the total up to 77 per cent (Jones, 1996, Table 6.1, p. 119; Saunders, 1987, p. 23). Thus the quantum of social expenditure devoted to the elderly has risen dramatically over time, and in ways that do not depend upon changes in longevity. Contrastingly, payments for families with children began to be means tested in the 1980s. Coverage was general for the young but low for the elderly in the first decades of the welfare state; in later decades it has been high for the elderly and a little less than general for the young.

David Thomson's analysis of New Zealand and Britain shows that taxes have been shifted dramatically from the older to the younger half of the population ('the redirection of taxes across the life cycle has been widespread, massive, radical and rapid') and that trends in spending have risen for the elderly and fallen slightly for the young (Thomson, 1996, pp. 52–84, 66). The Australian case is very similar. Thus consistency across time cannot be assumed and has not been maintained in the evolution of at least three social support systems. These welfare states began by favouring families with dependent children. They are now slanted against them. They need not have begun with that preference, nor need they have evolved in that way, but they did and they have. Once a certain pattern of horizontal distribution is established it needs to be maintained, since to vary policies is to hand windfall gains to some and unintended losses to others. Furthermore, visible variations undermine the social meanings implicit in social programs. The message across time has been to devalue parents' child-rearing role. This role was once seen as central and thus worthy of strong governmental support; now it is simply assumed to run a distant second to the claims of the retired.

For those tempted to suppose that these trends and problems are peculiar to English-speaking welfare states, here is American economist Lester Thurow, speaking of the situation in all OECD countries: 'Already the needs and demands of the elderly have shaken the social welfare state to its foundations, causing it for all practical purposes to go broke'. 'Everything else is being cut in government budgets to make room for the elderly'. 'Even with rapid economic growth and no new programs, government spending rises faster than tax revenues because of entitlements for the growing population of the elderly' (Thurow, 1996, pp. 97–99).

The lifetime perspective

I turn now to examine the lifetime experience of different cohorts under the welfare state. The task here is to follow typical families through life, estimating taxes paid and benefits and government services received at each stage of life, a calculation that culminates in lifetime balance sheets for model cohort couples. Can this be done? In 1991 David Thomson published the results of such a 'generational' analysis of the New Zealand case (Thomson, 1991). His findings were startling. Couples born in the period 1920 to 1940 benefited very greatly from their lifetime experience of state welfare. Couples born after 1945 have had a vastly different experience. My more recent analysis of the Australian story arrived at similar though somewhat less extreme conclusions. It is not possible here to explore the details of these analyses, either in their methodology or in their results, but Table 5.2 gives some indication of the magnitude of this issue.

In this analysis, typical average-income couples from two cohorts are tracked throughout their lives. Their taxes paid and benefits received in each year are converted into fractions of the average male wage for that year. The lifetime tallies are then expressed as 'years of average pay'. 'Average pay' is being used as an index of rising general standards of living. GDP per capita would do the same job and might do it better, but 'average pay' has the advantage of converting lifetime experiences into units that have some everyday meaning. The meaning that can be

Table 5.2 Lifetime income taxes, family benefits and age pensions for two cohorts: New Zealand and Australia

Cohort	Born 1930	Born 1950/55
New Zealand	+ 2.5	– 9.8
Australia	+ 1.9	– 7.2

Unit of measurement: 'Years of average pay'
Note: The table tracks model couples through life, tallying income taxes paid and family benefits and age pensions received, converting the net figure for each year of life into fractions of the average male wage for that year. Future calculations are based upon forward projections of current trends.
Source: For New Zealand, see Thomson, 1996, Table 6.2, p. 172. Thomson emphasizes that these figures minimize the generational disparity. For Australia, the calculations here are based upon Reserve Bank of Australia 1997.

drawn, somewhat crudely but not absurdly, from Table 5.2 is that couples born in the 1950s are likely to have to work ten, twelve or more years longer than their preceding generation if they are to make up for the net effect of changes in public policy in income taxation, family payments and age pensions. Thomson goes on to argue that the net impact of all taxing and spending – including education, health and housing expenditure but also expenditure on 'public goods' – results in a loss to the later generation (relative to their predecessors) of about 30 'years of average pay' (Thomson, 1996, Table 6.2, p. 172). My estimates for Australia are somewhat lower, about 15 years.

Three points can be made about these figures. First, the vast differences in lifetime experience are the product of continuous incremental changes in welfare and taxation policy and practice, changes each so small as to be almost insignificant, but which cumulatively amount to lifetime differences on a scale not even faintly suspected by any welfare theorist before Thomson undertook his calculations. Policy and practice have simply drifted in a certain direction. At the operational level, there was no mechanism in place to ensure that what each cohort took out of the system in any way matched what it had put into it.

Secondly, the cumulative cohort differences have no warrant in standard welfare theory. No welfare theorist advocates cross-generational redistribution. Nor can the benefits to today's elderly be construed as a cohort reaping what it sowed in early life: the value of age pensions in Australia today exceed the lifetime effective income taxes paid by today's older cohorts (taxes which also have to cover the costs of education, health and housing). The objection to windfall gains to early cohorts is not one of penny-pinching or accountancy for its own sake.

Rather, it is about ensuring that the members of each generation get their fair share of an arrangement in which all are compelled to participate. That is an ideal which all must accept, if welfare systems are to have any credibility.

Thirdly, it is recent cohorts raising children who have been the main losers in the generational sweepstakes. They simply had the misfortune to have been born at the wrong time. Today it does seem as though the welfare state is inimical to conventional family life. But this is a fact with an important history attached to it. There have been two quite different experiences of the welfare state. The first generation of welfare participants, today's elderly, who raised their children in the Youth State, are the principal beneficiaries of today's Elder State. Welfare preference has followed them through life, from the cradle of their children through to their own graves. The second generation, their children, the 'babyboomers', who are now in the middle of their working lives, have had a very different experience. For them there has been no net assistance with child-raising, at least not for two-parent families, and it is now very clear that they will enjoy in their old age only a fraction of the assistance now being enjoyed by today's elderly.

It remains an open question how widespread is the generational transformation described above. There is some evidence that the same story holds true of the United States. Kotlikoff and Gokhale have argued that 'lifetime net tax rates' (the average amount of taxes a cohort will pay minus the benefits it will receive, all divided by its lifetime income) have risen steadily throughout the century, 'from 22 per cent for the generation born in 1900 to 34 per cent for the generation born in 1991'. They add that these figures 'are likely to understate the generational differences in economic well-being generated by U.S. fiscal policy' (Kotlikoff and Gokhale, 1994, pp. 78–80). Shirley Burggraf has noted other dramatic changes in lifetime fortunes: 'People retiring in the 1980s could still expect to collect [from Social Security] from two to four times what the same contributions to a private insurance plan would pay ... By 1995, newly retired, single, maximum-earning workers could expect to get back *less* than what their contribution would have earned in a bank savings account; and AARP [the American Association of Retired Persons] estimates that the same workers retiring at age 66 in 2015 will have to live 47.1 years to get back what they paid into the system even if benefits are not reduced as they are, in fact, likely to be' (Burggraf, 1997, p. 92).

The evidence for Britain is more debatable. John Hills has carried out an analysis of generational transfers in the British welfare state. He concluded that 'those born between 1901 and 1921 will get more out of the welfare state than they put in, although even this generation will have 'paid for' 80 to 90 per cent of what they receive under most assumptions'; and that 'cohorts born between 1921 and 1966 will end up roughly breaking-even, generally making small gains' (Hills, 1995, pp. 60–61). If he is right, the British welfare state is an important exception to the trends seen in New Zealand, Australia, and the United States. However, the taxation side of Hills' estimates is far from convincing. As he acknowledges, 'There is remarkably little information on relative tax payments by age in Britain' (Hills, 1995, p. 47). Hills' procedure is to divide the bulk of taxes equally between all those aged between 20 and 59 (some taxes are also allocated to the over-60s). This equalization blurs generational differences very considerably, since it fails to factor in any changes in tax concessions for children and it fails to include changes over time in women's workforce participation. On the expenditure side, Hills makes the strange assumption that lifetimes are typically of 90 years' duration. A more realistic treatment of longevity might alter his conclusions.

Couples and ex-couples

The contemporary family, I have thus far sought to show, finds itself in a singular field of social forces: redistribution from young to old is taken for granted; for some decades policy trends have been unsympathetic to family interests; the accumulated gains of the first welfare generation have been followed by second-generation deficits. All of this has subjected the contemporary family to financial stresses which often go unnoticed but which are an important part of its social history. Commentators on the family agree that family change since the 1960s is historically unprecedented. The economic stresses of the Elder State offer a possible explanation of some of these trends. Here I will focus on issues to do with separation and divorce.

How should welfare systems respond to couples with children choosing the option of separation and divorce? Before tackling this question, some clarification is called for. The issue is not sole parenthood as such – never-married sole parents raise different questions. Nor are childless couples relevant here. The issue is horizontal equity between couples who stay together to bring up their children and couples who separate or divorce while raising children. The point is not one of personal morality, nor one of children's interests. It is simply the question of financial equity.

As they developed in the post-war decades, almost all welfare states took up responsibility for making regular support payments to the custodial half of separated couples, payments not made to still-married couples. The custodial sole parent was treated as comparable to a widow, someone unable to obtain a partner's support. The standard view of the matter was that sole parent payments are a form of income supplement to a household type that in many cases is incapable of being economically self-supporting. But how does separation reduce a couple's capacity to support their children?

Three questions arise here. One, what is an appropriate measure of need? Single-parent households are commonly income-poor. But in any plausible estimate, assets and taxes and time must be included alongside income. Two, how is household size to be factored in? Sole parent households are, by definition, one adult smaller than couple-family households, so payment systems require an equivalence formula which takes this into account. Three, should the non-custodial parent's economic position be included in society's calculation of need? Often he or she is not counted, for reasons that are unclear.

The comparison here is between two couples, one of which (for whatever reasons) has chosen to remain together and the other (for whatever reasons) has not. On the face of it, their economic capacities are equivalent, except for the more expensive, or less efficient, housing arrangements of the second couple. Welfare policy has commonly not taken this view. Rather, it has treated the separating couples as unrelated individuals, even though the key issue is their continuing support for their children. Treating them as a separated couple, with the same obligations to their children as they had before separation, involves compelling non-custodial parents to bear the same financial obligations to their children as they had before separation. In making child support payments by non-custodial parents compulsory, welfare policy in Britain and Australia and some American states has now come around to the view that the state should be neutral between couples who separate and couples who stay together. Compulsory child support accepts the principle that ex-couples are still couples as far as the costs of child-rearing are concerned. A more radical approach would be to give all couples with children a substantial pension account, which they could convert to regular payments on separation or invest in their non-separating relationship however they see fit. Either solution at least avoids the appearance of horizontal inequity between family types, and separation and divorce are not advantaged.

In practice, of course, compulsory child support by non-custodial parents has proven difficult to achieve, and sole parent families continue to rely heavily on state support. In Australia, fifteen years after the introduction of compulsory child support, the budget for sole parent families still runs close to that for all family allowances for all other families, even though children in these families outnumber children in sole parent beneficiary families by a factor of about ten to one. Thus, much of the family welfare budget goes to a smallish family type, and this creates the impression that public policy on family type is unbalanced, or even unjust.

Nor is policy consistent across time. Public support in Australia for the standard two-parent family with one average income and two children is today 10 per cent that of support for a sole parent family with two children; in 1965 it was 40 per cent. Similar trends are evident in other welfare states. David Thomson has shown that in New Zealand since 1971 the incomes of sole parent pensioners with two children have improved in real terms by 32 per cent while the incomes of single income families with two children have fallen by 18 per cent (Thomson, 1996, Table 5.7, p. 144). In short, much like the intergenerational story, the Australian and New Zealand stories on family support is one of inconsistency, expediency, and doubtful equitability.

Conclusion

I have sketched some trends and tendencies in four welfare states, and suggested that some similar features may be found in others. At the operational level, these four welfare states failed to devise measurements and control mechanisms to realize their ideals. This failure has emerged historically in the form of economic disadvantages for people – especially married couples – raising children in the later decades of the century. Public policy in these states has required more from and conceded less to such families than at any time previously in this century.

The dramatic shift from 'Youth State' to 'Elder State' described in this chapter corresponds closely to a process in which families based upon the permanency of marriage and with strong internal bonds are ceasing to be the norm, and in which the 'post-nuclear family', characterized by single parenthood or serial monogamy, is increasingly prevalent. It does not directly follow that family change has been driven by welfare dynamics. Other explanations of family change would need to be considered before that conclusion could be reached. Nevertheless, it can be said that the forces at work in welfare transformation are far greater than has been commonly supposed, even by those who favour the welfare-causation perspective. How exactly those forces have impacted on the family remains a topic for another discussion.

Bibliography

The Australian Bureau of Statistics (ABS) (1992) *The Effects of Government Benefits and Taxes on Household Income* ABS Catalogue No. 6537.0. ABS: Canberra.

Burggraf, S. P. (1997) *The Feminine Economy and Economic Man: Reviving the Role of the Family in the Post-Industrial Age* Reading, Massachusetts: Addison-Wesley Publishing.

Crystal, S. and Shea, D. (1990) 'The Economic Well-being of the Elderly', *Review of Income and Wealth* 36: 227–247.

Hills, J. (1995) 'The Welfare State and Redistribution Between Generations', in J. Falkingham and J. Hills, eds., *The Dynamic of Welfare: The Welfare State and the Life Cycle* New York: Prentice-Hall/Harvester Wheatsheaf.

Jones, M. (1996) *The Australian Welfare State: Evaluating Social Policy*, 4th edn. Sydney: Allen and Unwin.

Kotlikoff L. J. and Gokhale, J. (1994) 'Passing the Generational Buck'. *The Public Interest* 73–81.

OECD (1994) *New Orientations for Social Policy* Social Policy Studies No. 12. Paris: OECD.

Reserve Bank of Australia (1997) *Australian Economic Statistics: 1949–50 to 1995–96* Occasional Paper No. 8.

Saunders, P. (1987) *Growth in Australian Social Security Expenditures 1959–60 to 1985–86* Discussion/Background Paper No. 19, The Social Security Review: Canberra.

Thomson, D. (1991) *Selfish Generations? The Ageing of New Zealand's Welfare State* Wellington: Bridget Williams Books.

Thomson, D. (1996) *Selfish Generations? How Welfare States Grow Old* Cambridge: The White Horse Press.

Thurow, L. C. (1996) *The Future of Capitalism* Sydney: Allen and Unwin.

Travers, P. and Richardson, S. (1993) *Living Decently: Material Well-being in Australia* Melbourne: Oxford University Press.

Part Three

Challenging the State Framing of Social Issues

6

Black Families and Survival

Beverley Prevatt Goldstein

Introduction

This chapter is written from the perspective of an activist and practitioner as well as that of an academic. It is concerned with the survival and well being of black families in Britain. It is written in a tradition which represents black people as neither victim nor problem, but as agents engaged in an ongoing process of working on and against hostile prevailing ideological and material practices (Gilroy, 1987; Mama, 1995; Rassool, 1997). The historical record of the British state and the evidence of its failures to act in the best interests of black families provide grounds for characterizing the state as a major source of ideological and material practices inimical to the well being of black families (Luthra, 1997). The ideals and family practices that many black families have developed, and are developing, have been influenced by the need for strategies to manage and survive negative treatment, including the complex racism experienced in British society and the institutions of the state (Macpherson, 1999; Commission for Multi-Ethnic Britain, Parekh Report, 2000). These ideals and practices also draw on repertoires of ways of being that have been tried and tested in other historical periods, in the African and Asian diasporas and which are being reworked to fit their current contexts. In this chapter I will define the terms 'black' and 'families', explore some of the common ideals and practices of black families, look throughout at their interaction with the state and conclude by identifying the strengths and limitations of these ideals and practices and the role of the state in enabling the best elements within them to survive.

The term 'black' is used in this chapter to emphasize common experiences of racism and disadvantage and refers to 'Africans (continental and of the diaspora) and Asians (primarily of Indian subcontinental descent). All have a shared history of British colonialism and oppression' (Mama, 1984: 23). This inclusive use of the term 'black' has never been fully accepted and is becoming more highly contested (Baumann, 1996; Brah, 1992). Diverse histories, cultural identities, religions, historical, national and regional antagonisms continue to provide a competing discourse of difference and division. British state policies have contributed to the ethnicisation of minorities, for example, in immigration restrictions, in education policies, in housing allocation and in fostering competition between ethnic groups for funding based on ethnicity (Gilroy, 1987; Sivanandan, 1990). An academic postmodern discourse which rejects fixed identities and which meshes with a culture of individualism and choice has also encouraged the challenges to a unifying political term such as 'black' and the flourishing of competing terms such as Ethnic Minorities, Minority Ethnic, Black Minority Ethnic, Black and Asian. Each term has its supporters in government, academic and practitioner circles. This author subscribes to and uses the term 'black' as a unifying political discourse within which differences of class, ethnicity, gender etc are recognized. As Bonnett has suggested: 'It is important not to forget that within Britain "anti-racists" construction of blackness was designed to serve an important purpose: to establish and support a 'community of resistance' with and against a white racist society ... To dismantle blackness but leave the force it was founded to oppose unchallenged is to display both a political and theoretical naiveté' (1996: 99).

The term 'family' is only slightly less contentious than the term 'black'. In the mid-twentieth century sociologists talked of 'the modern family', meaning a nuclear family household of mother and father and children. This definition of family would not have suited many black groups. The definition used in the Caribbean publication Savacou: 'a household, a network of relationships of people, not necessarily living together within the same four walls, encompassing children' (Hodge, 1977) is more appropriate for many black groups retaining links with a scattered kin network. High rates of divorce and family regrouping in white British households have heightened wariness of presuming a particular sort of household constitutes a family. In British sociology, David Morgan (1996, 1999, 2002) has adopted the term 'family practices' to help refocus theorizing and research on the processes by which people come to define themselves as being a family and 'doing family'. There is now therefore a common open position from both black and white sources that can encompass the diversity of black and white families.

Interaction with the state

There is a considerable body of literature (Amin and Oppenheim, 1992; Berthould, 1997; Cashmore and McLaughlin, 1991; Gordon, 1990; Hills, 1995; Luthra, 1997; Model, 1996; Virdee, 1995, 1997; White, 1996) which lists challenges disproportionately faced by black families including racial attacks, unemployment, poverty, police suspicion and surveillance, deportation and immigration restrictions. Every black person does not equally feel the brunt of this catalogue of negative experience; there are differences due to class, ethnicity, age, sexuality, disability and gender. However, all black families live in the shadow of these challenges. In addition to physical and economic challenges, black families experience, in varying degrees, challenges on a cultural /spiritual level such as cultural racism, cultural isolation, minimalisation of spirituality/religion, and the imposition of European family lifestyles (Hylton, 1997). Political challenges include the undermining of political solidarity by individualism and the exacerbation of ethnic divisions (Sivanandan, 1983).

Some of these challenges can be traced directly to state activity, for example immigration policies, while others, for example, racial attacks, may partly be attributed to state inactivity. Interaction with the state is complex, as the state itself is a conglomerate of agents that not only lack coherence but also sometimes pursue contradictory practices. Some arms of the British state are empowered to mount attacks on the racism of other arms of the state, for example, the Commission for Racial Equality may formally challenge racism in state organisations and the Macpherson report's identification of institutional racism within British institutions, and most particularly within the Metropolitan Police Force, was endorsed by the Home Secretary (Travis, 1999). Some institutions, post Macpherson, are devising initiatives to ameliorate the situation of black families (Madge, 2001).

Those devising and operating state policies and initiatives that limit or damage the welfare of black people may not operate from conscious racism. Racialized concepts have long been integral to the conceptualisation of some British policies and institutions, for example, the framing of inner city crime and the debate on policies around asylum seekers and refugees. In some cases, negative effects on black families are an unintended consequence of policies and initiatives that have been devised without reference to the needs and strengths of black groups. Arguably, this is the case with respect to housing policies, child protection procedures, and community care legislation. The state policies and initiatives that impact negatively on black people may also be the result of the prejudices and inequalities built into the system to deter other groups, in which black people figure, from making onerous demands on the state, such as lone mothers, large families and working class young people.

Black family ideals and practices in the context of interaction with the state

Across a wide spectrum of literature documenting the experiences of African and Asian people in Britain and their prior colonial history, there are suggestions of some common ideals and practices of black family life that help sustain survival in the face of poverty, isolation and racism. This literature includes the British archival research of Fryer (1984) and the GLC (1986); the research and writings of Sudarkasa from an African and African-American perspective (1995); Williams from a West Indian perspective (1970); Kakar from an Asian sub-continent perspective (1994) and recent British research studies, notably that of Beishon et al (1998); Dosanjh and Ghuman (1996); Hylton (1997) and Modood et al (1994). Although these practices are constantly being modified (Gilroy, 1992), adapted (Dosanjh and Ghuman, 1996) or newly created (Bakare-Yusuf, 1996), their creativity and continuity can challenge negative perceptions of black people (Prevatt Goldstein, 2002).

Families extend across households and national boundaries

There is a wealth of research demonstrating that in conventional practices of 'doing family', black families extend across households, and that black communities are not limited to locality or country of residence. For example, Beishon et al found that 'all [African-Caribbean] respondents had family members living overseas. ... All were in contact with some family members living abroad. ... African Asian and Indian families maintained regular contact with members of their families in many different countries. Importantly there was an average of about one to two visits every two years to the homes of relatives abroad' (Beishon et al, 1998: 20, 41). The significance of the extended family can be challenged by the state, for example, in housing policies, in immigration policies, and in the fact that family responsibilities outside Britain do not qualify for tax exemptions. Conversely, this ideal and practice can be used by the state when economically convenient, such as in a lack of attention to services for older people because

'they look after their own' (Department of Health, 1998; Patel, 1990).
However, in some of its childcare policy and legislation, such as The
Children Act 1989, the state has moved to a definition of family that is
wider than that of the nuclear family though narrower than that
commonly understood by many black families.

Children are a vital part of a family

The ideal that children are a vital part of a family is not unique to
black people. However, differences in family ideals and practices
around the value of children are suggested by the continuing high
birth rate for some black groups compared to white groups in similar
socio-economic positions and the higher presence of children in
cohabiting families (Haskey, 1997; Murphy, 1996; Owen, 1996). Black
families can infer that the state does not value black young people
from the ongoing high rates of 'stop and search' by the police force
(eight times higher than similar white young people, Dodd and
Hopkins, 2003). Black families can also consider that there are some
state practices inimical to maintaining children within black families.
For example, there is some indication that black children are received
into the looked after system more readily and for less serious reasons
than white children (Barn, 1993). The challenge to the fostering and
adoption of black children by white parents has been couched both in
terms of good parenting and political survival as a community: 'the
most valuable resource of any ethnic group are its children ... the black
community cannot maintain any dignity in this country if black children are taken away from their parents and reared exclusively by
another race' (ABSWAP, 1983).

Nevertheless black families, like all families, receive support from the
state, for example, in employment, housing, education, income
support, child protection and family support even while the evidence
demonstrates that many black families continue to be disadvantaged in
some of these areas (Madge, 2001).

Adults and elders should be respected

This has been found to be a central feature among many black families
of all ethnicities:

'They [all black parents] talked of white children as not having respect
for their parents or elders and as being out of control' (Beishon et al,

1998: 77). 'I'm more concerned about their manners and how they are towards adults, family. That they show adults the respect that is due them' (African Caribbean respondent, Beishon et al, 1998: 27).

The significance of respect has been ignored in official assessment frameworks and guidelines on parenting (DoH, 2000) and its enforcement of respect in some black families has caused significant misunderstandings and conflicts in the area of child protection. There has been a failure of dialogue on this topic with some white professionals and some black families taking up defensive or hostile positions.

Religious practice is central

Religion plays a larger part in the family life of more black than white British families. Hylton identified spirituality as being central to respondents (1997: 10,13). Dosanjh and Ghuman highlighted that all Punjabi parents in their sample emphasized religion (1996: 141). Religious practice is becoming increasingly privatized in a secular society and the fear of fundamentalism coupled with a belief in individual choice has heightened a discomfort with strong religious beliefs being held and being passed on to children. The tension in the state's position can be seen in the acceptance in principle of diverse religions, for example, the forthcoming Employment Directive against discrimination based on religion in employment and training, alongside the fear of religion, most particularly Islam, entering the public domain (Modood, 1997).

Educational attainment is a key goal

Research also highlights the significance of education among many black families, (Dosanjh and Ghuman, 1996: 162). The campaigns to ensure that black children receive an adequate education include the campaign against wrongful placement in schools for those with special educational needs (Coard, 1971), campaigns against bussing (Baumann, 1996) against school exclusions (Bourne et al, 1991; Allen, 1994) and campaigns to establish separate schools suggest that some black parents have not found the state to be an ally in meeting their children's educational needs. The state has both identified low achievement amongst particular ethnic groups and initiated some measures to alleviate this (Race Relations Amendment Act, 2000). Nonetheless, it has also been wary of black parents' emphasis on educational attainment and support for supplementary education (Community Cohesion, Independent Review Team, Cantle Report, 2001).

While state intervention plays a complex and contradictory role in supporting black families' ideals and practices, the latter are themselves complex and contradictory. The concepts outlined above can be viewed as an 'ideal type' which many families aspire to, but do not completely achieve. For example, Beishon (1998) noted, 'There was unity among the minorities in their criticism of what they perceived as a lack of commitment to parenting amongst Whites', yet the high numbers of black children in the 'looked after' system, in the juvenile justice system, and disproportionate suicides among young South Asian girls (Butt and Mirza, 1996; Raleigh, 1996) suggest parenting deficits, as well as unfavourable socio-economic conditions and racism.

Some of these ideals and practices are being modified by some families, for example, 'parental authority and family cohesion have not yet been displaced from the centre of Asian cultural life ... yet within these limits the young people are seeking modifications' (Modood et al, 1994: 80). Others are not homogenously practiced, with differences between ethnic groups and within ethnic groups. For example, 'Nearly all Pakistani and Bangladeshi parents ensured that their children undertook some form of cultural and religious activity. ... Some Sikhs interpreted the influence of religion in negative terms ... a third of African-Caribbean children took part in activities related to church or religion' (Beishon et al, 1998: 71). Importantly, these ideals and practices are also found in some non-black groups. It is therefore essential to recognize that these ideals, which for many are 'the soul to hold you together' (Hylton, 1997: 11), are at one end of a continuum while practice stretches along the continuum so that we arrive at a position which eschews homogenizing while not minimizing the ideals and practices which offer some cultural unity, continuity and resilience in the face of negative or indifferent state practice.

Strengths and limitations

The reasons for changing ideals and practices are complex and include a healthy evolution in response to contact with other cultural norms and changing socio-economic and political conditions as well as a dilution of healthy norms as a consequence of hostility and lack of social support. The norms cited above have considerable strengths. They have enabled families to pool resources when state and commercial sources were denied them (Luthra, 1997); strong cultural and religious traditions have been a counterbalance to involvement in street crime; and education has been the ladder to success for some communities.

Beishon (1998) suggests that the black family is a protective force against racism. Gilligan (1998) acknowledges that these ideals and practices, family, culture, religion, education can be a significant source of resilience in adversity.

These ideals and practices also have weaknesses. For example, 'Families extending across households and national boundaries' can weaken the financial resources available to the less needy unit and can divert emotional attention from this unit. 'Children are a vital part of the family' can support elements of a culture that marginalize and deem women without children to be inferior, and can endorse large families where the financial and emotional resources are inadequate for this. 'Adults and Elders must be respected' can seem onerous and unfair to young people growing up in the wider youth centred culture and can encourage children's needs and wishes to be given low priority and abusive situations. Similarly a focus on religion and on education can be counter to children's wishes and aptitudes.

A role for the state

Is there a role for the state in supporting families to sustain their beneficial ideals and practices without the potentially damaging effects? It seems essential that a way is found as otherwise we risk:

- Loss of protective and beneficial ideals and practices. This can be identified in the decreasing academic aspirations of some African Caribbean young men and by the increasing growth of drug misuse among young South Asians as they become less embedded in family, religion and culture.
- Antagonism by some black families towards potentially helpful state intervention as it is viewed as wholly negative and damaging to black families. Bernard's research has identified how black children can remain unprotected by the state from child sexual abuse because of racism and disablism by the state or/and because of parents' fear of racism by the state (1997).
- Continuation by some black families of negative practices, such as physical punishment, as they are held on to defensively as 'cultural' against a hostile state, deemed damaging to the continuing existence of black cultural groups.

We need to move towards the position found by researchers such as Dosanjh and Ghuman (1996), where parents retain beneficial ideals and practices with adaptations to improve them. For example, these authors write 'it is abundantly clear that the second generation Punjabi mothers have changed their attitudes to the development of independence in generally helping [their children] to develop their personal interest. However they are more like their first generation counterparts in giving and receiving affection, in giving rewards and praise, in the dislike and disapproval of the use of physical punishment and in the 'co-sleeping arrangement of babies, infants and children' (Dosanjh and Ghuman, 1996: 115).

Recommendations for change

In order to support the retention and development of ideals and practices that are benefical to its constituent communities, the state needs to improve its practice and image and draw back from its fear of cultural difference, as evidenced in the Cantle Report (2001), and enter into a dialogue where the communities and state can hear each other. This requires that the state is seen as a partner in combating disadvantage and discrimination. The Macpherson Inquiry, 1999, and subsequent Race Relations Amendment Act 2000 were good beginnings but there is some suggestion that the impetus has waned with reports of 100% increase in emergency calls to the Monitoring Group on Racism in the last year. Suresh Grover from the group concludes:

'We are in a worse situation than pre-Macpherson. There is a massive increase in race and religion-based attacks. There is a war on asylum seekers by the media, politicians and by violent thugs. Black Communities are under developed, suffering more deprivation, poverty and marginalisation' in Dodd and Hopkins, 2003.

The state needs to take seriously the issues of concern to black families, not only the poverty, unemployment, lack of opportunities and vulnerability to attack and abuse they experience with so many others, though to a disproportionate degree, but also their children's experience of bullying at school, racist attacks, educational underachievement, haphazard child protection (Barter, 1999; Dutt and Phillips, 1996). Ways forward need to be found in partnership rather than postponed for continual research and consultations, or imposed. One example of good practice is Hackney's 'Child Protection Procedures' where racist abuse is incorporated in the definition of abuse (Bond, 1999).

The state needs to ensure that its provisions, such as, the recent government initiatives in Britain (the Early Years, family support, child protection, fostering and adoption, Sure Start and Connexions[1]) incorporate the positive ideals and practices of all communities. The importance of identity, of education, of the wider family is being incorporated to some degree but without acknowledging or valuing their origin in the ideals and practices of black families. Appropriate and acknowledged integration of positive ideals and practices fosters their retention and development in the originating communities, facilitates use of the mainstream services by these communities, offers something additional to all communities, and challenges cultural racism.

The state also has a role in limiting practices that are known to be negative, rather than merely different. This is much more likely to be successful if the above two measures are put in place. Additionally, there is a skill in doing this that includes not assuming these practices are widespread in a particular community and only in this community. For example, challenges to a culture of physical punishment in some black families need to draw on those black families which do not use physical punishment, admit that this is an issue in many families, black and white and use the good practice that has been developed in working with white families, for example, working with the psychological and socio-economic reasons and offering alternative methods of dealing with behaviour as well as challenging the defensive cultural stereotypes offered by some black families.

The state needs to move to the position recommended in the Parekh Report (2000) where it values communities of individuals and communities of communities. It thus promotes equality for all, while enabling healthy ideals and practices of all groups to enter into the public domain. The dialogue on 'what is healthy' needs to be an open one based on evidence to which all can contribute and in which everyone is listened to. In this way the best ideals and practices of black families can be sustained and influence the mainstream while black families move from being perceived as victims and problems, to being acknowledged as leaders in the area of resilience in children and families.

Conclusion

This brief exploration of some of the ideals and practices which black families have developed to survive, their interaction with the state, their strengths and their limitations have led to recommendations for a different type of state intervention. This 'partnership' approach is likely to happen, if at all, slowly, incrementally and with difficulty. It is therefore essential that this is encouraged and monitored by black families and communities, and complemented with action by these families and communities to assess the strengths and weaknesses of their ideals and practices, and to identify and put in place mechanisms for sustaining them without damaging effects. It is imperative therefore that black families do not see themselves as victims or problems but as agents working within and with the state to secure their survival physically, economically and culturally.

Note

1 The impact of a number of these initiatives is also raised in the chapter by Selman. The Early Years programme was launched in a National Childcare Strategy Green Paper: 'Meeting the Childcare Challenge' in May 1998. It proposed that plans for establishing and developing early years and childcare services should be drawn up and implemented at local level by Early Years Development and Childcare Partnerships, bringing together local authority, private and voluntary providers. The Government's vision was that childcare and pre-school education are interlinked and interdependent. One-hundred and fifty partnerships in England were in operation in 2002/3 and thirty-two in Scotland. Sure Start was also launched in 1998 to help enhance the possibility of children having a 'sure start' in life by tackling disadvantage and 'social exclusion'. In Scotland this programme was local-authority led but in England and Wales it was more centrally managed. Connexions was launched in 2002 in England and Wales. This service is also provided through local partnerships and includes help-line and email services and 'Personal Advisors' offering a range of guidance and support, including career guidance, for young people who are up to 19 years old. Scotland has retained a separate career guidance service (Careers Scotland, relaunched in 2002 as an all age service), and in-school guidance systems.

Bibliography

Amin, K. and Oppenheim, C. (1992) *Poverty in Black and White* London, Child Poverty Action Group/Runneymede Trust.

Allen, E. (1994) *A Summary of the Research relating to the school experiences of young African-Caribbean males* London, Positive Images Education Project.

Association Of Black Social Workers And Allied Professionals (1983) *Report to the House of Commons* London, ABSWAP.

Bakare-Yusuf B. (1997) 'Raregrooves and Raregroovers' in Mirza, H. S. ed., *Black British Feminism* London: Routledge.

Barn, R. (1993) *Black Children in the Public Care System* London: Batsford.

Barter, C. (1999) *Protecting Children from Racism and Racial Abuse* London: NSPCC.

Baumann, G. (1996) *Contesting Culture* Cambridge: Cambridge University Press.

Beishon, S., Modood, T. and Virdee, S. (1998) *Ethnic Minority Families* London: Policy Studies Institute.

Bernard, C. (1997) 'Black Feminist Perspectives of Childhood Sexual Abuse' in Fawcett, B., Galloway, M., and Perrins, J. eds'. *Femimism and Social Work in the Year 2000: Conflicts and Contradictions* Bradford: Bradford University Press.

Berthould, R. (1997) 'Income Protection, Inclusion and Exclusion' in Hirsch, D. ed., *Social Protection and Inclusion: European Challenges for the United Kingdom* London: York Publishing Service.

Bond, H. (1999) Fighting racism is more than child's play, *Community Care* 8–14.4.99, pp. 24–5.

Bonnett, A. (1996) Anti-Racism and the critique of white identities. In *New Community* 22: 97–110.

Bourne, J. Bridges, L. and Searle, C. (1991) *Outcast England: How Schools Exclude Black Children* London: Institute of Race Relations.

Brah, A. (1992) 'Difference, Diversity and Differentiation' in Donald, J. and Rattansi, A. eds., *Race, Culture and Difference* London: Sage.

Butt, J. and Mirza, K. (1996) *Social Care and Black Communities* London: HMSO.

Cashmore, E. and McLaughlin, E. eds. (1991) *Out of order? Policing Black People* London: Routledge.

Coard, B. (1971) *How the West Indian Child is Made Educationally Subnormal in the British School System* London: New Beacon Books.

Commission for the Future of Multi-Ethnic Britain (2000) *The Future of Multi-Ethnic Britain, The Parekh Report* London: The Runnymede Trust.

Community Cohesion, Independent Review Team (2001) *Report of the Independent Review Team, Cantle Report* London: Home Office.

Department of Health (1988) *They Look After Their Own, Don't They : Inspection of Community Care Services for Black and Ethnic Minority Older People* London: The Stationery Office.

Department of Health (1989) *The Children Act* London: HMSO.

Doh, Dfee, Home Office (2000) *Framework for the Assessment of Children in Need* London: The Stationery Office.

Dodd, V. and Hopkins, N. (2003) 'Momentum in fight against racism wanes', *Guardian* 19.4.2003.

Dosanjh, J. S. and Ghuman, P. A. S. (1996) *Child-Rearing in Ethnic Minorities* Clevedon: Multilingual Matters Ltd.

Dutt, R. and Phillips, M. C. (1996) 'Race, Culture and the Prevention of Child Abuse', *Childhood Matters: Report of the National Commission of Inquiry into the Prevention of Child Abuse. Vol. 2, Background Papers* London: Stationery Office.

Fryer, P. (1984) *Staying Power* London: Pluto Press.

Gilligan, R. (1998) 'Beyond permanence: The importance of resilience in child permanency planning' in Hill, M. and Shaw, M. (eds), *Signposts in Adoption* London: BAAF.

Gilroy, P. (1987) *There ain't no black in the Union Jack* London: Hutchinson.

Gilroy, P. (1992) 'The end of anti-racism' in Donald, J. and Rattansi, A. eds., *Race, Culture and Difference* London: Sage.

Gordon, P. (1990) *Racial Violence and Harassment* London: Runneymede Trust.

Greater London Council Ethnic Minorities Unit (1986) *History of the Black Presence in London* London: Greater London Council.

Haskey, J. (1997) Population Review 8: The ethnic minority and overseas born populations of Great Britain, *Population Trends* 88:13–30, London: Office of National Statistics.

Hills, J. (1995) *Joseph Rowntree Foundation Inquiry into Income and Wealth 2* York: Joseph Rowntree Foundation.

Hodge, M. (1977) Young women and the development of stable family life in the Caribbean Savacou: Trinidad.

Home Office (2000) *Race Relations Amendment Act, 2000* London: The Stationery Office.

Hylton, C. (1997) *Family Survival Strategies: Black Families Talking* London: Exploring Parenthood.

Kakar, S. (1994) *The Inner World of the Indian Child* New Delhi: Oxford University Press.

Luthra, M. (1997) *Britains Black Population* Aldershot: Arena.

Madge, N. (2001) *Understanding Difference, the Meaning of Ethnicity for Young Lives* London: National Children's Bureau.

Mama, A. (1984) 'Black women, the economic crisis and the British State', *Feminist Review* 17: 21–35.

Mama, A. (1995) *Behind the Masks* London: Routledge.

Model, S. (1996) 'Ethnic Inequality in England: an analysis based on the 1991 census', *Ethnic and Racial Studies* 22: 966–90.

Modood, T., Beishon, S. and Virdee, S. (1994) *Changing Ethnic Identities*. London: Policy Studies Institute.

Modood, T. (1997) *Church, State and Religious Minorities* London. Policy Studies Institute.

Morgan, D. H. J. (1996) *Family Connections: An Introduction to Family Studies* Cambridge, Polity Press.

Morgan, D. H. J. (1999) 'Risk and family practices: accounting for change and fluidity in family life' in E. B. Silva and C. Smart (eds.), *The New Family?* London, Sage, 13–30.

Morgan, D. H. J. (2002) 'Sociological perspectives on the family' in A. Carling, S. Duncan and R. Edwards (eds.), *Analysing Families: Morality and Rationality in Policy and Practice* London: Routledge.

Murphy, M. (1996) 'Household and Family Structure among ethnic minority groups' in Coleman, D. and Salt, J. eds., *Ethnicity in the 1991 Census 1* London: HMSO.

Owen, D. (1996) 'Size, structure and growth of the ethnic minority populations' in Coleman, D. and Salt, J. eds., *Ethnicity in the 1991 Census 1* London: HMSO.

Patel, N. (1990) *A Race against time? Social Services Provision to Black Elders* London: Runnymede Trust.

Prevatt-Goldstein, B. (2002) 'Black Perspectives' Davies, M. (ed.), *The Blackwell Companion to Social Work*, Oxford: Blackwell.

Raleigh, S. (1996) 'Suicide Patterns and Trends in People of Indian sub-continent and Caribbean origin in England and Wales', *Ethnicity and Health* 1: 55–63.

Rassool, N. (1997) 'Fractured or Flexible Identities: Life Histories of Black diasporic women in Britain' in Mirza, H. S. ed., *Black British Feminism* London: Routledge.

Sivanandan, A. (1983) *A Different Hunger: Writings on Black Resistance* London: Pluto Press.

Sivanandan, A. (1990) *Communities of Resistance* London: Verso.

Sudarkasa, N. (1995) *The strengths of our mothers* Trenton, N. J. Africa World Press.

Travis, A. (1999) 'Stephen Lawrence's Legacy: confronting racist Britain', *Guardian* 25.2.99.

Virdee, S. (1995) *Racial Violence and Harassment* London: Policy Studies Institute.

Virdee, S. (1997) 'Racial Harassment' in Modood, T., Berthould, R., Lakey, J., Smith, P., Virdee, S. and Beishon, S. eds. 1997, *Ethnic Minorities in Britain: Diversity and Disadvantage* London: Policy Studies Institute.

White, R. (1996) *Racist Violence and the State* Harlow: Longman.

Williams, E. (1970) *From Columbus to Castro, The History of the Caribbean 1492–1969* London: Deutsch.

7

And One Man in His Time Plays Many Parts: the Five Ages of Impairment

Tom Shakespeare and Nick Watson

Introduction

Whilst William Shakespeare defined seven ages of man, for the purposes of this chapter we will concentrate on five life stages of a disabled person. By adopting a life course approach and reconceptualizing the impaired foetus, the impaired child, the impaired adult, the impaired parent and the impaired older person, we will be able to adopt both a horizontal and a vertical analysis, highlighting two dimensions of the disabled experience which are often neglected in the literature. In addition, we will be able to highlight a major area of neglect in research into families, namely that of disability. Disabled people are often researched as if they are not part of a family or they are seen as being part of 'special families'. This is despite the fact that disability is a significant area of state intervention into families. We write from the perspectives of sociologists, disability theorists and activists, and draw on a range of empirical and theoretical work to construct our argument about societal oppression of disabled people and the role of the state within this.

By adopting a horizontal analysis, we will show how, by decontextualising and individualising the experience of disability, the disabled person has become abstracted from the family context. Conversely, when the family becomes the focus of the study, the disabled person is absent from the analysis, the emphasis instead being placed on the effects of having a disabled person within the family. In both these cases, the disabled person becomes conceptualized as a burden, someone who requires support fiscally, both in health and social care terms, and who makes demands in terms of emotional and caring labour. The disabled family member is presented in terms relating to the physical, psychological and emotional problems that he or she presents to other family members. Whilst this emphasis on the efforts and stresses involved in caring may be useful for the management of disabled people by professionals, and the state more widely, any notion of reciprocity, or what De Swaan (1990) terms 'interdependencies' are lost.

Second, through observing the life course as a whole a vertical analysis can emerge, allowing the examination and exploration of social processes that serve to exclude people with impairment at different stages of the life course. By drawing upon the insights of the disability studies perspective, we will put forward a conceptualization of disabled people, family and the state that is based upon civil rights and disability equality. The development of the disabled people's movement worldwide since the 1970s, based on the principle of self-organization, has led to new developments in the sociology of disability, which move beyond the chronic illness approaches associated with medical sociology (see Bury, 1997). The Union of Physically Impaired Against Segregation's Fundamental Principles of Disability (UPIAS, 1976) set out the main elements of what Oliver (1983) termed the social model of disability. The social model underpins the majority of the writings associated with the disability studies paradigm. Put briefly, this approach regards disability as a social construction, or as Oliver phrases it, a social creation. People with impairment are disabled, not by their bodies, but by a society which fails to include them. Being disabled by society is about the twin processes of discrimination (Barnes, 1991) and prejudice (Shakespeare, 1994), which restrict individuals with impairment. This is a structural analysis, based on the notion of disabled people as an oppressed minority group, and disablement as a collective experience. Disability is viewed as a problem located within society and the way to reduce disability is to alter the social and physical environment. As Finkelstein writes:

'Once social barriers to the reintegration of people with physical impairments are removed, the disability itself is eliminated.' (1980: 33)

It closely follows Marxist and feminist paradigms of social relations. Thus when feminists distinguish sex and gender (Oakley, 1972), disability studies separates impairment and disability, the former physical and the latter social and cultural. Much of the research in this area focuses on the disabling environment – the physical and social barriers which exclude disabled people and render them powerless and voiceless. The social model provides an important alternative to the traditional individualist accounts of living with impairment, which locate the problem in the deficits of the disabled person and their body. These accounts could be said to 'blame the victim', and to make public issues into private problems.

There is a danger that presenting disabled people as a social group, as the social model approach demands, can deny diversity. Disabled people are not a monolithic block of likeminded people defined solely by the presence of an impairment. For example, not all disabled people are impaired throughout their whole life-time and there may be significant differences between people with congenital impairments, those who become impaired through injury or disease in young adulthood or middle age, and those who develop impairments as a result of the ageing process or in later life or through chronic illness. Similarly, the disability experience may be altered through gender, sexuality, ethnicity and class. Disabled people comprise an enormous range of social groups and the recognition of heterogeneity is, as we shall argue below, important. However, we believe that the notion of presenting disabled people as a social group and examining the experiences of that group through the life course is a useful, heuristic device that allows for a conceptualization of the disabled family, and enables us to trace the continuities in the way disability is conceptualized and dealt with.

Background

There is general agreement that, in the UK, the experiences of disabled people have changed rapidly as a direct result of social transformations in the past two decades. Continuing changes in the labour market, as well as more recent changes in social security, have led to a reappraisal of the categories of 'disability' and 'incapacity' and disability policy generally. Recent legislation restricts access to, for example, income maintenance benefits, thereby increasing demand for means tested benefits, while a Disabled Person's Tax Credit will reduce disincentives to work. Under the New Deal for Disabled People (NDDP) a system of personal advisors to assist disabled individuals to secure employment will run in conjunction with schemes supported by the Employment Services under the National Disability Development Initiative (NDDI).

These initiatives come in the wake of other developments in the policy arena regarding disabled people in general. Recent changes in legislation such as the Community Care Act (1993), the Disability

Discrimination Act and its recent amendment (1995 and 2001), the Further and Higher Education Acts in both Scotland and the rest of the UK, the Children's Act (1989), the Children (Scotland) Act (1995) and The Children (Northern Ireland) Order (1995) will all affect the rights and prospects of disabled people. These emphasize the rights of disabled people, prioritising their inclusion in every aspect of social, economic and political life. For example, local authorities and other agencies now have a duty to provide services which minimize the adverse effects of disability, enabling disabled people to achieve full citizenship. Proposals within the New Deal for Disabled People reinforce these processes through an emphasis on work as a route to inclusion as well as independence from welfare.

While the emphasis on citizenship and inclusion underpinning current policy must be welcomed, these do in themselves present a danger. They could be taken to suggest that disabled people who are not capable of work, of producing anything deemed to be of value, do not have a right to full citizenship. Such rights should guarantee substantive independence as unconditional on employment or family circumstances, but there is a danger that a focus on citizenship can ignore material and social inequalities. Citizenship has become equated with independence; it is only through being what modern culture has decreed 'independent', that an individual can achieve full citizenship. This denial of citizenship is reinforced through other social policy. Both Hahn (1986) and Stone (1985) have argued that disability is defined by policy: disability is whatever policy says it is. The dominant policy discourse, in the UK, presents disability as a tragedy and disabled people as people who need help and treatment (Oliver and Barnes, 1998). Consequently disability is presented as a welfare problem; issues of rights are ignored. The disabled people's movement have argued against such policy discourse, demanding that issues of discrimination and civil rights become part of the political discourse. We will emphasize the issue of civil rights and anti-discrimination as we explore how disability is conceptualized within what we have described as the five ages of impairment, starting with the foetus and moving on through childhood, adulthood, parenting and on to old age.

The disabled foetus

There is a profound irony that, for the first time in human history, a combination of changing attitudes, civil rights, technological support, and medical expertise has meant that having an impairment need be no obstacle to a high quality life and the achievement of social goals. For, just as this achievement becomes possible for many disabled people in the west, so the knowledge and practices arising from genetic medicine promise the elimination of some impairment. An approach based on the idea that impairment should be avoided at all costs, and that what medicine cannot cure it would be better to prevent, leads to the espousal of screening programmes to detect chromosomal, genetic, and developmental impairments in utero, and to provide the option of termination to pregnant women and their partners or preimplantation diagnosis.

Implicit in this approach is the idea that to be impaired is inevitably to experience a poor quality of life – a life not worth living – and to be a burden to one's family and to society. Extensions of screening programmes are explicitly advocated in terms of the financial savings which will accrue to the National Health Service (Wald, 1992); although the notion of individual choice for parents is used as a way of separating genetic screening from the coercion associated with past eugenic programmes. The rhetoric of disability as suffering is used to justify selective termination, despite evidence that abortion has serious negative emotional consequences for many who opt for it. Moroever, the whole discourse is framed in terms which are individualist and rely on a 'medical tragedy' definition of disability.

As disabled people have pointed out, the main barriers to disabled people are a lack of social and economic opportunity, not the problems of impairment. Rather than genetic engineering, it is social improvement which is needed. The key determinants of a disabled person's quality of life are issues such as socio-economic circumstances and the disabling effects of society, not the extent of physical limitation. If the prospective parents are in receipt of effective income; if their housing and the surrounding areas are accessible; if schooling is inclusive; then continuing a pregnancy affected by impairment is far more of an option than if these equality criteria are not met. Yet, an outdated view of what it is to be disabled is dominating discourses on genetics. Of course, the majority of medical professionals and non-disabled people do not understand what being disabled is about; they have been socialized to think of disability as a tragedy best avoided.

The information received by those considering screening does not provide a full picture of what it is to be disabled either. It concentrates on the genetic causes, and the clinical implications, rather than including testimony from the best experts on disability – disabled people themselves. This, together with the implicit influence of medical professionals, may contribute to decision-making outcomes which are not as open or considered as they should be. We are not arguing here that people should not be able to control their fertility, or opt for termination if they desire it, within the constraints of law and ethics. But we are suggesting that the current choice is not an informed one, that current counselling is neither adequate nor non-directive, and that the idea of genetics as a panacea for the problem of impairment may be misguided (Shakespeare, 1998). This, we would suggest, is the key challenge for the future; if, as seems likely, the use of genetic screening expands, there is an urgent need to ensure free and informed decision making based on a balanced appraisal of the family impact and quality of life in disability.

Disabled children

Much of the prevailing literature on disability tends to be dominated by non-disabled people discussing disabled people. In the case of disabled children, this imbalance is combined and reinforced because, like much of the prevailing research on childhood, this is work where adults are discussing children. Further, disabled children are presented within a paradigm that medicalizes and individualizes impairment (Shakespeare and Watson, 1998). We know from previous social policy research that families with disabled children experience a range of social and economic difficulties. However, there is a danger that this work also pathologizes disabled children. The contemporary research agenda (and research funding) continues to be dominated, in the main, by medical and epidemiological studies. Thus, the bulk of research into the lives of disabled children has been led by a preoccupation with impairment. This has been true not only for traditional forms of medical research but also for research apparently targeted at social issues. This work tends to be little more than catalogues of medical conditions, service directories or guidance notes on the 'handling' of children with impairments (Priestley, 1998). From the 'social model' perspective, the disadvantage experienced by disabled children is not a consequence of impairment but rather a failure of social structures and institutions to accommodate them on equal terms (Oliver, 1983; Barnes, 1991).

The advent of the disability movement, coupled with the development of disability studies, has radically changed the way that disabled people view themselves (Hasler, 1993) and the research agenda on disablement (Oliver, 1992a). At the same time a paradigm shift has taken place within academic and policy approaches to childhood. The UN Convention on the Rights of the Child, and its adoption by the UK government, the Children Act (1989) and Children (Scotland) Act (1995) all place emphasis on children as free agents, giving children a right to be consulted and heard on decisions affecting them. In academia, the new social studies of childhood, which originates from a children's rights perspective, has reinforced this view with its focus on children as social actors who play an active part in their own representation (Prout and James, 1997; Jenks et al, 1998). Both these approaches demand that children's testimonies are taken seriously.

There has, however, until recently, been little attempt to combine these new perspectives on childhood and on disability. The voices of disabled children themselves are largely absent from disabled childhood research. So Baldwin and Carlisle (1994), in their review of the literature, write:

'We found no studies focusing in detail on the disabled child's daily life and the way disability affects her.' (Baldwin & Carlisle, 1994, 33)

Priority is given to the views of health professionals, educationalists, policy makers and parents, with little attempt to gain the views of disabled children themselves.

From a disability studies perspective, it seems fairly clear that a major problem for disabled children is that they live in a disabling society. For example, whilst disabled children are no longer abandoned or killed at birth (in most cases), emphasis is placed on ensuring that disabled children are not born at all (Shakespeare, 1998). If, however, a child does slip through this screen, a whole array of technologies have been set up to measure and assess the child. Universal, standardized developmental targets are used to remind both the child and his or her parents that they are different. It is within this value system that disabled children have to grow up, as Middleton writes:

'All these efforts to make a child normal by stimulating brain waves, hanging them upside down, pushing, pulling and cajoling, mean that the child receives the very clear message that there is something about them that nobody likes. Chances are that they will learn not to like it either. Since it is likely to be something about which, realistically, they can do little or nothing, this overemphasis is likely only to create a sense of failure or even of self-hate.' (Middleton, 1996, 37)

These developmental targets and medical technologies equate impairment with disability and there is little recognition that such targets may themselves be socially or culturally defined (Davis et al, 2000).

This is combined with prejudiced cultural representations of disability which again serves to remind disabled children of the status society accords them (Integration Alliance, 1995). Traditional stories – such as The Secret Garden, or Heidi, or Tiny Tim – and charitable interventions – Children in Need, Action Research for the Crippled Child – reinforce these images. A disabled child is portrayed as one who needs sympathy, one who is 'tragic but brave' and in need of public support. Disabled children come to be seen as in-valid, dependent and incapable. The prevailing prejudice towards disabled children is also reflected in the poor provision of education for disabled children which limits them in their later lives (Fulcher, 1999). Disabled children are also under constant surveillance (Allan, 1996) and are prevented from developing social skills and self-confidence (Morris, 1997). They are further disadvantaged by disabling barriers in the built environment, housing and transport (see Barnes, 1991).

Whilst this disability studies analysis is important in that it points out the social factors that lead to disability, its material focus suggests that disabled children may not be capable of affecting the structures that impact on their lives and presents disabled children as an homogeneous group (Shakespeare and Watson, 1998). Recent research with disabled children, which, whilst broadly supporting the disability studies approach, has emerged from the new social studies of childhood, and points to the fluid and diverse nature of their lives (Watson et al, 1999). This work shows how many teachers, and other adults who work with disabled children, emphasize how different disabled children are from other children and that they do not understand things in the way that other children do (Davis et al, 2000). The researchers describe how the teachers often talked about the children as if they were not there, denying the children privacy and reducing the child to little more than their impairment. Being disabled subsumed all other identities in the eyes of teachers and other professionals, becoming the dominant identifier for many of these children (Davis and Watson, 2001). Importantly, however, this work also shows that the children are not passive in the face of this oppression. The children adapted their behaviour with different adults and in different settings (Davis et al, 2000). They often attempted to negotiate their own choices, constructing their own childhoods and identities

(Priestley et al, 1999). Their ability to resist and challenge stereotypical representations (Davis and Watson, 2002), and how disabled children negotiate structural and material aspects of their lives (Davis et al, 2000) are also highlighted.

Work by Priestley et al (1999) shows how bullying was identified as a major issue by many of the disabled children they worked with. Indeed some of the children in that study, when asked what the word disabled meant to them, replied 'we all get bullied'. Further, many of the children in special schools said that they were there because of being bullied, that they could not cope in the mainstream with the constant intimidation that they faced (Watson et al, 1999). This raises a number of questions: first, why are the bullied excluded, not the bully; second, what is going to happen in the future when these children leave school and have to re-enter a world of non-disabled people; and, third, why can't the processes leading to bullying be altered? These are concerns that children themselves raised. Segregation and special education are short-term solutions and fail to tackle the real problem of discrimination against disabled people; indeed it might be argued that it reinforces and legitimizes it.

Much of the work on disabled children presents depressing findings. However thinking of these children as victims or tragedies, either of their impairment or of society, must be avoided. As Shakespeare and Watson (1998) argue, many disabled children lead happy and fulfilling lives. The way that the children themselves have resolved the problems that they face point the way forward (Davis et al, 1999). While the social model should guide our analysis, and the principle of disability equality should inform our values, the ultimate commitment must be to the views of disabled children themselves. As researchers, as social workers, or any professionals providing services for disabled children, the task becomes clear: listen to what disabled children say about their lives; respect their wishes; and support their choices.

Disabled adults

There are three points that we wish to make in relation to disabled adults: first, disability is a social and not a medical problem. This is not to suggest that disabled people do not need medical care and attention, all people do. However, for disabled people the overriding problems that we face in our daily lives are the result of social, cultural and environmental factors. Oliver argues that disability arises through both, what he terms, the mode of thought of society and the mode of production (1990; 32). By this he means that disability is the product of not just capitalist production but also individualism, the medicalization of society and the societal view of disability as a 'personal tragedy'. Bio-engineering and rehabilitative medicine, with their emphasis on normality, by changing the individual rather than society merely serves to increase disabled people's oppression. This view of disability is the product of the social relations of capitalism (1990; 132). It is society that has to change, and this will only be achieved by political action, not through social policies initiated by the establishment or individualized treatments and interventions (Oliver, 1996). We could cite, for example the Disability Discrimination Act, a piece of legislation that was introduced because of political agitation by disabled people despite government assertions that it was unworkable (Doyle, 1996). This legislation, despite its many loopholes, is the first comprehensive bill for disabled people ever introduced by a British Government. It is too early to tell if this legislation will affect employment for disabled people, but, as Doyle (1996) points out, law has an ideological as well as instrumental impact. The 1990 Americans with Disabilities Act, by clearly stating that the major problems disabled people faced were social in origin helped in the creation of a stronger constituency, which in turn strengthened legal provision and the enforcement mechanism.

The radical rhetoric of the social model has invigorated the disabled people's movement. Disabled people have defined themselves. No longer are disabled people represented by organizations 'for disabled people' but 'of disabled people' (Hassler, 1993). Through political demonstrations by for example the Direct Action Network, disabled people have challenged the notion that they are docile, they are demanding 'rights not charity', equality of access and accessible transport. The problem of disability is relocated to environments and structures, not bodies and minds.

Second, impairment does not equal dependency. The tradition of seeing disabled people as dependent arises out of the denial of autonomy to disabled people, because they are seen as being unable to survive independently. Dependency suggests that an individual is unable to perform certain tasks for themselves, relying upon others to carry out these tasks. To be independent suggests that people do not require assistance in their day to day lives. In reality no one is independent, and whilst the dependence of disabled people is quantitatively different from that of non-disabled people, it is not qualitatively different and should not be a feature used to mark disabled people out as different from the rest of the population. Professional definitions of independence tend to focus on the ability to perform self-care activities such as washing, toileting and so on. Disabled people, however, define independence as an ability to take decisions for themselves, to be in control, rather than performing tasks without help (Morris, 1993). This distinction between physical dependence and social dependence is critical. Disabled people can take far more responsibility for their own lives than has ever been allowed to them, historically.

The Independent Living Movement, whose philosophy is based on the social model coupled with a belief that disabled people have a right to participate fully in society and are capable of exerting choices, shows how disabled people can lead independent lives. The provision of independent living schemes, administered through direct payments and providing sufficient funds to employ Personal Assistants can enable those with even the most severe impairments to contribute to society (Barnes, 1993) They can allow the attainment of normative social goals.

Third, disabled people are denied access to citizenship, in the public domain, and also to ordinary adult rights in the private domain. Again, this relates to the picture of disabled adults as 'child-like' and 'innocent', requiring protection. Particularly relevant here are issues of sexuality, and of parenting. Recent research by Shakespeare et al (1996) and others has clearly demonstrated that disabled people are regarded as asexual and denied a right to relationships or family life. For example, sex education is often not provided to disabled people. People living in institutions may not have the freedom or privacy to develop sexual partnerships. Leisure and social spaces may be inaccessible to disabled people, either because of physical barriers, or because gate-keepers and members of the public do not expect disabled people to be there, or actively prevent them being there. The barriers to disabled people's sexual expression are not physical incapacity, impotence etc, as the prevailing stereotypes would suggest. Instead, it is social barriers, lack of sex education, low self-esteem and segregation which contribute to the emotional marginalization of disabled people.

Disabled parents

Both a cause and a consequence of this exclusion is the perceived problem of disabled people as parents. That is to say, fear of disabled people reproducing may underlie a reluctance to enable the sexual expression of disabled people, and that the barriers to disabled people forming relationships may prevent them being able to have children and family life. After all, up until recently it was common for people with learning difficulties, for instance, to be sterilized without their consent. In the same way that the disabled adult is denied sexual rights, so the disabled adult is denied reproductive rights. The powerful ideology of disabled people as dependent and passive is supplemented by the notion that they must be the cared for rather than the care givers. For example, in a recent study, one of the participants, a woman with cerebral palsy, described how, when she went for assisted conception, the consultant asked her if she thought that she would make a suitable mother, if she felt that she would be able to care for her child (Watson, 2000). It was recommended that she should go away and reconsider her position – this despite it having taken two years for her to get the appointment. Fitness to parent is only asked of some social groups.

Disabled people who choose to have children are seen as being both selfish and irresponsible. Disabled people who wish to be parents are asked not only if they can cope with the physical and emotional demands of parenthood, but their ability to meet many of the practical demands are also raised. For example Wates (1997) describes how disabled parents are questioned about their ability to meet the extra financial costs associated with parenthood and are also asked to consider their own future health. She further argues that:

> 'Disability is so closely associated with dependence and social isolation that it is hard for people to imagine a disabled person at the centre of family life in the role of primary carer.' (1997; 2)

Keith and Morris (1996) point out how some literature on disabled parents is written in such a way as to suggest that the very idea of disabled people having children is seen as exploitative of the children. For example, they quote the work of Aldridge and Becker (1993) who describe children of disabled parents as 'young carers' and go on to argue that 'the roles have been reversed so that the child becomes the parent of the parent' (p. 58).

If disabled parents do rely on their children as carers, it is not because they wish to, but because society has failed to provide them with adequate social support. Children with disabled parents do indeed sometimes find themselves in the position of having to help their parents, however, as both Parker (1994) and Wates (1997) argue this is generally the result of inadequate support or when support systems have broken down. As Keith and Morris (1996) argue, children who find themselves in a position in which they have to provide care and support that is inappropriate to their age and strength, do so because of poverty, disabling professional attitudes, disabling environments and disabling communities. It is the media and some social scientists, who, by presenting these as the norm, further propagate the image that disabled people are unsuitable to be parents by laying the blame on the parents themselves. All parents have to negotiate issues around help in the home with their children, again there may be a quantitative difference here for disabled parents, but qualitatively, there is no difference.

For disabled parents, what is needed is a recognition that many of the problems that they face are the product of a society that either fails to include them because of disabling barriers, or fails to provide them with adequate social support.

Disabled older people

Next to nothing is known about ageing with a disability (Zarb, 1993). With the exception of work by Zarb and Oliver (1993) and Walker and Walker (1998) there is little research in the area of disabled older people. This is despite the fact that, with improvements in medical technology, more disabled people are surviving into old age and that the majority of disabled people are over pensionable age. Walker and Walker (1998) suggest that this lack of research arises because disability is seen as a 'natural' part of the ageing process, and, consequently, there is no need to explore the issues that arise through ageing with an impairment. However, as disabled people age there are issues that may be particular to disabled people. For example, Zarb and Oliver (1993) report that older disabled people are even more likely to be separated from family and friends than their non-disabled peers. Whilst many older people are likely to experience some loss of independence, for disabled older people this appears to be more exacerbated than that found in the general ageing population. Zarb and Oliver argue that there are two key issues for disabled older people; first, many feel that their needs are overlooked and, second, many are anxious about maintaining their independence which they see as being threatened by a lack of appropriate and supportive services. Their research suggests that what services are available create and reinforce older disabled people's dependency through the lack of recognition of the needs of older disabled people, a lack of knowledge of the medical consequences of ageing with a long term disability, a lack of acceptable living options and inadequate pension provision.

Drawing on Oliver and Zarb's work, we would like to explore disabled older people in three ways. First, the social ascription of incompetence and senility to older people, their portrayal as childlike, as dependent, as a burden, presents a cultural stereotype of older people similar to that experienced by disabled people. All older people are devalued and marginalized, and, in a similar way to disabled people, they are treated as objects of pity. As Warnes (1993) clearly demonstrates, writings on older people in general, have, over the last couple of decades, tended to focus on older people as a burden, especially the financial demands that older people place on society and the demands that they place as recipients of care. Older people present a fiscal crisis, a demographic time bomb. The political demands for yet further reductions in public expenditure and the assertion that older people are responsible for the increase in healthcare costs have set the agenda for this debate. There is little recognition of the social creation of dependency in old age (Walker, 1980) and this mirrors the lack of a recognition of the social creation of disablement. Oliver (1992b) makes the point that whilst it is important to explore the links between ageism and disablism, they are experienced simultaneously, not as parallel forms of oppression.

This leads us onto our second point; whilst the views of user groups have become a key perspective within other areas of social policy, we would argue that this has not occurred within old age. Old age is biologized, older people are objectified in a way that no other group experiences. In issues of care, the research agenda and policy tend to focus on the burdens that the older person places on the carer, giving primacy to the position of the provider of the care. The views of the providers of care are privileged with little attempt to understand the experiences of the recipients of care, what it is like to be disabled, sick or receiving care. Morris (1996) has pointed out that much of the feminist literature on informal care takes the side of middle-aged women who are the care givers. The views of the care receivers, many of whom will also be women, are for the most part absent. Drake (1999; 165) reports two studies that he carried out in Wales on disabled and nondisabled older people. He argues that the prime concerns of older people, both disabled and nondisabled, 'rested with the fabric of their communities and with their abilities to participate in the ebb and flow of everyday life rather than expressing any desire for greater "welfare" interventions.' (165–166). The issues that the older people identified centred on crime prevention, the environment, housing, access, transport and domestic support services. They are not interested in services which attempt to ameliorate the impact of impairment, the traditional focus of much welfare provision for older disabled people.

Third, older people in general are subjected to material and social deprivation. They face poverty, not just because of poor welfare provision but also due to structural factors that legislate against their ability to work (Walker, 1980). For disabled older people this effect can be even more apparent. Many disabled people are denied access to work and through this a private pension scheme; consequently, in old age their incomes are inadequate. Zarb and Oliver (1993) make the point that ageing, for disabled people, is associated with increases in expenditure on, for example, house maintenance, domestic support, personal assistance and transport. They suggest that two thirds of those in their sample had an income that was inadequate, with almost half having a severely inadequate income.

We would argue, following Zarb and Oliver (1993), that there is a need to establish a framework of rights and entitlements for older disabled people. Disabled people must be listened to in the development and delivery of services, discriminatory stereotyping must be challenged and older disabled people provided with an adequate income to ensure that they are not forced into a life of dependency.

Conclusion

The life course approach that we have adopted in this chapter has allowed the juxtaposition of different literatures through which themes and continuities showing the same processes at each stage have emerged. At the same time, a horizontal analysis has enabled us to present literature that is specific to particular stages in the life course. Two important elements have emerged from this. Firstly the primacy of structural issues in the lives of disabled people, the way that the social impacts on those with impairments. Disabled people have, since the 1970's, been demanding that disability be seen as a social and political issue, not a medical problem. What we have shown in this chapter is how these structural issues impact on disabled people throughout their life course. Secondly, it may be argued that the majority of research on disability concerns issues of agency; how people cope with, or come to terms with an impairment, or how people come to terms with or cope with having a family member who is impaired. Whilst this work is of value, as we have argued in the case of disabled children, there is a danger that such work can ignore the structures which form and shape disabled people's experiences

(Williams, 1996). This focus tends to blur what we see as the real issues in disability research. Its bottom up approach runs the danger of neglecting important structural issues. What we are arguing for is a focus on civil rights, on justice and on humanity. This implies a research agenda that does not decontextualize the experiences of disabled people, but one which analyses these experiences in the light of structural issues. It is only then that the impact of the state and its associated institutions can be thoroughly understood.

Bibliography

Alan, J. (1996) 'Foucault and Special Educational Needs: A box of tools for analysing children's experiences of mainstream', *Disability and Society* 11(2), 219–233.

Aldridge, J. and Becker, P. (1993) *Children who Care: Inside the World of Young Carers* Department of Social Sciences, University of Loughborough.

Barnes, C. (1991) *Disabled People in Britain and Discrimination* London: Hurst and Co.

Barnes, C. (1993) *Making Our Own Choices: Independent Living, Personal Assistance and Disabled People* Belper: British Council of Organisations of Disabled People.

Baldwin, S. and Carlisle, J. (1994) *Social Support for Disabled Children and Their Families: a Review of the Literature* London: HMSO.

Bury, M. (1997) *Health and Illness in a Changing Society* London: Routledge.

Davis, J. and Watson, N. (2001) Where are the children's experiences. Analysing social and cultural exclusion in 'special' and 'mainstream' schools. *Disability & Society* 16(5), 671–688.

Davis, J. and Watson, N. (2002) 'Challenging the Stereotypes: disabled children and resistance' in Corker M. and Shakespeare T. eds., *Disability and Postmodernity* London: Cassell.

Davis, J. Priestley, M. and Watson, N. (1999) 'Dilemmas of the field: What can the study of disabled childhoods tell us about contemporary sociology?' Paper presented at the 1999 BSA conference *'For Sociology'* University of Glasgow, 6–9 April 1999.

Davis, J. Watson, N. and Cunningham-Burley, S. (2000) 'Learning the Lives of Disabled Children' in Christensen, P. and James, A. eds., *Research with Children: Perspectives and Practices* London: Falmer Press.

De Swann, A. (1990) *The Management of Normality* London: Routledge.

Doyle, B. (1996) *Disability Discrimination: The New Law* London: Jordans.

Drake, R. (1999) *Understanding Disability Politics* Basingstoke: Macmillan.

Finkelstein, V. (1980) *Attitudes and Disabled People*, New York: World Rehabilitation Fund.

Fulcher, G. (1999) *Disabling Policies? A comparative approach to education policy and disability* Sheffield: Philip Armstrong.

Gregory, S. (1976) *The Deaf Child and His Family* London: George Allen Unwin.

Hahn, H. (1986) 'Public Support for Rehabilitation Programmes: an analysis of US disability policy', *Disability, Handicap and Society* 1(2) 121–138.

Hasler, F. (1993) 'Developments in the Disabled People's Movement' in Swain, J. Finkelstein, V. Oliver, M. and French, S. eds., *Disabling Barriers – Enabling Environments* London, Sage.

Integration Alliance (1995) *Invisible Children: Report of Conference* London: Integration Alliance.

James, A. and Prout, A. eds. (1997) *Constructing and Reconstucting Childhood: contemporary issues in the sociological study of childhood* London: Falmer.

Jenks, C. James, A. and Prout. (1998) *Theorising Childhood* Cambridge: Polity.

Keith, L. and Morris, J. (1996) Easy Targets: a disability rights perspective on the 'children as carers' debate in Morris, J. ed., *Encounters with Strangers: Feminism and Disability* London: Women's Press.

Middleton, L. (1996) *Making a Difference: Social Work with Disabled Children* Venture Press, Birmingham

Morris, J. (1993) *Independent Lives: community care and disabled people* Basingstoke: Macmillan.

Morris, J. (1996) *Encounters with Strangers: Feminism and Disability* London: Women's Press.

Morris, J. (1997) 'Gone Missing: Disabled children living away from their families', *Disability and Society* 12(2) 241–258.

Parker, G. (1994) *With this Body: Caring and Disability in Marriage* Milton Keynes: Open University Press.

Oakley, A. (1972) *Sex, Gender and Society* London: Maurice Temple Smith.

Oliver, M. (1983) *Social Work with Disabled People* Basingstoke: Macmillan.

Oliver, M. (1990) *The Politics of Disablement* Basingstoke: Macmillan.

Oliver, M. (1992) 'Changing the Social Relations of Research Production', *Disability, Handicap and Society* 10(3) 261–279.

Oliver, M. (1992b) 'Societal Responses to Long Term Disability in Whiteneck', G. ed., *Ageing with a Spinal Cord Injury* New York: Demos Publication.

Oliver, M. (1996) *Understanding Disability: from Theory to Practice* Basingstoke: Macmillan.

Oliver, M. and Barnes, C. (1998) *Disabled People and Social Policy: from Exclusion to Inclusion* London: Longman.

Priestley, M. (1998) 'Childhood Disability and Disabled Childhoods: agenda for research', *Childhood* 5(2) 207–233.

Priestley, M. Corker, M. and Watson, N. (1999) Unfinished Business: disabled children and disability identity, *Disability Studies Quarterly* 19(2).

Shakespeare, T. (1994) 'Cultural Representations of Disabled People: dustbins for disavowel', *Disability and Society* 9(3) 283–301.

Shakespeare, T. (1998) 'Choices and Rights: eugenics, genetics and disability equality', *Disability and Society*, 13(5) 665–682.

Shakespeare, T., Gillespie-Sells, K. and Davis, D. (1996) *Untold Desires: the Sexual Politics of Disability* London: Cassell.

Shakespeare, T. and Watson, N. (1998) 'Research with Disabled Children' in Robinson, C. and Stalker, K. eds., *Growing Up Disabled* London: Jessica Kingley Press.

Stone, D. (1985) *The Disabled State* London: Macmillan.

UPIAS (1977) *The Fundamental Principles of Disability* London: Union of the Physically Impaired Against Segregation.

Wald, N. (1992) 'Antenatal Maternal Screening for Down's Syndrome: results of a demonstration project', *British Medical Journal* 305: 391–394.

Walker, A. (1980) 'The social creation of dependency and poverty in old age', *Journal of Social Policy* 9: 49–75.

Walker, A. and Walker, C. (1998) 'Normalisation and "Normal" Ageing: the social construction of dependency among older people with learning difficulties', *Disability and Society* 13: 125–143.

Warnes, A. (1993) Being Old, Old People and the Burdens of Burden, *Ageing and Society* 13: 297–338.

Wates, M. (1997) *Disabled Parents: dispelling the myths* Cambridge: National Childbirth Trust.

Watson, N., Shakespeare, T., Cunningham-Burley, S. and Barnes, C. (1999) *Life as a Disabled Child* Final Report to the ESRC, Department of Nursing Studies, University of Edinburgh.

Williams, G. (1996) Representing Disability: some questions of phenomenology and politics in Barnes, C. and Mercer, G. eds., *Exploring the Divide: Illness and Disability* Leeds: Disability Press.

Zarb, G. (1993) 'The Dual Experience of Ageing with a Disability', in, Swain J., Finkelstein V., Oliver M. and French S. eds., *Disabling Barriers – Enabling Environments* London: Sage.

Zarb, G. and Oliver, M. (1993) *Ageing With a Disability: what do they expect after all these years* London: University of Greenwich.

8
Scapegoating and Moral Panics: Teenage Pregnancy in Britain and the United States

Peter Selman

> *'Public policies on adolescent pregnancy...have frequently misdescribed the problem and misled as to the solution'.*
>
> Deborah Rhode (1993)

Introduction

Changes in the last 40 years of the twentieth century mean that patterns of family formation and dissolution are now very different from the mid-twentieth century: higher divorce rates; lower marriage rates; a growth in non-marital cohabitation; more births outside wedlock; an increase in the number of lone parent families; more mothers in paid employment (Selman, 1996b). Most of these changes are represented to a greater or lesser extent in all 'western' capitalist democratic nation states: from Sweden to Ireland; from North America to Australia; and also in the newly industrialized countries of South East Asia. Van de Kaa (1987) has referred to this cluster of changes in Europe as a 'second demographic transition'. In most of these countries birth rates have fallen again after a 'baby-boom' in the 1960s and the median age of childbearing has been rising. In Northern European countries, the number of births to teenagers fell dramatically in the 1980s (see Table 8.1), but in Britain and the United States adolescent fertility rates, although substantially lower than in the 1960s (Selman, 1996a; Arai, 2003), rose from the mid-1980s and remain much higher than in mainland Western European countries (UNICEF, 2001). This is despite a reversal of the upward trend in the US in the 1990s and in Scotland[1] where the rate has remained fairly stable since the 1996 and declines in England & Wales since 1999.

Table 8.1   Teenage fertility rates (births under 20 per 1000 women aged 15–19) 1970–1999: USA, England and Wales and other European countries

Country	1970	1980	1990	1995	1998/99*
United States	66.1	53.3	59.4	58.2	50.5*
Bulgaria	71.5	81.0	73.9	54.0	45.1
Romania	66.0	73.0	66.0	40.5	40.9
Hungary	50.5	69.0	41.2	29.9	26.5
England & Wales	50.8	30.9	33.3	29.7	31.1*
Greece	36.2	52.6	26.3	13.0	11.8
Finland	29.8	18.9	12.4	9.8	9.2
Denmark	29.3	16.8	9.8	8.8	7.9
France	27.7	17.8	9.1	7.9	9.3
Sweden	34.6	15.8	12.7	7.8	6.5
Italy	27.1	15.4	9.6	6.8	6.6
Netherlands	22.2	9.2	6.4	5.6	6.3

Source: UN Demographic Year Books (1975; 1986; 1992; 1997; 1999); Eurostat Demographic Statistics; UNICEF (2001)

In both countries young single mothers have been the subject of much hostility from the media and politicians, as symptomatic of a decline in morality and the collapse of the traditional family. Although government concerns in this area increased under the conservative administrations of Reagan and Thatcher, they were maintained through the Clinton presidency in the USA and the 1997 New Labour administration in the UK, both of which launched new programmes to tackle the 'problem' (National Campaign to Prevent Teen Pregnancy, 1999: Social Exclusion Unit, 1999). The development of these programmes will be discussed further in the conclusion to this chapter.

Young mothers as scapegoats: moral panics about adolescents in Britain and the United States

This chapter examines these concerns over teenage pregnancy by looking at media and political representations in both countries. In particular it analyses the scapegoating of young single mothers as both symptom and cause of the collapse of the family, and the moral panics engendered by media reports on irresponsible sex and welfare scroungers. I use the term 'scapegoating' to refer to a discrediting routine by which people move blame and responsibility away from themselves towards a target group (Males, 1996; Scapegoat Society, 1999) and 'moral panics' to refer to a collective over-reaction to a perceived social problem (Cohen, 1980; Goode and Ben-Yehuda, 1994; Thompson, 1998), a process akin to what Ryan (1971) has termed 'blaming the victim'. The idea of moral panics has been criticized by Norman Dennis (1993) who has written that '*the fate of two-year-old James Bulger* [the British toddler beaten to death by two older children, also boys] ... *dealt the death blow to the 'moral panic' school ... a pernicious theory and a cant phrase was given its last airing*'. But Thompson (1998) argues that the Bulger case represented a further manifestation of such panics.

My aim is to review the available evidence to challenge the scapegoating and moral panic surrounding teenage pregnancy, making use of demographic data; media coverage; the comments of individual politicians; and government policy and rhetoric. I shall argue that the punitive attitudes to teenage mothers are hard to justify and have been counter-productive, distracting from the need to come to terms with long term changes in the family (Kamerman, 1990) and doing nothing to help with the immediate problem of unwanted teenage conceptions.

Public hostility to young mothers in the UK in the 1990s

In the early 1990s, government ministers were involved in an 'orchestration of public hostility towards young single mothers, much of which was focused on their abuse of welfare' (Sinclair, 1994). At the Conservative Party Conference in October 1992, Peter Lilley, then Minister for Social Security, spoke of '*young ladies who get pregnant just to jump the housing list*', and a few months later, John Redwood delivered a speech in Cardiff, where he talked of young women having children '*with no apparent intention of even trying marriage or a stable relationship with the father of the child*'. In July 1993, Sir George Young , Minister of Housing, asked how he was to explain to responsible young couples who were waiting for a council house before they started a family that they could not be rehoused ahead of '*the unmarried teenager expecting her first, probably unplanned, child*'.

This was followed by a hostile campaign in the popular press culminating in 1995 with reports linking teenage mothers to the collapse of family life in Britain (Selman, 1996b: 2). The Sun Newspaper called on its readers to express their views on a 16-year old from Aberdare in Mid-Glamorgan who was expecting her third baby, a situation described by Tory MP Sir Teddy Taylor as '*a sad reflection of the way in which this country has declined*'.

Young single mothers continued to hit the headlines with Margaret Thatcher's call for them to be sent to convents (Daily Express,

21/11/98) and Jack Straw's suggestion that they give up their children for adoption (Daily Mail, 26/1/99). On August 28 1999, the Star had a banner headline *'GIRL 12 IS A MUM'*; five days later the Daily Mirror followed this with the headline *'NEW MUM AGED 12'*. In an 'exclusive' interview in the Observer of 5 September 1999, the Prime Minister, Tony Blair, said that he was appalled by the two cases which *'should be a matter of anxiety and concern to everyone who cares about the future of this country'*. Births to girls as young as this are very rare, but in the following weeks the media scoured the country for more twelve-year-old 'mums' to interview.

An epidemic of teenage pregnancy in the United States

Concerns about teenage pregnancy have been around much longer in the United States. In 1975, US Congress began its hearings on teenage pregnancy, which was described as *'the most serious and complex problem facing the nation'*. A year later the influential Alan Guttmacher Institute (AGI, 1976) produced a pamphlet entitled *11 Million Teenagers: what can be done about the epidemic of adolescent pregnancies in the United States?* – the 11 million referring neither to the number of teenage births that year (about 600,000) nor the number of pregnancies (1 million) but the estimated number of sexually active adolescents, male and female (Furstenberg, 1998; Vinovskis, 1988). This culminated in the passing in 1978 of the Adolescent Health Services and Pregnancy Prevention and Care Act, which encouraged the provision of abortion and contraceptive services for young people.

By the 1980s the agenda had shifted under President Reagan as a reaction set in and the Act was superseded in 1981 by the Adolescent Family Life Act which became known as the 'chastity bill'. The failure to reduce teenage birth rates was seen to discredit the liberal approach of the 1978 Act. Welfare bills for young mothers were growing rapidly and teenagers themselves were seen as deliberately having children to get welfare payments. Adolescent birth rates rose throughout the 1980s and by the early 1990s, there were growing calls for new action. The *Progressive Policy Institute* described teenage pregnancy as a 'preventable calamity' (Sylvester, 1994) and argued that *'teenage welfare mothers symbolize the tragedy of our nation's failed welfare policy and the unravelling of our nation's social fabric'* (Sylvester, 1995). The Republican Party's 1994 *Contract with America* proposals to end welfare payments to unmarried mothers under eighteen gained widespread support and were soon emulated by a Democrat president fighting for re-election (Luker, 1996; Rhode, 1993; Selman, 1998c). The rhetoric became reality with the Clinton welfare reforms which are discussed in more detail later in this chapter.

Males (1996) notes that in the United States adolescents have been scapegoated for many other things, from drug-taking and crime to drinking and smoking. Similarly in Britain there have been concerns over wider aspects of adolescent – and indeed of pre-adolescent – behaviour (Macdonald, 1997).

Reactions to teenage parenthood in Europe

In contrast, attitudes to young single mothers in mainland Europe seem not to carry the same attitude of condemnation as in Britain and the USA. Klett-Davies (1996) has noted that in Germany lone mothers are viewed rather as *'helpless and innocent victims who are justified in receiving welfare state's assistance as long as the child requires this'*. In Scandinavian countries there is concern about teenage pregnancy (Knudsen, 1997), for which abortion is the most common outcome, but no targeting of young mothers for criticism and no suggestions of any withdrawal of state support.

The paradox of concerns over teenage births in Britain and the USA

In both Britain and the United States media and political concern over adolescent births reached a peak when numbers and rates were substantially lower than in the 1960s (Luker, 1996; Selman & Glendinning, 1996). In England & Wales in 1995 the total number of teenage births was less than half the total recorded thirty years earlier in 1966 (see Table 5.2 below). There has been a steady growth in the proportion of these births that occur outside marriage – from 20% in 1961 to 90% in 2001 – but most of these are registered jointly with the father (and half by couples sharing the same address): the number of births registered by the mother alone has fallen (Selman, 1996a). The increase in joint registered births matches the decline in pre-maritally conceived 'legitimate' births; indeed the overall number of births *conceived* outside marriage had fallen by a third by 1995.

The high level of teenage births in the mid-1960s was not seen as a major concern, because a third of the births were to women who were married before conceiving and most single pregnant teenagers either married before the birth, had a back street abortion, or relinquished their child for adoption (Selman, 1996a). Of those women having an extramarital birth in England & Wales in 1996, less than

Table 8.2   Teenage fertility, England and Wales: selected years, 1966–2001

	1966	*1991*	*1996*	*2001*
Total Births	86,746	52,996	44,667	44,189
Birth Rate[1]	*47.7*	*33.0*	*30.0*	*28.0*
Births inside marriage	66.164	8,948	5,365	4,640
Premarital conceptions	*36,761*	*3,267*	*1,567*	*1,086*
Births outside marriage	20,582	43,448	39,302	39,549
Sole registration	*16,600*	*15,200*	*12,900*	*11,669*
Joint Registration	*4,000*	*28,200*	*26,400*	*27,880*
Rate[1]	12.3	28.0	26.4	25.4
Ratio[2]	237	805	880	895
Births conceived outside marriage	57,343	46,715	40,869	40,635

Source: ONS Birth Statistics Series FM1
1 – per 1000 women aged 15–19: 2 – per 1000 live births

1 in 30 had their child adopted, in contrast to an estimated 1 in 3 in the late 1960s (Kiernan, 1980). A similar reduction in the number of adoptions has occurred in the United States (Bachrach, 1986; Miller, 1999).

The number of teenage *births* in England & Wales fell from the late 1960s following the 1967 Abortion Act, but the number of conceptions to women under age 20 reached a peak of 132,700 in 1971. In that year, out of every 100 pregnant teenagers, 18 had a legal abortion; 63 had a birth in marriage and 19 had a birth outside marriage. Twenty-five years later, the number of conceptions had fallen to 94,900 and the pattern of outcome had changed dramatically; out of every 100 pregnant teenagers, 37 had a legal abortion; only 9 had a birth in marriage; and 44 had a birth outside marriage (Office of National Statistics, *Conceptions in England & Wales, 1996*, FM1 98/1).

In the United States the teenage birth rate in 1960 (91 per 1000 women aged 15–19) was much higher than in 1990 (61.7), despite the rise in the 1980s (Luker, 1996). In 1960, fifty per cent of all marriages were to teenage brides, half of whom were pregnant at the time of marriage. The teenage birth rate fell to a low point of 51.3 in 1986 but then rose to 63.5 in 1991, the highest level since 1972, but has subsequently fallen again to 54.4 in 1996, a level similar to the mid-1970s and less than 60 per cent of the 1960 rate (Cheeseborough et al, 1999). By 2000 it had fallen further to 48.7.

Against this demographic background, the 1990s have seen more verbal attacks on teenage mothers than ever before and we need to ask the question why teenage mothers are targeted by the media and politicians and what does this tell us about the relationship between the family and the state? The demographic evidence from the two countries offers no compelling reason for a rising concern over teenage pregnancy in the 1990s, even if this is equated with under-16 conceptions which were marginally more frequent than in the 1970s (Department of Health, 1992; Henshaw, 2001).

If we are to understand the scapegoating and moral panics which surround teenage pregnancy in Britain and the United States, it is important to explore whether the concerns are not so much about early pregnancy and parenthood itself as about the fact that most births occur outside marriage; that pregnancies to younger girls highlight an ever earlier onset of sexual activity; that a growing number of pregnancies end in abortion; and that young mothers are seen as a current and potential welfare burden. In exploring these issues, we shall also need to look at the relationship between moralising about the family and political gain for those who do this, which raises further questions about the relationship between the family, young people and the state.

Is illegitimacy the real concern?

Debates about the underclass and the 'culture of dependency' flourished in Britain and the US under Reagan and Thatcher (Fitzpatrick, 1999; Macdonald, 1997). Charles Murray (1984) had argued that in the United States a major contributor to the rise of the underclass had been the welfare state and its implicit approval of non-marital fertility. Later, he identified illegitimacy, single parenthood and youth unemployment as key factors in an emerging British underclass and argued that immediate action was needed to reverse these trends (Murray, 1990).

On 11 July 1993 the Sunday Times proclaimed '*Once illegitimacy was punished; now it is rewarded*', implying that any solution must limit welfare support and reintroduce shame and stigma. A year later in the USA, Sylvester (1994) argued that '*it is wrong, not simply foolish or impractical, for women to make babies they cannot support emotionally or financially ... unmarried teen childbearing is morally wrong because of its costs for children and society*'.

The association of illegitimacy with welfare provision is not a new idea. An article in Social Forces entitled '*The Amazing Rise of Illegitimacy in England'* (Hartley, 1966) charted the rise of 'illegitimacy' ratios in the early 1960s and saw the increase as encouraged by the availability of social assistance for unmarried mothers. But Males (1996) has pointed out that for the last thirty years the United States has been punishing unwed, divorced and poor young mothers for their childbearing, *'thus creating the very conditions that breed more of it'*. Certainly the history of moral condemnation of young single mothers in both countries is a good example of the way in which the 'state' attempts to abrogate responsibility for the social conditions which its economic policy promotes by blaming individuals rather than social processes (Ryan, 1971).

In England & Wales the proportion of teenage births occurring outside marriage rose from 60 per cent in 1960 to 89 per cent in 1997, a similar rise occurred in births to mothers of all ages. Teenage out of wedlock births represent only a small – and diminishing – proportion of all non-marital births (17 per cent in 1995 in contrast to 33 per cent in 1971). If 'illegitimacy' is the problem, older age groups would more logically be the target for criticism.

In the United States non-marital fertility rates for women under 20 rose from 22.4 in 1970 to 42.5 in 1990. Rates for black teenage mothers fell from 96.9 in 1970 to 89.3 in 1985, but then rose again to 110.1 in 1990; rates for white teenagers rose steadily throughout the period from 10.9 in 1970 to 29.5 in 1990. By 1990, 58 per cent of teenage births occurred outside marriage – a smaller proportion than in Britain (80 per cent) – but teenage non-marital births accounted for less than a third of all births outside marriage, fewer than in 1970 when half of all such births were to women under 20 (Luker 1996).

When marriage is deferred, teenage births increasingly occur outside wedlock, but there is no clear pattern associating the level of teen birth rates with overall levels of non-marital fertility. Sweden and Denmark with high levels of non-marital fertility have low teenage birth rates, while Greece and Portugal, with higher but falling teen birth rates, have low rates of births outside marriage.

Is the concern really about teenage sexuality?

Reading the concerns over teenage pregnancy, it becomes apparent that one thing that separates these out from pregnancies to older women is that they are seen as the outcome of inappropriate sexual behaviour: for example, in July 1997, the Sun carried a report on a twelve year old mother, headlined *'SEX at 11; MUM at 12: a story to shock Britain'*. If this is so, falls in teenage pregnancy or birth rates will not diminish the concerns, unless accompanied by a reduction in levels of teenage sexual activity. Although the focus is often on under-age sex, hostility is generalized to all extra-marital sexual activity by teenagers – as in the Daily Mail headline (13 March 1999 '*SHOCK TRUTH ON TEENAGE SEX*'), which reported that one in five girls aged *16–19* admitted having multiple partners.

Luker (1996) points out that the increased sexual activity in teenagers should put some context on the failure of US teenage pregnancy rates to fall. However, there is no evidence that such an increase was unique to the USA. In Britain the median age of first sexual experience has fallen sharply in the last 40 years (Wellings, 1994) and this appears to be equally true of those countries that experienced greater declines in birth rates. In all countries the highest rates of teenage births occurred when the number of sexually active teenagers was much lower than today.

The Netherlands is frequently cited as a country with a unique pattern of low teenage birth rates achieved with less recourse to abortion as a resolution than in most other countries. Dutch commentators (David & Rademakers, 1996; Ketting, 1994) attribute this to the highly effective use of contraception by sexually active couples of all ages, although critics (see e.g. Daily Mail, 23/1/99) have argued that this is a result of the greater 'shame' attached to young motherhood in Dutch society. In the Netherlands, sex education typically starts earlier than in Britain and, for older teenagers, there is a continuing media provision of information, such as the TV programme *Sex with Angela*. They also argue that this approach has deferred age of first intercourse – a view supported in the extensive literature review by Grunseit & Kippax (1994). This pragmatic approach to teenage sex is also evident in the Scandinavian countries (David, 1990; Jones, 1986) – with similar success, albeit with more reliance on abortion.

In the United States, progress towards better contraceptive service for young people has been threatened by panics over teenage pregnancy, which argued that sex education and contraceptive availability encouraged adolescent sexual activity. Federal funding for contraceptive services was substantially reduced in the 1980s and there have been attacks on sex education programes that incorporate contraceptive advice (Lawson & Rhode, 1993; Luker, 1996). Instead there were calls for abstinence-based programs, which were specifically encouraged in the final clauses of the 1996 *Personal Responsibility and Work Opportunity Reconciliation Act*, (Selman, 1998c). Yet many critics (Males,

1996) have argued that such rhetoric is unrealistic, especially as much under-age sex is the result of rape by older men (AGI, 1994; Boyer & Fine, 1992).

Under President Bush, abstinence promotion has become a key component of the strategy to reduce rates of teenage pregnancy with a goal of 'parity' in federal funding for contraceptive services and abstinence education (Daillard, 2002). However emerging research suggests that the effectiveness of abstinence-only messages is not scientifically proven and that those breaking the pledge were less likely to use contraception than sexually active teenagers in 'safer sex' programs (Daillard, 2002). Meanwhile the number of under 18s using federal Title X family planning services rose by less than 2 per cent between 1995 and 2001, compared to an 8 per cent rise in overall use (Alan Guttmacher Institute, 2002).

In Britain, the provision of contraceptive advice to those under 16 was affected by the Gillick judgement in 1982 (Durham, 1991; Selman, 1998a). This was reversed in the late 1980s, but there continues to be much confusion over the issue of confidentiality (Francome, 1993) and it was not until 1990 and the publication of the *Health of the Nation* (DoH, 1990), with its target of halving the under 16s pregnancy rate by 2000, that serious attention was paid to improving access to contraception for younger teenagers. Sex education also provoked much opposition: in March 1994 the Health Education Authority announced a new publication, *Your Pocket Guide to Sex,* labelled by its critics 'an explicit sex guide for teenagers'. Health Minister, Brian Mawhinney called for its withdrawal, describing it as 'smutty'. In the same month Education Minister John Patten condemned a school nurse who had discussed oral sex and 'Mars bar parties' in a sex education class. In 1998, the Scottish *Sunday Post* (18/10/98) carried headlines exposing plans for school nurses to make emergency contraception available and attacked proposals to open a contraceptive clinic for young people in a chemist's in central Glasgow under the headline *Schoolgirl Sex Clinic at Boots*, which led to a call from local anti-abortion groups to boycott the store at Christmas.

The experience of the Nordic countries makes a strong case for pressing for earlier sex education with a stronger emphasis on practical contraceptive advice, but it is important to remember that one finding of Jones' study was that an open attitude to sex was a key correlate of low teenage birth rates (Jones, 1996). The confused handling of sex education issues in Britain and the USA suggests that such openness is far from present for either country and that explicit sex education will continue to be viewed with suspicion. Furstenberg (1998) has argued that 'unless and until its citizens come to terms with teenage sexual behaviour, the United States will probably continue to lag behind other developed countries in limiting teenage fertility'.

The Social Exclusion Unit Report (1999) argues that one key factor in the high rates of teenage pregnancy in Britain is the 'mixed messages' received by teenagers (Selman, 2000). On the one hand, the media 'bombards teenagers with sexually explicit messages and an implicit message that sexual activity is the norm'; on the other hand, access to contraception is denied and explicit sex education condemned. Media coverage of the 'twelve year old mums' exemplified this with the front page headlines mentioned earlier, juxtaposed with approving images of adult sexuality: in the Star a picture of a full-breasted Geri Halliwell (ex 'Spice Girl') under the slogan *'HEAVY BAGS, GERI'*; In the Mirror a picture of Nick Faldo (golfer) and his new girl-friend captioned *'FALDO'S KISSING LESSON FOR SON'*. The problems over sexuality seem to lie with those who condemn teenage mothers, rather than the mothers themselves!

Teenage pregnancy and the abortion debate

Goode and Ben-Yehuda (1994) have noted that 'concern over abortion has helped to fuel ... moral panics'. Certainly in the USA opposition to liberal sex education has been associated with the pro-Life movement and for such groups abortion is the worst manifestation of teenage pregnancy. Continued restriction on public funding of abortions has had an effect on teenagers' access to legal termination of pregnancy and a majority of states now require parental notification or consent before girls under 18 can get an abortion (AGI, 1994; Solinger, 1998). Clinton's welfare reforms rewarded states for reducing illegitimacy rates but only if this were done without increasing abortions (Lewin, 1998), a policy which has failed so that the so-called 'illegitimacy bonus' has now been scrapped. In the 1980s, the proportion of teenagers having abortions fell as pregnancy rates rose, accelerating rises in birth rates, but in the 1990s the teenage abortion rate fell more rapidly than the birth rate (Henshaw, 2001). Teenage abortions still account for only a small proportion of all terminations. Meanwhile in the UK the proportion of conceptions ending in abortion has risen from 42.4 per cent in 1999 to 46.0 per cent in 2001.

In Scandinavia, there are no continuing acrimonious debates about abortion and a majority of teenage pregnancies end in a termination.

In Denmark in 1991 there were nearly two abortions for every teenage birth and of 54 recorded pregnancies to girls under 15, only two resulted in a live birth (UN Demographic Yearbook, 1995). Similar high levels of abortions are found in Sweden, but not in Holland (David & Rademakers, 1996; Ketting, 1994).

In England & Wales , a majority of pregnancies to older teenagers end in a maternity, and even for those aged 13–15, the proportion ending in abortion was only 51 per cent in the mid 1990s, while in poorer areas, a majority of under 16s opted for a live birth. Revelations that the Catholic Church in Scotland had given £5000 to a pregnant twelve year old girl who had decided to 'keep' her baby provoked angry reactions from 'pro-choice' groups. The importance of the availability of legal abortion was highlighted in the Irish Republic by the High Court's refusal to allow a 14 year old rape victim to travel to England for a termination (Francome, 1991).

Bitter divisions over the question of abortion have hindered rational solutions to the high rates of teenage pregnancy in Britain and the United States. This has even extended to the issue of 'emergency contraception' which is seen by pro-Life groups as a variation on abortion rather than an effective way of preventing pregnancy after unprotected intercourse.

Teenage parenthood and the welfare debate

Many of the previously cited attacks on young single mothers touched on issues of their access to council houses and other welfare benefits. Concentration on young parents rather than older single mothers suggests that the real issue may be the welfare costs. Is the concern over teenage parenthood justified at least in relation to its cost to the state through welfare payments? Unmarried teenage mothers are likely to be dependent on means-tested benefits and many continue to be on welfare for many years after they leave their teens. However what has given the welfare debate a particularly problematic twist in both Britain and the USA has been the assertion that young women are deliberately getting pregnant in order to get benefits or subsidized housing and that the progressive reduction in benefits to this group will, therefore, both reduce the costs to the taxpayer directly and have a significant impact on the number of births to teenagers (Murray, 1992; 1994a).

The welfare debate in the United States

Debates on the role of welfare in teenage pregnancy have been raging in the USA for many years, fuelled by a belief that the benefits system is contributing to the creation of a dependent underclass. It has been estimated that half of all families on welfare in the early 1990s began with a teenage mother, although teenagers account for less than 10 per cent of those on welfare at any time (Alan Guttmacher Institute, 1995). However, the central concern is that the welfare system perpetuates the very problem it was set up to solve – that it leads to an increase in the number of single mothers and hence of poor families. Pragmatic concerns blend with moral concerns. Welfare is seen as encouraging people, specifically teenage women, to have babies they would not otherwise have had. This view often sits uneasily with the view of young mothers as feckless and ignorant, but such contradictions run through all debates on the underclass and the culture of poverty.

Males (1996) has argued that 'the notion that generous public assistance promotes single motherhood is one of the most easily disproved myths of the welfare reform debate'. If welfare benefits encourage teenage births, we should expect more young single mothers in Sweden where the social welfare system is generous rather than the USA which provides less support for single mothers than any other industrialized country (Luker, 1996). There appears to be no correlation within the USA between the level of benefit and the level of out-of wedlock births in individual states (Wilcox et al, 1996) and the real value of welfare benefits has declined throughout the period during which non-marital births to teenagers have been rising (Luker, 1996).

However, Conservative claims – despite all findings to the contrary – appealed to 'a public worried about two different things – the cost of welfare and changing family structures – in a way that knits these two concerns together' (Luker, 1996: 180). The *Personal Responsibility and Work Opportunity Reconciliation Act*, signed by President Clinton on 22 August 1996, addressed both issues, 'ending welfare as we know it', but also proclaiming that 'marriage is the foundation of a successful society' and providing grants for 'abstinence' programmes. The Act, which replaced AFDC with a new programme of *Temporary Assistance for Needy Families* (TANF), starts with a section of 'findings' about the costs of teenage mothers, and proceeds to a series of punitive measures: prohibiting assistance to mothers under 18 unless they are living at home or in an approved adult-supervised setting; refusing additional grants for girls having a baby while already on welfare; and cutting their benefit if they do not declare the name of their father's child (O'Connor, 1998; Selman, 1998c).

The Bush administration has now introduced a new welfare bill (H.R.4, the Personal Responsibility, Work and Family Promotion Act of

2003), which reauthorizes TANF and seeks to 'encourage the formation of healthy 2-parent married families, encourage responsible fatherhood, and prevent and reduce the incidence of out-of-wedlock pregnancies' and proposes measures to reduce the disincentives to marriage in means-tested aid programs.

The welfare debate in the UK

In Britain, lone parents who have never married are more likely to be dependent on state benefits. This group is also the fastest growing category incorporating as it does those who become single parents following the breakdown of cohabitation (Haskey, 1998; Berthoud et al, 1999). Most single parents in this category are not teenagers, but Burghes and Brown (1996) have shown that about half the mothers first gave birth as unmarried teenagers. Sinclair (1994) concludes that a major factor in public hostility towards young single mothers lies in the fact that they do not work and are held to be culpable for their non-employment.

Yet the assumption that there are many teenagers cynically seeking a council house or welfare payments remain unsubstantiated and most studies show teenagers to be amazed at such suggestions or to be largely unaware of such possibilities (Allen, 1998; Phoenix, 1993). The Social Exclusion Unit report notes that there are only 2000 tenants under age 18 in council houses and the reality is that any young mothers who are re-housed ahead of other 'more deserving' cases are likely to be placed in poor accommodation on sink estates. Mothers under 16 are not eligible for income support and single mothers under 18 receive lower rates of benefit, so that the thought of these as incentives to parenthood seems inherently implausible (Selman & Glendinning, 1996; Wilcox et al, 1996), a view endorsed by recent research under the ESRC Household & Change Programme (Allen et al, 1998; Berthoud et al, 1998, 1999; McRae, 1999).

The scapegoating of young single mothers described above became increasingly evident in the later years of the last Tory government, culminating in decisions to freeze lone parent premium and one parent benefit, a policy change endorsed by the New Labour government from 1997 onwards. Statements from government ministers seemed to indicate a continuing concern that welfare encourages teenage parenthood – as when Jack Straw, then Home secretary, spoke of the benefit system having '... *created an environment in which the natural checks that existed before on teenagers having children and keeping them has gone ...*' (The Observer, 1 February 1998).

The government has shown concern to reduce the level of teenage – and in particular under-age parenthood – and in 1998 referred the matter to its new Social Exclusion Unit, whose report was published in June 1999. The report itself provides an impressive analysis of the issues involved and few would argue with its analysis (Social Exclusion Unit, 1999: 7) of the three main reasons for Britain's high rate of teenage pregnancy: low expectations; ignorance of contraception; and the mixed messages referred to earlier. But the recommendations do not always match up with the analysis – and the issue of underlying social inequalities is largely ignored. Although the Teenage Pregnancy Report dismisses the welfare incentives thesis, Prime Minister, Tony Blair chose to launch the report in the Daily Mail of 14 June 1999 under the headline '*Why we should stop giving lone teenage mothers council homes*', and was quoted as saying that this 'could send out a signal to young teenagers that having a baby is a fast track to their own flat and the symbols of adulthood'.

However, other government initiatives under *welfare into work* could prove helpful in encouraging higher expectations in young people and helping young mothers to rebuild their lives. The *National Child Care Strategy* promises high quality childcare for all who need it; the *New Deal* and the *Working Families Tax Credit* offer help to older teenagers; and *Sure Start Plus* programmes are funded to offer support to young mothers and their children, as well as advice to pregnant teenagers. But here too there are conflicting views on whether single mothers should be encouraged to work or helped to be good 'stay-at-home' parents (Morgan, 1996).

Adoption as a solution – back to the stigma of the sixties

In suggesting that historical checks 'on mothers keeping the child' had weakened, Jack Straw raised the spectre of a return to a time when poverty and stigma led many young mothers to relinquish their babies for adoption. In January 1999, speaking at a conference organized by the Family Policy Studies Centre on the government's Green Paper, *Supporting Families,* Straw attacked 'well-meaning but misguided' social workers for encouraging single mothers to keep their children and spoke of an 'anti-adoption culture'. The Daily Mail picked up his speech with a headline on 26 January '*Give up babies pleas to single mothers*': with a sub-heading '*Teenagers who cannot cope with children should opt for adoption*'. The Mail's leading article applauded Straw's speech and the next day the paper launched '*The Great Debate: Should teenage mothers give up their babies for adoption?'* giving pride of place to a positive response from a woman who had chosen to give up her baby in the sixties. Once again teen mothers were the target of both political and media hostility.

Supporters of Straw looked back to the 'good old days', when adoption was the preferred solution in more than 1 in 5 'illegitimate' births in England in the years before the 1967 Abortion Act (Selman, 1976). Such adoptions are rare today in Britain, although there has been a rise in the number of adoptions of older children, often against the wishes of their mothers many of whom were teenage parents (Mason & Selman, 1997).

However, in recent years it has become more fashionable to advocate adoption as a solution to the problem of teenage parenthood, which at the same time re-inforces the rights of 'proper' parents to have children. In Britain, Patricia Morgan (1998) has called for a greater use of adoption to place babies of young single mothers in stable two-parent families, while in the United States, Charles Murray (1994a) has supported the withdrawal of benefit from teenage mothers as likely to lead '... *many young women who shouldn't be mothers to place their babies for adoption. This is good!'* In 1997, President Clinton launched *Adoption 2002*, which called for a doubling of the number of adoptions in five years. Although ostensibly focused on the need to move older children from state foster care to new families, the campaign has also become linked to plans for pregnant teenagers to be given more information about adoption as an alternative to abortion or motherhood. Following the introduction of the *Adoption & Safe families Act* 1997, the goal of a 50 per cent increase in adoptions from public care was achieved and there were indications of a rise in adoptions of the children of teenage parents, fuelled by strong promotion from pro-Life groups. A new *Adoption & Children Act* has been passed for England & Wales in 2002, which has similar aims of increasing the number of adoptions from care, but has not been linked to any pressure on young pregnant women.

An alternative solution, which was seen as rescuing children from inadequate parenting, was put forward in the United States by Republican Newt Gingrich, who proposed that orphanages be established for children whose mothers cannot take care of them and Katherine Sylvester's call for 'second-chance homes' has been incorporated into the Clinton welfare reforms (Sylvester, 1995). In Britain Virginia Bottomley, as Secretary of State for Health in the last

Conservative administration, called for hostels for single mothers, an idea revived and elaborated by former Prime Minister Margaret Thatcher who emerged from retirement to suggest that young unmarried mothers should be sent to convents (Daily Express, 21 November 1998). On 12 June 1999 the Daily Mail anticipated the Social Exclusion Unit Report's recommendation, that young mothers under age 18 should be provided with 'supported' housing if unable to live with family or partner, with the headline *'Lone mothers' hostel plan'* reprinting this alongside the Prime Minister's launch referred to above (p. 116), adding that *'Blair must stick to this bold proposal'*.

Such proposals are reminiscent of the Mother & Baby Homes which flourished in Britain the 1960s and often encouraged the adoption of the child. Evaluations of 'second-chance homes' (Sylvester, 1995) have indicated that unmarried mothers entering them are more likely to relinquish their children for adoption. The Daily Mail (26 January 1999) linked Jack Straw's speech on adoption with Mrs. Thatcher's earlier call for 'convents' with the headline *'Straw echoes Maggie with adoption appeal'*. But pressures on unmarried teenage mothers to relinquish their babies for adoption seem unlikely to have more than a marginal effect today and would do so – as in the past – only at great cost to the mothers (Howe, 1992). The reasons for the decline in domestic adoption are much more complicated than Murray, Morgan or Straw will allow. It has occurred throughout the Western world and the adoption of young babies is now virtually unknown in Northern Europe (Hoksbergen, 1986).

Many of the mothers who gave up their babies for adoption in the sixties would have opted for abortion in the eighties. A study at the end of the twentieth century by Allen (1997) found that young mothers were more likely to have considered abortion as an alternative rather than adoption. One of the strongest responses to Straw's statement came from the British Pregnancy Advisory Service who commented that adoption was 'an entirely inappropriate solution to teenage parenthood' and called for more attention to the provision of contraceptive services to prevent teenage pregnancies. However, the call was welcomed by the pro-Life movement and childless couples and there were fears that the proposed 'pregnancy advisors' under Sure Start Plus[2] (Social Exclusion Unit, 1999: 101) would come under pressure to persuade pregnant teenagers to opt for adoption rather than abortion. In 2003, Sure Start Plus is being piloted in 20 areas of England and evaluations are underway but there is no indication that pressure to opt for adoption is playing a major role.

The social origins of teenage pregnancy

Much of the debate on adoption assumed that teenage single parenthood is a cause of many problems – from child abuse to rising crime (Dennis, 1993) – and is a cause, rather than a consequence, of poverty and school dropout. But it is increasingly clear that girls who become mothers in their teens often bring to that a prior experience of poverty, school drop out and educational failure (Stern, 1997; Hosie & Selman, 2001). If this is so, deferred childbearing may have only a marginal effect on a woman's life chances. (Babb, 1994; Botting et al, 1998; Furstenberg, 1998; Geronimus, 1997). It is also clear that there is need for much better support for young single mothers, most of whom show a strong desire to be 'good' mothers but face immense problems in achieving this in the face of poverty and prejudice (Aarvold, 1998; Phoenix, 1991).

In both Britain (Babb, 1994; Botting, 1998) and the USA (Luker, 1996) teenage motherhood is associated with poverty. The Alan Guttmacher Institute (1994) found that 38 per cent of young people aged 15–19 were living in poverty; but this figure rose to 85 per cent of those who became mothers in their teens. There are wide geographical variations in the incidence of teenage pregnancy in Britain which point to a strong association with poverty (Selman & Glendinning, 1996; Selman, 1998a).

Table 8.3 shows local and regional variations in conception rates for under 18s in England & Wales in 1998 and 2001. The highest rates are found in the poorest regions and districts and are associated with

Table 8.3   Under 18's conception rates, England, regions and top-tier local authorities, 1998 and 2001 [per 1000 women aged 15–17]

Local Authority Area	1998	% leading to maternity	2001	% leading to maternity
Kingston upon Hull	83.9	68%	73.7	69%
Sandwell	71.8	61%	63.8	60%
Manchester	67.8	72%	72.4	63%
West Midlands	60.6	61.%	50.5	55%
England	47.0	58%	42.3	54%
East of England	37.9	56%	34.1	53%
Hertfordshire	31.7	53%	29.1	44%
Surrey	28.0	50%	26.8	39%
Windsor & Maidenhead	26.1	38%	25.0	37%

Source: ONS Conception data for top-tier Local Authorities, 1998–2001 March 2003

higher proportions continuing with the pregnancy. In Scotland a frequently quoted study on Tayside (Smith, 1993) showed that the teenage pregnancy rate for girls in poor neighbourhoods was 6 times that for girls in more affluent areas and that girls in poor areas were more likely to reject abortion. Murray (1994) takes this as evidence of an emerging British underclass which is rejecting the idea of marriage and in which children are being brought up without fathers with what he sees as the inevitable consequence of rising crime. However, it seems more likely that the high rates of teenage births are a result of deprivation, in which case further reductions in teenage birth rates in Britain may depend on New Labour's success in spreading educational and job opportunities, linked to better child care provision, rather than any changes in the welfare system. Yet the scapegoating of young parents continues and there are clearly tensions in New Labour policies and contradictions in their rhetoric.

Blaming the victim: the social costs of scapegoating

In both Britain and the USA, there has been a growing tendency to blame young single mothers for many of society's failures and to see the problem of teenage pregnancy as a consequence of immorality rather than poverty, stemming from '*cultural permissiveness, a decline in parental authority and a weakening of community sanctions against illegitimacy*' (Rhode, 1993). Talk of scapegoating is dismissed by such critics as ignoring the manifest need to bring back the stigma which once led to a reluctance to enter into or remain in dependent parenthood. It is argued that to suggest that attacks on teenage mothers are 'blaming the victim' ignores the fact that getting pregnant and bearing a child is voluntary behaviour; and to suggest that poverty causes early childbearing is to miss the point that most poor women do not become pregnant. Murray (1992) cheerfully acknowledging that his proposals are 'horribly sexist', argues that the only way to ensure that women actively avoid getting pregnant and '*once again demand marriage from a man who would have them bear a child*' is to ensure that childbearing entails economic penalties for a single woman. Such solutions are unlikely to have any major impact on pregnancy and birth rates but will certainly make the situation of young mothers and their children even more marginal. The arguments are viewed with horror by most people in mainland Europe (e.g. Knudsen, 1997) who recognise the need for a determined attack on the occurrence of unwanted adolescent pregnancy, but also sympathetic support for the small number of young women who do become mothers in their teens.

Neglected realities of teenage pregnancy

I do not wish to argue that teenage pregnancy is unproblematic – but rather that in Britain and the United States its presentation by the media and the use of young mothers as scapegoats for wider problems was at best unhelpful and at worst a distraction from the real issues. The emphasis on welfare carried with it the assumption of perverse incentives and cynically planned pregnancy and ignored the fact that most pregnancies to younger teenagers are unplanned, many are unwanted and some clearly the result of sexual abuse and violence (Boyer and Fine, 1992). Taylor et al (1995) cite national surveys in The United States which revealed that a majority of women who had sex before the age of 15 reported that they had coerced sex and the Alan Guttmacher Institute study, *Sex and America's Teenagers*, found that 43 per cent of those of such age said their only sexual experience was of being raped (AGI, 1994). In such a context, the prime issues for policy must be of support for these young women and attention directed at the often much older men who have abused them.

Teenage pregnancy is traditionally defined by the age of women, but in Britain and the US a majority of the men involved are not teenagers themselves. In California in 1996 two thirds of the fathers of children born to teenage women were aged twenty or over – and 17 per cent were over 25. As Males (1996) argues, most teen pregnancy is a result of teen-adult sex although this is less true of under 18 births in Britain, where most fathers seem to be only a few years older at most. Most of the scapegoating is very gendered and does not touch the power of patriarchy but rather reinforces it (Lees, 1993).

Concentration on the removal of perverse incentives from welfare – and the introduction of clear incentives to seek work – may lead to a neglect of other barriers to independence such as the high cost and limited availability of good quality child care. For schoolgirl mothers the challenge is to ensure that pregnancy does not mean an end to education, building on the success of supportive educational units, such as Ashlyns School in Newcastle (Aarvold, 1998), and to tackle the reality that school failure and drop-out *precedes* pregnancy in most cases (Hosie & Selman, 2001).

Summary and conclusion

A successful family policy must address the issues raised by changes in the family. I have argued elsewhere (Selman, 1996b) that a policy which acknowledges the irreversibility of many of these changes and seeks to minimize their costs is more likely to succeed than one which seeks to turn back the clock and reverse the changes. However, the persistence of high rates of teenage fertility in Britain and the United States, when elsewhere rates have fallen alongside a general deferment of childbearing, raises interesting questions about why these two countries have had such a different demographic profile compared to other industrialized countries. In both countries media reports and irresponsible politicians have linked adolescent pregnancy to what is portrayed as a more general collapse of the family, marked by falling marriage rates, rising divorce and an increase in out-of-wedlock births, all of which have been equally present in countries with very low teen birth rates. Much of the public discussion of teenage pregnancy has been very damaging and runs counter to a rational solution.

If we see teenage pregnancy as a symptom rather than a cause of social malaise, then the scapegoating of young mothers is not unexpected as a means of diverting attention from the inequalities that underlie the phenomenon. As Luker (1996) has written: *'Society should worry not about some epidemic of "teenage pregnancy" but about the hopeless, discouraged and empty lives that early childbearing denote'*. Early motherhood is often an effort to escape from a life of violence and bleakness and this can only be tackled by a determined attack on social deprivation and major improvements in sex education and contraceptive provision. Family policy must move forward on a broad front – tackling child poverty and embracing the rights of all to reproductive freedom and sexual health – and not narrowly focused on bolstering the traditional family (Selman, 1998b).

In the United States the teenage birth rate has been falling for nearly a decade (Henshaw, 2001), although it remains the highest in the developed world (Unicef, 2001). The birth rate for women under age 20 peaked at 63.5 in 1991 and has subsequently fallen to 48.7 in 2000. This decline was most rapid in black teenagers (from 115.5 to 79.2). In 2000 the highest rate was found in Hispanics (94.4); the lowest in Asian groups (21.8). The rate for white teenagers fell from 43.4 in 1991 to 32.8 in 2000. The birth rate for women aged 15–17 peaked at 37.8 in 1992 and has subsequently fallen to 33.8 in 1996 and to 28.7 in 1999; the abortion rate fell from 23.1 to 17.4 in the same period (Henshaw, 2001). Debates over the key factors in the declining teenage birth rates continue but the emerging consensus is that both a reduction in sexual activity rates and the use of more effective contraceptive methods have played a part (Alan Guttmacher Institute, 1999).

In Britain targets for reduction in under-age pregnancy set in the early 1990s (Department of Health, 1992) were not achieved, as initiatives on sex education and contraceptive provision met media opposition and ministerial doubts. For older adolescents, the emphasis on young mothers getting pregnant to get a council house has distracted from the vast majority who had not wanted to conceive in the first place and has hindered efforts to ensure adequate support for this vulnerable group and their children.

In 1999 the Social Exclusion Unit's report set new targets for a national campaign: 'to halve the rate of conceptions among under 18 year olds in England by 2010' and to reduce the risk of long term social exclusion for teenage parents and their children by getting more parents into education, training or employment. Many feared that if policy priorities focused on welfare disincentives, the provision of 'hostels', encouragement of adoption, the pursuit of fathers for maintenance and a continued condemnation of young single mothers, without any real improvement in educational and job opportunities, it was likely that the targets would be missed yet again and that a heavy price would be paid by the next generation of young mothers and their children. However, if the Social Exclusion Report's analysis led to a determined attack on social deprivation and a transformation of sex education and contraceptive services, linked to improved support for young mothers, the targets could well be achieved and the position of young people would certainly be improved whatever the demographic outcome.

By 2003 the ten-year national Strategy for England & Wales set out in the SEU Report was on its way to being implemented, starting with the establishment of a Teenage Pregnancy Unit within the Department of Health. An initial £60m investment package had been delivered and all but two of 30 'action' points were completed by the end of 2002 (Department of Health 2002). The aim of an interim reduction of 15% in the under 18s conception rate by 2004 was on target with figures available in 2003 showing that the rate had fallen from 47.0 in 1999 to 42.3 in 2001 (a fall of 10 per cent). A strong media campaign with the intention of discouraging teenage pregnancy was underway through teenage magazines and radio programmes. Developments in supported accommodation for teenage mothers were slow but seemed to be avoiding 'hostels' with more emphasis on what has been termed 'floating support'. Assessing the impact of all initiatives was not yet possible. For example, the impact of the Sure Start Plus programme and the more universal, Connexions, a government initiative aimed at helping young people in the transition to adulthood, remained uncertain.[3] However, there was evidence that programmes to counter the educational disadvantage typically associated with teenage parenthood were having some success (Hosie & Selman, 2001; Selman et al, 2001; Department of Health, 2002). The eventual outcome of the overall package of British government strategies remains uncertain. The move away from universalism towards market welfare, with its emphasis on the importance of paid work and a concern about public spending (Lister, 1998), can easily be translated into a scapegoating rhetoric. It is not clear that the British government has managed to break free from the influence of US models of strengthening the family through welfare reform and abstinence education although the New Labour government has been making efforts to address the underlying social inequalities that Luker identified as the key route to radically reducing US teenage pregnancy.

There seems to be a continuing tension between the British government's anti-poverty strategy and the temptation to scapegoat young, single mothers, which is still being played out in the early years of this century. The tabloid newspapers have continued to challenge government strategies that eschew a punitive approach and attempt to tackle disadvantage. There are still denouncing headlines about teenage sex and sceptical headlines in response to services for teenagers with babies. On 22 February 2001 the Daily Express responded to a plan to provide full-time child-minders for young mothers returning to school with the headline '*Fury Over Free Childcare for Teenage Mums*' and there has been renewed criticism of sex education programmes for encouraging premature sexual activity and increasing the incidence of sexually transmitted infections.

The decline in teenage birth and conception rates suggests some impact from current campaigns in both countries, but these should be placed in the context of declining birth and conception rates at all ages. Rates remain much higher than in most Western European countries and to achieve a reduction to these levels will require more attention to the structural causes outlined above. Support services are still in need of more investment and the long term impact on education, training and employment remains uncertain.

Notes

1 The tables given in this chapter focus on the majority population of Britain in England and Wales but the trends in Scotland are broadly similar. Detailed Scottish figures are provided by the Information and Statistics Division (ISD Scotland), part of the Common Services Agency for NHS Scotland, and in 2003 figures were placed on the web pages: http://www. show.scot.nhs.uk/isd/sexual_health/Teenpregs/Teenpregs_homepage.htm

2   Sure Start was the name given to a government initiative launched in 1998 which aimed to help enhance the possibility of children having a 'sure start' in life by tackling disadvantage and 'social exclusion'. In Scotland this programme was local authority led but in England and Wales it was more centrally managed. In 2000 in England and Wales Sure Start Plus was the name given to programmes focusing on pregnant teenagers.

3   Connexions is another new service set up by the government in England and Wales with the broad aim of tackling disadvantage and social exclusion by helping young people during the transition to adult life. It offers a range of guidance and support for young people who are up to 19 years old. It has taken over the role of careers guidance and aspects of personal guidance. The service is provided through local Partnerships which run help line and email services and employ 'Personal Advisors' offering a range of guidance and support. Scotland retained a separate career guidance service (Careers Scotland, relaunched in 2002 as an all age service), and an in-school guidance systems and has no exact equivalent to Connexions.

Bibliography

Aarvold, J. (1998) 'Risk, sex and the very young mother' in B. Heyman ed., *Risk, Health and Health Care* London: Edward Arnold.

Alan Guttmacher Institute (1976) *11 Million Teenagers; What can be done about the Epidemic of Adolescent Pregnancies in the United States?* Washington: AGI.

Alan Guttmacher Institute (1994) *Sex and America's Teenagers* New York: AGI.

Alan Guttmacher Institute (1995) 'Teenage Pregnancy and the Welfare Reform Debate', *Issues in Brief* Washington: AGI.

Alan Guttmacher Institute (1999) *Why is Teenage Pregnancy Declining? The Roles of Abstinence, Sexual Activity and Contraceptive Use* New York: AGI.

Allen, I., Dowling, S. and Rolfe, H. (1998) *Teenage Mothers: Decisions and Outcomes* London: Policy Studies Institute.

Arai, L. (2003) 'British Policy on Teenage Preganancy and Childbearing' *Critical Social Policy* 23, 1: 89–102.

Babb, P. (1994) 'Teenage conceptions and fertility in England & Wales, 1971–1991', *Population Trends* 74: 12–17.

Bachrach, C. (1986) 'Adoption Plans, Adopted Children and Adoptive Mothers', *Journal of Marriage and the Family* 48: 243–253.

Berthoud, R., Rowlingson, K. and McKay, S. (1998) 'The Growth of Lone Parenthood: Diversity and Dynamics', *ESRC Research Results* [Population and Household Change Research Programme], No. 9.

Berthoud, R., McKay, S. and Rowlingson, K. (1999) 'Becoming a single mother' in S. McRae, (ed.) 1999, *Changing Britain: Families and Households in the 1990s* Oxford: Oxford University Press.

Botting, B. (1998) 'Teenage mothers and the health of their children', *Population Trends* 93: 19–28.

Boyer, D. and Fine, D. (1992) 'Sexual abuse as a factor in adolescent pregnancy and child maltreatment', *Family Planning Perspectives* 24: 4–11.

Burghes, L. and Brown M. (1995) *Single Lone Mothers: problems, prospects and policies* London: Family Policy Studies Centre.

Cheesebrough, S., Ingham, R. and Massey, D. (1999) *Reducing the rate of teenage pregnancy: An international review of the evidence: USA, Canada, Australia* London: Health Education Authority.

Cohen, S. (1980) *Folk Devils and Moral Panics* Oxford: Martin Robertson.

Daillard, C. (2002) *Abstinence Promotion and Teen Family Planning: The Misguided Drive for Equal Funding* New York: AGI.

David, H. P. (1990) 'United States and Denmark: different approaches to health care and family planning', *Studies in Family Planning* 21–1.

David, H. and Rademakers, J. (1996) 'Lessons from the Dutch Abortion Experience' *Studies in Family Planning* 17: 341–343.

Dennis, N. (1993) *Rising Crime and the Dismembered Family* London: Institute of Economic Affairs.

Dennis, N. and Erdos, G. (1991) *Families without Fatherhood* London: IEA.

Department of Health (1992) *The Health of the Nation: A Strategy for Health in England* Cm 1986, London: HMSO.

Department of Health (2002) *Government Response to the First Annual Report of the Independent Advisory Group on Teenage Pregnancy* Department of Health (with DfES, DWP, Home Office and Office of Deputy PM), June 2002.

Durham, M. (1991) *Sex and Politics: the family and morality in the Thatcher Years* London: MacMillan.

Fitzpatrick, T. (1999) 'Cash Transfers' In J. Baldock, N. Manning, S. Miller and S. Vickerstaff eds., *Social Policy* Oxford: Oxford University Press.

Francome, C. (1991) *If You Ever Go Across the Sea to England* Enfield: Middlesex Polytechnic.

Francome, C. (1993) *Children Who Have Children* London: FPA.

Furstenberg, F., Brooks-Gunn, J., Morgan, S. P. (1987) *Adolescent Mothers in Later Life* New York: Cambridge University Press.

Furstenberg, F. (1998) 'When will teenage childbearing become a problem? The implications of western experience for developing countries', *Studies in Family Planning* 29: 246–253.

Geronimus, A. T. (1997) 'Teenage childbearing and personal responsibility: an alternative view', *Political Science Quarterly* 112.

Goode, E. and Ben-Yehuda, N. (1994) *Moral Panics: the Social Construction of Deviance* Oxford: Blackwell.

Gress-Wright, J. (1993) 'The contraceptive paradox', *The Public Interest* 113: 15–25.

Grunseit, A. and Kippax, S. (1994) *Effects of Sex Education on* Young *Peoples Sexual Behaviour* Geneva: WHO.

Hartley, S. F. (1966) 'The amazing rise of illegitimacy in England', *Social Forces* 44–4.

Haskey, J. (1998) 'One-parent Families and their Dependent Children in Great Britain', *Population Trends* 91, 5–15.

Henshaw, S. (2001) *US Teenage Pregnancy Statistics* New York: AGI.

Hoksbergen, R., (1986) *Adoption in Worldwide Perspective* Swets and Zeitliger.

Hosie, A. and Selman, P. (2001) *Teenage Pregnancy in Young Women of School Age; an Exploration of Disengagement from the Education System* Paper presented at SPA Annual Conference, Belfast, 24–26 July, 2001.

Howe, D. et al (1992) *Half a Million Women* London: Penguin.

Jones, E. F. (1986) *Teenage Pregnancy in Industrialized Countries* New Haven: Yale University Press.

Van De Kaa, D. (1987) 'Europe's second demographic transition' *Population Bulletin* 42: 1–59.

Kane, R. and Wellings, K. (1999) *Reducing the Rate of Teenage Pregnancy: An International Review of the Evidence; Data from Europe* London: Health Education Authority .

Ketting, E. (1994) Is the Dutch abortion rate that low? *Planned Parenthood in Europe* 23: 29–32.

Kamerman, S. (1990) 'Family change and family policy: lessons from the industrialized west', Paper presented at the Sino-American-British conference on Social Policy, Taiwan, July 1990.

Kiernan, K. (1980) 'Teenage motherhood – associated factors and consequences – the experiences of British birth cohort', *Journal of Biosocial Science* 12: 393–405.

Klett-Davies, M. (1996) 'Single mothers in Britain and Germany: an underclass or escaping patriarchy', Paper presented to SPA annual conference, *Social Policy in Europe: Convergence or Diversity?* University of Sheffield, 16–18 July 1996.

Knudsen, L. (1997) *Birth Control and Pregnancies among Teenagers in Denmark* Paper presented at EAPS International Conference, Cracow, Poland, 11–13 June 1997.

Lawson, A. and Rhode, D. (1993) *The Politics of Pregnancy: Adolescent Sexuality and Public Policy* New Haven: Yale University Press.

Lees, S. (1993) *Sugar and Spice; Sexuality and Adolescent Girls* London: Penguin Books.

Lewin, T. (1998) 'Report Tying Abortion to Welfare is Rejected' *New York Times,* Monday, June 8th 1998.

Lister, R. (1998) From equality to social inclusion: New Labour and the welfare State', *Critical Social Policy,* 18–2, 215–25.

Luker, K. (1996) *Dubious Conceptions: the Politics of Teenage Pregnancy* London: Harvard University Press.

Lundberg, S. and Plotnick, R. D. (1995) 'Adolescent pre-marital childbearing: Do economic incentives matter?' *Journal of Labour Economics* 13: 177–200.

Macdonald, R. (1997) (ed.) *Youth, the Underclass and Social Exclusion* London: Routledge.

Males, M. A. (1996) *The Scapegoat Generation: America's War on Adolescents.* Monroe: Common Courage Press.

Mason, K. and Selman, P. (1997) 'Birth Parents' experience of contested adoption', *Adoption and Fostering* 21: 21–28.

McRae, S. (ed.) (1999) *Changing Britain: Families and Households in the 1990s* Oxford: Oxford University Press.

Miller, B. and Coyle, D. (1999) 'Adolescent pregnancy and childbearing in relation to infant adoption in the United States', Paper presented at the *International Conference on Adoption Research* Minneapolis, August 1999.

Moffit, R. (1992) 'Incentive effects in the U.S. welfare system: a review', *Journal of Economic Literature* 30: 1–61.

Morgan, P. (1996) *Who Needs Parents? The Effects of Child Care and Early Education on Children in Britain and the United States* London: IEA.

Morgan, P. (1998) *Adoption and the Care of Children: the British and American Experience* London: IEA.

Murray, C. (1984) *Losing Ground: American Social Policy, 1950–1980* New York: Basic Books.

Murray, C. (1990) *The Emerging British Underclass* London: IEA.

Murray, C. (1992) 'Welfare and the family: the U.S. experience', *Journal of Labor Economics* 11: 224–262.

Murray, C. (1994) *Underclass: The Crisis Deepens* London: IEA

Murray, C. (1994a) *Testimony before the House Ways and Means Subcommittee on Human Resources* July 29, 1994.

National Campaign to Prevent Teenage Pregnancy (1999) *National Campaign Fact Sheet,* http://www.teenpregnancy.org

O'Connor J. (1998) 'US social welfare policy: the Reagan record and legacy', *Journal of Social Policy* 27: 37–61.

Office of National Statistics, *Conceptions in England & Wales 1996*, FM1 98/1.

Phoenix, A. (1991) *Young Mothers?* Cambridge: Polity Press.

Plotnick, R. D. (1990) 'Welfare and out-of-wedlock childbearing: evidence from the 1980s', *Journal of Marriage and the Family* 52: 735–746.

Plotnick, R. D. (1993) 'The effect of social policies on teenage pregnancy and childbearing', *Families in Society* (June): 324–328.

Rhode, D. L. (1993) 'Adolescent pregnancy and public policy' in A. Lawson and D. Rhode *The Politics of Pregnancy: Adolescent Sexuality and Public Policy* New Haven: Yale University Press.

Ryan, W. (1971) *Blaming the Victim* London: Orbach and Chambers.

Scapegoat Society (1999) *The Scapegoat Society Web Site.*

http://www.scapegoat.demon.co.uk/

Selman, P. (1976) 'Patterns of Adoption in England and Wales since 1959', *Social Work Today* 7: 194–197.

Selman, P. (1996a) 'Teenage motherhood then and now: a comparison of the pattern and outcome of teenage pregnancy in England and Wales in the 1960s and 1980's in H. Jones and J. Millar, eds., *The Politics of the Family* Aldershot: Avebury.

Selman, P. (1996b) 'The Relationship Revolution: Is the family collapsing or adjusting to a new world of equal opportunities?' in R. Humphrey ed., *Families behind the Headlines* Department of Social Policy, University of Newcastle upon Tyne.

Selman, P. (1998a) 'Teenage fertility, poverty and the welfare debate in the United States and Europe', Paper presented at the Cicred Seminar on *Poverty and Family Planning* Mexico City 2–4 June 1998.

Selman, P. (1998b) 'Adolescent pregnancy, sexuality and the welfare debate in Britain and the United States', Paper presented at Youth Support Conference on *Adolescent Health* London, 22–23 October 1998.

Selman, P. (1998c) 'Teenage pregnancy and welfare reform in Britain and the United States', Paper presented at ESRC seminar on *Adolescent Sexuality.* London, 30 November 1998.

Selman, P. (2000) *Mixed Messages; Teenage Pregnancy, Social Policy and the Welfare Debate in Britain and the United States* Paper presented at Social Policy Association Annual Conference, University of Surrey, Roehampton, 18–20 July 2000.

Selman, P. and Glendinning, C. (1996) 'Teenage pregnancy: do social policies make a difference?' in J. Brannen and M. O'Brien *Children and Families: Research and Social Policy* London: Falmer.

Selman, P. and Clarke, L. (2000) *Teenage Pregnancy in Northumberland. A Statistical Analysis* Newcastle upon Tyne: Department of Sociology and Social Policy, University of Newcastle.

Selman, P., Richardson, D., Hosie, A. and Speak, S. (2001) *Monitoring of the DfES Standards Fund Teenage Pregnancy Grant* Final Report to DfES, Newcastle upon Tyne: Department of Sociology and Social Policy, University of Newcastle.

Sinclair, S. P. (1994) 'Public Hostility Towards Young Single Mothers', Paper presented at SPA annual conference, University of Liverpool, 12–14 July.

Smith, T. (1993) 'Influence of socio-economic factors in attaining targets for reducing teenage pregnancies', *British Medical Journal* No. 6887.

Social Exclusion Unit (1999) *Teenage Pregnancy* Cm 4342. London: HMSO.

Solinger, R. (ed.) (1998) *Abortion Wars: a Half Century of Struggle 1950–2000* Berkeley: University of California Press.

Stern, C. (1997) 'Teenage pregnancy as a social problem: a critical perspective', Paper presented at XXIII General Population Conference, Beijing, 11–17 October 1997.

Sylvester, K. (1994) *Preventable Calamity; Rolling Back Teen Pregnancy* Washington: Progressive Policy Institute.

Sylvester, K. (1995) *Second-Chance Homes: Breaking the Cycle of Teen Pregnancy* Washington: Progressive Policy Institute.

Taylor, J. M., Gilligan, C., and Sullivan, A. M. (1995) *Between Voice and Silence: Women and Girls, Race and Relationship* Harvard University Press.

Thompson, K. (1998) *Moral Panics* London: Routledge.

Unicef (2001) *A League Table of Teenage Births* Florence: Innocenti Research Centre.

Vinovskis, M. (1988) *An Epidemic of Adolescent Pregnancy? Some Historical and Policy Considerations* New York: Oxford University Press.

Wellings, K. (1994) *Sexual Behaviour in Britain* London: Penguin Books.

Wilcox, B., Robbennolt, J., O'Keefe, J., and Pynchon, M. (1996) 'Teen Nonmarital Childbearing and Welfare: the gap between research and political discourse', *Journal of Social Issues* 52: 71–90.

9
Youth, Dependence and the Problem of Support

Gill Jones

Introduction

There has been very little research on the parenting of young people: what it involves, who does it, how it is offered and received, or how it changes with age and over time. Equally, while there has been an increasing policy emphasis on supporting families (latterly as a means to combating social exclusion), the emphasis has been on the parenting of young children. UK Government policies affecting the family lives of young people thus draw on a blank sheet, largely uninformed by research evidence. This was clear from the Green Paper 'Supporting Families' (Home Office, 1998), which followed the existing research agenda in concentrating on the parenting of younger children, but focused only on those aspects of youth defined as social problems, targeting such issues as teenage pregnancy, offending and truancy. Even in the changed policy environment of the post 1997 Labour Governments, the family context in which young people become adult has been largely ignored (Social Exclusion Unit, 2000) . While those identified as socially excluded and/or living in poor neighbourhoods have received policy and research attention, the everyday problems of the majority remain, in both research and policy, within the 'black box' of family life.

In this chapter, I am going to shift away from the policy focus on young people as a social problem, to examine some of the problems that young people face. I will first present a conceptual framework for understanding youth as a period (for most) of extended dependence involving new difficulties and new needs; next consider the role of parents and the state in supporting the transition to independence; and then address some of the problems with making assumptions about youth. To conclude, I will discuss the problems young people face when needing to access state or family support, and consider how some young people cope without support. The relationship between young people, their families and the state is complex, involving individual transition, family and/or state support, and a changing family/state relationship which impinges on the whole process of transition to adulthood (Figure 9.1).

The changed nature of 'youth'

It is sometimes regarded as politically incorrect among those working with young people to focus on their transitional status, as though young people are only *'becoming'*, rather than *'are'*. But there are equal if not greater dangers in focusing on the 'here and now' and not recognising that, during their youth, young people are developing their individual identities, asserting their increasing independence, and building their futures in both the wider world and the private world of family life. Research on children in local authority care has indicated that too great a focus on current welfare has led to neglect of education and training for the future (Biehal, Clayden, Stein and Wade, 1995). It is, however, the concept of youth as a static stage in life, occupied by homogeneous age groupings, which is embedded in state policy. As a result, it is assumed – in social security regulations for example – that transitions to adulthood are so linear and age-structured that young people's needs can be determined by their age alone. Thus, changes to the social security regulations in the 1980s were structured around the premise that 'at the age of 18 the majority of claimants are not fully independent, and that the great majority of claimants above the age of 25 are' (the 1985 Green Paper, quoted in Jones and Bell, 2000).

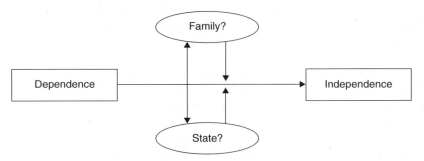

Figure 9.1 Support for the transition?

It is more appropriate and accurate to think of the period of 'youth' as one of process, rather than as a static stage in life. It is a part of the life course which has been extended and changed: by policies opening up access to education and training; by the virtual loss of the youth labour market; and by the welfare policies of the 1980s and 1990s which removed much of the safety net from young people who 'failed' to get jobs. If adulthood is defined as the achievement of economic independence, then adulthood has been deferred in policy terms. However, as we shall see, young people are active agents, not simply puppets reacting to policy constructions.

The period of transition has not just been extended but has also become more complex. It is no longer a simple linear process in two stages – only a generation or two ago, it was for most people a matter of leaving school, starting work and saving money in the first stage, followed later by leaving home to marry and start a family. There were class and gender differences, with working class and female transitions more contracted and those of the middle class and males more extended (Jones, 1988). The economic transition embodied in the starting work, saving money element underpinned the later household and family formation elements of this linear transition to adulthood. Indeed, Willis (1984) saw the wage as the 'golden key' to adulthood, without which young people would be excluded from the adult world. In the same vein, Wallace (1987) found that young people with experience of unemployment were likely to defer household and family formation. But the increase in youth unemployment in the 1980s created new tensions for young people and new coping strategies developed. Adulthood was not simply deferred: the transition to adulthood was instead adapted. Willis himself argued that one such adaptation was the achievement of independence through motherhood (see also Payne, 1989, on unemployment and fertility among young men). Harris (1987) suggested that in contrast to the research emphasis at the time on the school-to-work transition, leaving home was becoming more significant as a means of achieving adult identity, and more recent research (including Jones, 1995b) confirms this. Similarly, it has been argued that young people who are unable to obtain jobs may nevertheless have economic power as consumers, though it is debatable whether visible consumption represents power or is merely a response to other constraints (Jones and Martin, 1999; Jones and Wallace, 1992). So perhaps we should recognize that though the normative pattern of transition was linear, its patterns and timing varied between social groups and is capable of adaptation when not underpinned by economic stability.

It is now more useful to think of the transition to adulthood as having different strands or dimensions, and to recognize that the process is not only more protracted but also more complex (see Figure 9.2). Rather than following a normative ordering along one pathway, there are several strands of transition, each of which can involve backtracking. The ways in which young people follow these paths vary, but these are no individualized transitions. Clear polarization has developed between those with and those without socioeconomic advantage (Bynner et al, 2002; Jones, 2002). And the 'destinations' of each pathway are by no means clear: the concept of adulthood has become ever more problematic.

What I am suggesting here is no deconstructionist, postmodern perspective on youth, but a changed and more refined conceptual framework for understanding youth, needed because youth has itself changed (Furlong and Cartmel, 1997). It becomes imperative that a holistic approach is taken, and also one which recognizes the processes involved in transitions to adulthood (Coles, 1995). Young people are defined here as between the ages of 16 and 25 because in the UK this is the period between the minimum school-leaving age and the age at which they are eligible for adult rates of welfare benefit, in other words the period of 'youth' as constructed in policy terms. As working definitions, let us therefore think of childhood as a period of economic dependence (on parents or other carers) and adulthood as the achieve-

TRANSITION	CHILDHOOD →	YOUTH →	ADULTHOOD
School to work	School →	Course or scheme →	Labour market?
Family	Child in family →	Cohabiting/ Single parent →	Partner-Parent?
Household	Parental home →	Intermediate non-familial →	Independent home?
Housing	Home-ownership or council tenancy →	Transitional housing →	Home-ownership or council tenancy?
Income	Child income →	Youth income →	Full adult income?
Economic independence	Dependence →	Semi-Dependence →	Independence?

Figure 9.2 Extended transitions to adulthood

ment of economic independence. These are simplifications which hold more meaning in policy terms than in everyday life, where people may resist fitting into simple constructions of what they are meant to be. There are children who though classified as 'dependants' have an important social and economic role in their families as earners or carers: research on children working in family businesses (Song, 1994, on Chinese takeaways; Wallace, 1991, on farming families), or children as carers (Dearden and Becker, 2000) or contributors to the domestic economy (Morrow, 1996) indicates that though constructed as dependants in policy terms, children often begin their transitions to economic independence from an early age. Equally, economic independence is not 'automatically' achieved with adulthood, as I shall show. Nevertheless, youth appears to be an expanding period of transitional semi-dependence, driving a widening wedge between childhood and adulthood (Jones and Bell, 2000). The ways in which this happens and the ages at which transitions occur vary between social groups. In other words, young people's experiences during their youth may vary considerably, including by social class, gender, ethnicity and disability (Jones, 2002).

The period of childhood has also been extended in policy terms. Although the school leaving age currently remains at 16 years, policies affecting access to welfare provisions such as Income Support, Unemployment Benefit, together with the erosion of the 'traditional' youth labour market and its replacement with extended education and training, mean that 16/17 year olds are effectively not recognized as individual citizens in welfare terms, but as the dependants of citizens and deriving their rights by proxy through them. It is as though the school leaving age had been raised to 18 years, since at 16 and 17, young people are expected to be in education and training. Most young people are semi-citizens: not until the age of 25 does an 'adult' gain full adult social citizenship in terms of welfare entitlement. Youth incomes, from whatever source, do not generally of themselves allow a young person to move away from the parental home and live independently, to work, study or raise a family. This means that most young people cannot support themselves through the period of their youth: they are dependent on others at least to supplement their incomes. Yet the 'others' on whom they need to be dependent may not easily recognize their needs. Youth has changed so significantly since parents – or policy makers and care providers – were themselves young, that those who might be offering more support to young people may have little experience to draw on and little knowledge of the problems that young people currently face (an issue explored elsewhere with regard to young people migrating from rural communities, Jones 1999, and in the author's current research).

Unchanging policy assumptions

In all, there is a growing mismatch, it seems, between policy constructions and the practice of youth. I want to consider ways in which the analytic model of extended transition to adulthood shown in Figure 9.2 should provide a framework to allow us to call into question some of the assumptions which continue to underlie approaches to youth policy. In its new forms, youth creates new problems for young people, for their families and for policy-makers. Among these, there is the problem of identifying and targeting those at risk, there is the problem of defining 'success' and 'failure', and there is the continuing problem of assuming that young people make choices on the basis of economic rationality. Finally, I want to highlight the danger of policy-makers and parents ignoring the power of the major dynamic in youth, that is the dynamic of a young person's own quest for independence.

The first issue is identifying vulnerability. The extension of the period of dependent youth creates a series of transitional statuses inhabited by young people. There are now more likely to be intermediate stages between school and entry into the labour market, between living in the parental home and having a home of one's own, and (perhaps) between being a child in a family and being a parent or partner in one. Each of these intermediate statuses is, however, potentially problematic and difficult to sustain. Some of these situations represent new adaptations and may be imbued with risk – young people are increasingly living as householders, alone or with their peers, between the parental home and the partnership home, for example, and we know very little about this group (Heath and Kenyon, 2001). Some commentators argue that risk has become endemic in the postmodern world (Beck, 1992). However, risk is inherent in youth, since risk-taking is part of growing up and identity construction. This makes it difficult to set criteria which can distinguish between vulnerability which needs intervention, and vulnerability which does not, risks which are acceptable, and risks from which young people need protection.

The only kind of safety net which could offer support for those in transitional statuses would be a *universal* safety net. There is however little state support for the intermediate stages in which young people increasingly appear to find themselves: young people are actively discouraged from leaving home or becoming parents at ages which are deemed 'too young', (Jones, 1995a; Phoenix, 1991). Young people in these transitional statuses can be targeted for discriminatory policies, and in the early 1990s this occurred within the rhetoric of an 'underclass' (Murray, 1990). Those perceived to have failed in their attempt to become independent, such as the homeless or jobless, were blamed for their circumstances (Walker, 1990; Hutson and Liddiard, 1994; Jones, 1997; MacDonald, 1997). Even those in 'acceptable' transitional statuses, students and trainees, had their incomes reduced and their debts increased, so that the age group as a whole became impoverished in relation to the rest of society. Though there has been a policy shift under post-1997 Labour Governments towards emphasizing social inclusion through the extension and expansion of education and training, particularly through the New Deal, age discrimination against young workers was institutionalized in the Minimum Wage Act 1998 (which failed to cover under-18s and ensured only a 'transitional rate' for 18–21 year olds).

The next problem is defining success and failure. This issue is important, when current debates about welfare are stressing the value of rewarding success rather than appearing to reward failure. The end product of youth – adulthood – is less clearly defined than ever, and also less secure: position in the labour market, access to an independent home, and a secure family life are all more in doubt than before. The idea of lifelong careers has been replaced with the notion of lifelong learning. Workers are expected to retrain with transferable skills, to meet employer needs, and to follow – even geographically – the needs of the labour market. This might affect their ability to maintain instrumental kinship links. 'Flexibility' may be the name of the game, but insecurity may be its net effect. So what constitutes a successful transition to adulthood, when there is no point of arrival?

The third issue is 'economic rationality'. The discussion above about whether transitions can only occur if they are economically underpinned becomes important in relation to state policies which were, under Conservative Governments, attempting to change behaviour through economic means. There is no longer a normative ordering between pathways (a successful school-to-work transition providing the economic foundation for a household-and-family-formation transition). There are now many different ways in which the strands of transition interact, and 'progress' to adult independence may involve back-tracking (returns to education or training, returns to the parental home, and tentative partnership formation and cohabitation, for example). Some backtracking is an inevitable result of experimentation; some may represent failure. Nevertheless, there appears still to be a policy assumption that the second set of transitions will follow the first – thus that young people will not leave home or form partnerships until they are established in the labour market with incomes that will support these transitions. It appears to be this 'economic rationality' assumption that informed Conservative Government policies to combat homelessness or teenage parenthood in the early 1990s (so that the withdrawal of economic 'incentives' will prevent young people from leaving home or having babies). Removing 'incentives' to leave home does not stop young people from leaving home, and far from preventing homelessness, may in practice increase it. Young people are leaving home earlier than they used to, mainly because they need to leave home if they are to make the most of education and training opportunities. Many more may now return to live in their parental homes again; this may be one strategy to cope with housing problems and avoid homelessness, though the option of returning home is not open to the vast majority of homeless young people (Jones, 1995b).

Which brings us to the role of individual agency manifested in the principal dynamic in youth – the dynamic which takes a young person from dependence on parents to adult independence and subsequent responsibility for the next generation. Young people want more independence as they grow up whether or not they are able to gain it through earning a wage. This powerful dynamic is likely to prevail despite the lack of supporting structures, with or without state support, and with or without family support. Thus, young people leave home despite the lack of affordable housing and the risk of homelessness, because they need to show that they can be independent (Jones, 1995b) and they may resort to new strategies of household formation in order to achieve the transition to independent living (Pickvance and Pickvance, 1994). Thus the intermediate transitional statuses shown in Figure 9.2 may be partially structured by government policies, and family responses to them, but they are also partially structured by young people themselves.

Support for the transition

If we can maintain a conceptual distinction between the expressions 'youth', meaning a process and a part of the life course, and 'young people', meaning a very heterogeneous grouping of individuals broadly distinguished by age, we can think more clearly about what youth and its parenting involve, how support for the transition to adulthood could be provided, and how it might be shared between different actors and institutions. The 'parenting of youth' here refers therefore to the role of parents (and those acting *in loco parentis*) in the light of recent changes to the structure of youth, as evidenced in Figure 9.3 below.

Young people have suffered from a loss of income opportunities – especially of the level of income which would allow them to be self-supporting during their transition to adulthood. Their partial or 'component' incomes (borrowing a term from Siltanen, 1994) need economic subsidies from someone. However, when it comes to support for young people, as with other dependent groups, the boundary of responsibility between the family and the state is being re-drawn (by the state, not presumably by parents). In a series of measures started under previous governments and continued under Labour, welfare has been restructured and much of it 'privatized' onto families. The state safety net now has gaping holes which 'families' seem to be expected to fill (Jones and Bell, 2000). As indicated, more young people are on youth incomes, whether from wages, student grants, trainee allowances or welfare benefits, and they are expected to turn to their parents for support. This has considerable implications for young people as it

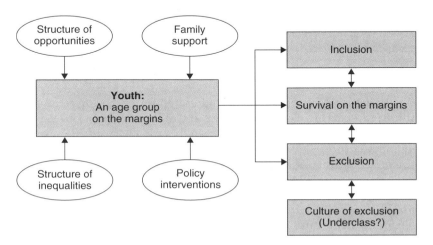

Figure 9.3 Family and state interventions

means that, at a time when they need to live independently if they are to capitalize on education, training and employment opportunities, when their income needs have increased, their right to have these needs recognized and met has been withdrawn. It also has considerable implications for parents who may be struggling with the competing demands emanating from their children, their parents and their own needs to pay off debts and prepare for their retirement. A study of family support for young people leaving the parental home in the 1990s (Jones, 1995a, b) suggests little consensus among young people over who they should be able to turn to for support. While 'Terry' thought that all young people over 16 years of age should be entitled to welfare benefits in their own right, 'Jill' thought that it was the responsibility of parents to help them until they could support themselves:

> Terry: (*Students*) are out to better themselves. And their parents – why should they support them after they're 16? I mean, fair enough until you're 16, because you're at school and you're supposed to support your kids. But after 16, I think – even 18 when they leave school (*then*) – I think you should get something to yourself.

> Jill: I think if you have a kid you should be prepared to keep him, nae just till his 16th birthday, but till they ready to go on their own.

It is worth considering for a moment why young people appear not to have access to state support, and why despite this they may still not get help from their families. I am going to focus on the issue of rights and responsibilities of young people vis-à-vis firstly the state, and secondly their parents.

Problems of access to state support

The transition to adulthood is encapsulated in the notion of citizenship, a proposition explored in Jones and Wallace (1992). Citizenship rights and responsibilities are conferred in a somewhat haphazard and inconsistent way according to age, in Britain (with some variation between Scotland, and England and Wales in this respect) (see Jones and Bell, 2000). While the legal age of majority is 18 years, young people are deemed responsible for criminal actions much younger, but not entitled to adult welfare rights (in terms of full adult rates of social security benefit) until they are 25 years of age. The link between rights and responsibilities in youth has never been a close one – in the case of National Insurance, responsibility preceded rights, as there has always been a gap between a young person's responsibility to pay National Insurance and their right to benefit from it (Harris, 1989). It is unclear how the current emphasis on earning one's rights is understood by young people, or how it squares with a more appropriate notion that reciprocity (between the individual and the state) would normally occur over the individual life course rather than 'here and now'. In the drive to reduce welfare dependency, there is now a strong policy emphasis on the need for rights to be balanced with responsibilities, and benefits thus involve contractual obligations. In the context of Labour's New Deal, this can be seen in the contracts young people have to sign to indicate their willingness to work before they can be offered training. Current citizenship education in schools stresses the need to demonstrate being a good citizen, focusing on responsibilities rather than rights.

If reciprocity is meant to be immediate, and rights to be balanced with responsibilities synchronically, rather than over time, then young people are very disadvantaged. They are only just emerging from the 'black box' of family life into independent roles in the public sphere. Many of the contributions that they make will be hidden from view, within their families. They may not yet have been able to be taxpayers and thus contributors to welfare schemes. They may, however, have been involved in different forms of work, including domestic work (caring for parents or siblings), or just plain – but perhaps undervalued – school homework, or contributing to the domestic economy through employment outside the home, or in family businesses. For some reason they still tend to be seen by policy-makers and the media as inactive, not contributing, and therefore (it seems) needing to be taught about citizenship and to be recruited for community service and volunteering. Many of the arguments that have been made in respect of women's contributions (such as wages for housework) could be used in relation to young people too, but it seems that so far it is not enough to make a private contribution: to be seen is to be believed. Hence we put the spotlight on children and young people who do good or brave deeds, but leave the rest in the shadow, characterized as lazy, good-for-nothing, and 'undeserving'. According to one prevailing notion, community service – Citizens' Service – was the way forward to allow young people to make a positive contribution to society and 'earn' their citizenship. In practice they may have been doing this already.

If it really is essential to recognize young people's contribution before according them the rights of social citizenship, including welfare provision, then there are two ways of doing this: the first is to accept that even young people who need our support now, can make a visible contribution to society over their life course; the second is to accept the level of contribution young people may make in an invisible way in the privacy of their families. Of course there is also a third way, which is to create full-waged jobs.

Problems of access to family support

Let me move on to the question of whether young people can get support from their families. State policy has been to increase and extend the economic, social, moral and legal responsibility of parents for their children. Finch, in Chapter One, has drawn attention to the fallacy that governments could regulate people's family lives, especially in Britain, where she pointed to a clear distinction which has prevailed through history between family roles (such as father, mother) and the family relationships which are only loosely attached to these roles. Her argument (developed in relation to laws relating to inheritance) was that there is no consensus about roles (or about obligations attached to them) and no single model of family life. Relationships are 'ego-focused, flexible, and affective'. She argued that the resulting variability is not a recent phenomenon stemming from post-modernism (c.f. Beck, 1992; Giddens, 1991), but that it has long historical roots (quoting MacFarlane, 1978). Finch used this thesis to argue that governments should not legislate for family relationships (except in protecting the vulnerable) and cannot make assumptions about how families 'ought' to work.

Young people are caught up in these contradictions. To define the dependency of one family member might be expected to re-define the obligations of another. Despite Finch's caveat, it is nevertheless curious that the extension of dependence in youth created by youth policies has not been paralleled with an extension of parental responsibility in family policy (see the extended review of youth and family policy in Jones and Bell, 2000). Research on family obligations has equally tended to neglect responsibility for 16–25 year olds, and has focused more on the responsibility for the elderly or for younger children (Finch, 1989; Finch and Mason, 1993; Millar and Warman, 1996). Most of the research undertaken (e.g. Allatt and Yeandle, 1992; Hutson and Jenkins, 1987; Jones, 1995b) has been on working class families, or families where there have been particular problems of marital breakdown and/or unemployment. We know very little about how the extended support now implicitly expected of parents may be negotiated between young people and their parents in other family types, although earlier research (Bell, 1968; Harris, 1987) has indicated that there are significant social class differences in the extent to which families provide economic support to older children and young adults, and also in the nature of such support (i.e. that middle class families are more likely to provide extended financial support while working class families are more likely to provide help in kind).

There are many cases where parents cannot or will not help their adult children, and it is likely that many parents are not even aware that their children may need to be able to be dependent on them for longer. Where there are no legal requirements that parents should help, family support for a young person may depend on the parents' recognising the need for support, and also on the quality of the parent-child relationship. But parental support is sometimes not forthcoming because young people may find it too difficult to ask for it (Jones, 1995b). It is demeaning to young people who are trying to assert their adult independent identities to have to act as dependants again, to ask for help. Finch and Mason (1993: 167) argued that 'claiming rights is definitely not seen as a legitimate part of family life. Even where one person accepts a responsibility to help, the other does not have the right to claim, or even to expect, assistance'. There may thus be a number of levels on which asking for help is difficult for young people. In the following quotations (drawn from Jones 1995a, as before), young people describe how family support is – like state support – conditional, with strings attached, and that asking for help is difficult when, as indicated earlier, the main dynamic is towards staying independent:

Amy: I've got too much pride aboot asking people for money. I just wouldnae ask them, like my dad or my grandparents. But I knew I could have got it, but I wouldnae ask for it. (...) I'm so independent I want to do it all myself. I don't want anybody turning roond and saying: 'Do you remember we got you this flat?' or 'Who got you this or that?' – *casting it up* to me.

Denise: See, if I've nae money, absolutely really skint, I'll no go near him. It *feels like begging* even when you're going to your ain faither, ken. I dinnae like going and saying 'I've nae money. I need food, ken'.

Roscoe: I won't ask and I'm just *too much myself to ask* somebody for anything like that, especially my ma, so she offers and I refuse and she offers it again and I refuse. And this goes on for ages before I go 'OK, OK, I'll take it'.

Kevin: If I need something I wouldnae do to my da' 'Oh I need this, I need that', or my granny or my sister or whatever – *but if I get offered* – but really I wouldnae ask.

Yet government policies have assumed that the longer-standing middle class patterns of extended financial support can be applied to working class families among whom this has not in the past been common practice. Furthermore pressure is being put on parents precisely at a time when there is increased likelihood of marital breakdown, and an increased chance that young people will not be living with their two biological parents (McRae, 2000). The problem is not simply that the responsibilities of step-parents may be unclear, but also that parental divorce can mean the loss of whole kinship networks which might have been able to provide alternative support. Policy expectations of extended parental support can increase the strain on both marital and parent-child relations, particularly (perhaps) in reconstituted families. Young people with step-parents tend to leave home earlier than those with both their biological parents, are more likely to leave home because of relationship problems, are less likely to receive financial support for leaving home, and are more likely to become homeless. Those without families to draw on for support, such as many care-leavers, face an even greater risk of homelessness (Jones, 1995a).

So youth policies have been implemented without regard to their effect on families, and family policies have been implemented without regard to their effect on the young people in them (Jones and Bell, 2000). State policies (growing welfare budget, extension of education and training) and changes in family life (greater likelihood of parental divorce, migration, unemployment) both impact on young people as they grow up, and the tensions between the state and the family are likely to be detrimental. If the state and the family simultaneously pull back their sides of the safety net, then young people are increasingly likely to fall into the chasm of poverty, joblessness, and homelessness.

Strategies for coping alone

Let me return to the question whether the extension of dependency and deferring of full adult citizenship results in young people increasingly being trapped in a state of limbo. The answer has to be 'no', for the majority of young people at least, for the following three reasons: first, because the achievement of adulthood is not solely along one dimension, but along several (see Figure 9.2), so that 'failure' in one respect may not mean failure in another; second, because, as Finch inferred, social policy has only a limited effect in regulating family and individual behaviour; and third because the transition to independence is a powerful dynamic, so that where there are obstacles and constraints, strategies emerge to deal with them. These may be reactive strategies of survival or resistance (for a discussion on the use of the term strategy, see Wallace, 1993; Crow, 1989). They may be short term, adaptive strategies. They may not be available to all, and even where they can be called into play, they may involve longer-term problems.

Strategies are not limited to young people. We can think of strategies of the state: the emphasis on parental responsibility for young people can be seen as a strategy intended to achieve two aims simultaneously: to reduce the welfare budget and to deal with the perceived law and order problem. But the strategy may not be successful where other players in the game have strategies of their own. Finch (1989) comments on some earlier unanticipated consequences of government policy. In the 1930s, the Household Means Test was imposed and household income was defined as the sum of individual incomes, on the basis that these were pooled; the result was that households containing employed young people were penalized and so some left home so that their parents could claim a higher rate of benefit. This had not been intended by the policy, which was based on false assumptions about family economic practices. Currently, we can see situations where parents evict their adult children rather than accept responsibility for them (Jones, 1995a; Smith et al, 1998) – and in Scotland it is perfectly legal for parents to do this when a child reaches the age of 16. More pressure on parents to extend their responsibilities does not mean that parents will obediently accept government policy and continue to offer their adult children a home or financial support. They may not currently even be aware that more responsibility is expected of them.

Young people have their own strategies for coping or resistance. I have indicated here some of the ways in which they may continue to seek independence despite the economic constraints. But poverty brings its own strategies. A study of youth poverty in Edinburgh (Kirk, Nelson, Sinfield and Sinfield, 1991) found that young people had adopted a 'poverty of expectations' and lowered their aspirations accordingly. There was much talk in the 1990s of a growing underclass in Britain

(Wilkinson and Mulgan, 1995), and it is likely that some of the young people who are increasingly identified as socially excluded – not just from jobs and housing, but also from family life – may indeed form cultures of resistance, perhaps even along the lines of an 'underclass' (MacDonald, 1997). We should think very hard about the policies which now need to be put in place to ensure that young people are not marginalized and excluded from society. As long as the policy focus is on universal early interventions to help children, but on targeted policies for the control rather than care of young people over 16 years, then there will be more young people who will suffer. When young people resort to strategies of resistance in order to cope with a lack of family/state support, they are likely to be vilified, to become the subjects of a 'moral panic'. It is thus imperative that the family context in which young people are living is taken into account by policy makers and researchers alike. Only then can the problem of support be resolved.

Bibliography

Allat, P. and Yeandle, S. (1992) *Youth Employment and the Family: Voices of Disordered Times* London: Routledge.

Beck, U. (1992) *Risk Society: Towards a New Modernity* (trans. M. Ritter) London: Sage.

Bell, C. (1968) *Middle Class Families: Social and Geographical Mobility* London; Routledge and Kegan Paul.

Biehal, N., Clayden, J., Stein, M. and Wade, J. (1995) *Moving On: Young People and Leaving Care Schemes* London: HMSO.

Bynner, J., Elias, P., McKnight, A., Pan, H. and Pierre, G. (2002) *Young People's Changing Routes to Independence* York, Joseph Rowntree Foundation.

Coles, B. (1995) *Youth and Social Policy* London: UCL Press.

Crow, G. (1989) The use of the concept of 'strategy' in recent sociological literature. *Sociology* 23(1): 1–24.

Dearden, C. and Becker, S. (2000) *Growing Up Caring: Vulnerability and Transition to Adulthood – Young Carers' experiences* Leicester, Youth Work Press and the Joseph Rowntree Foundation.

Finch, J. (1989) *Family Obligations and Social Change* Cambridge: Polity Press.

Finch, J. and Mason, J. (1993) *Negotiating Family Responsibilities* London: Routledge.

Furlong, A. and Cartmel, F. (1997) *Young People and Social Change: Individualization and Risk in Late Modernity* Buckingham: Open University Press.

Giddens, A. (1991) *Modernity and Self Identity* Cambridge: Polity Press.

Harris, C. C. (1987) *The Family and Industrial Society* London: George Allen and Unwin.

Harris, N. S. (1989) *Social Security for Young People* Aldershot: Avebury.

Heath, S. and Kenyon, L. (2001) 'Young single professionals and shared household living', *Journal of Youth Studies* Vol. 4 No. 1 p. 83–100.

Home Office (1998) *Supporting Families: a consultation paper* Green Paper. London: Home Office.

Hutson, S. and Jenkins, R. (1989) *Taking the Strain: Families, Unemployment and the Transition to Adulthood* Milton Keynes: Open University Press.

Hutson, S. and Liddiard, M. (1994) *Youth Homelessness: the Construction of a Social Issue* Basingstoke: Macmillan.

Jones, G. (2002) *The Youth Divide: Diverging paths to adulthood* York, Joseph Rowntree Foundation.

Jones, G. (1999) 'Trail-blazers and path-followers: social reproduction and geographical mobility in youth' in S. Arber and C. Attias-Donfut (eds.), *Changing Generational Contracts* London: Routledge.

Jones, G. (1995a) *Family Support for Young People* London: Joseph Rowntree Foundation and Family Policy Studies Centre.

Jones, G. (1995b) *Leaving Home*. Buckingham: Open University Press.

Jones, G. (1991) 'The cost of living in the parental home', *Youth and Policy* 32: 19–29.

Jones, G. (1988) Integrating process and structure in the concept of youth: a case for secondary analysis, *The Sociological Review* 36(4): 706–732.

Jones, G. and Bell, R. (2000) *Balancing Acts? Youth, Parenting and Public Policy* York, York Publishing.

Jones, G. and Martin, C. D. (1999) 'The "Young Consumer" at home: Dependence, resistance and autonomy', in J. Hearn and Roseneil (eds.), *Consuming Cultures: Power and Resistance* Basingstoke: Macmillan.

Jones, G. and Wallace, C. (1992) *Youth, Family and Citizenship* Buckingham: Open University Press.

Kirk, D., Nelson, S., Sinfield, A. and Sinfield, D. (1991) *Excluding Youth: Poverty among Young People Living Away from Home* Edinburgh: Centre for Social Welfare Research, University of Edinburgh.

MacDonald, R. (ed.) (1997) *Youth, the 'Underclass' and Social Exclusion* London: Routledge.

MacFarlane, A. (1978) *The Origins of English Individualism* Oxford: Blackwell.

MacRae, S. (ed.) (1999) *Changing Britain: Families and Households in the 1990s* Oxford, Oxford University Press.

Millar, J. and Warman, A. (1996) *Family Obligations in Europe* London: Joseph Rowntree Foundation and Family Policy Studies Centre.

Morrow, V. (1996) Rethinking childhood dependency: children's contribution to the domestic economy *Sociological Review* 44(1): 58–77.

Murray, C. (1990) *The Emerging British Underclass* Choice in Welfare Series No. 2, Institute of Economics Affairs, London: IEA Health and Welfare Unit.

Payne, J. (1989) 'Unemployment and family formation among young men', *Sociology* 23(2): 171–191.

Phoenix, A. (1991) *Young Mothers?* Cambridge: Polity Press.

Pickvance, C. and Pickvance, K. (1995) 'The role of family help in the housing decisions of young people', *Sociological Review* 42: 123–149.

Siltanen, J. (1994) *Locating Gender: Occupational Segregation Wages and Domestic Responsibilities* London: UCL Press.

Smith, J., Gilford, S. and O'Sullivan, A. (1998) *The Family Background of Homeless Young People* London: Family Policy Studies Centre.

Social Exclusion Unit (2000) *Young People: National Strategy for Neighbourhood Renewal* Report of Policy Action Team 12, London, Stationery Office.

Song, M. (1999) *Helping out: Children's Labour in Ethnic Businesses* Philadelphia: Temple University Press.

Walker, A. (1990) Blaming the victims. Commentary in (C. Murray) *The Emerging British Underclass*, Choice in Welfare Series No. 2, Institute of Economics Affairs. London: IEA Health and Welfare Unit.

Wallace, C. (1991) Young people in rural south-west England. *Youth and Policy* 33: 10–17.

Wallace, C. (1993) Reflections on the concept of 'strategy', in D. Morgan and L. Stanley (eds.), *Debates in Sociology* Manchester: Manchester University Press.

Wallace, C. (1987) *For Richer for Poorer: Growing Up In and Out of Work* London: Tavistock.

Wilkinson, H. and Mulgan, G. (1995) *Freedom's Children: Work, Relationships and Politics for 18–34 year olds in Britain today* London: Demos.

Williamson, H. (1997) *Youth and Policy: Contexts and Consequences* Aldershot, Ashgate.

Willis, P. (1984) 'Youth unemployment', *New Society* 29 March, 5 April and 12 April.

Index

n/ns indicates note(s)